indaba!

A Way of Listening, Engaging,
and Understanding
across the Anglican Communion

Paula D. Nesbitt

Church Publishing
NEW YORK

Church Publishing
19 East 34th Street
New York, NY 10016
www.churchpublishing.org

Cover design by Jennifer Kopec, 2Pug Design
Typeset by Denise Hoff

Library of Congress Cataloging-in-Publication Data

Names: Nesbitt, Paula D., 1948- author.
Title: Indaba! : a way of listening, engaging, and understanding across
    the Anglican communion / Paula D. Nesbitt.
Description: New York : Church Publishing, 2017. | Includes bibliographical
    references.
Identifiers: LCCN 2016041236 (print) | LCCN 2016049192 (ebook) |
    ISBN 9780819233172 (pbk.) | ISBN 9780819233189 (ebook)
Subjects: LCSH: Church controversies--Anglican Communion. |
    Reconciliation--Religious aspects--Anglican Communion. |
    Conflict management--Religious aspects--Anglican Communion.
Classification: LCC BX5005 .N47 2017 (print) | LCC BX5005 (ebook) |
    DDC 283--dc23
LC record available at https://lccn.loc.gov/2016041236

Printed in the United States of America

~ CONTENTS ~

INTRODUCTION V

1 : *Indaba* as an Anglican Communion Adventure 1

2 : Preparing for the Journey:
The Continuing Indaba Project .29

3 : Touching Ground Zero:
The Search for Common Ground
in New York, Derby, and Mumbai 51

4 : Siblings in a Global Family:
Toronto, Hong Kong Sheng Kung Hui,
and Jamaica and the Cayman Islands.
                              —*Joanna Sadgrove* 77

5 : Unity in Diversity:
A *Safari* across Differences in Saldanha Bay,
Ho, and Mbeere.
                              —*Mkunga H. P. Mtingele* 101

6 : "If I Had a Cow like That . . .":
A Quest for Mutual Mission in Western Tanganyika,
El Camino Real, and Gloucester 125

7 : Reflections on the Journey:
Insights, "*Indaba* Moments," and
Meaningful Conversation 151

8 : Other *Indabas* across the Anglican Communion 183

9 : *Indaba* and the Future 209

APPENDIX   About the Evaluation Research:
Continuing Indaba and
Mutual Listening Project 231

BIBLIOGRAPHY 243

ABOUT THE AUTHOR AND CONTRIBUTORS 261

~ INTRODUCTION ~

IMAGINE YOURSELF ON A JOURNEY. Differing viewpoints, customs, language, and culture confound your sense of order. At first you feel curious. But at some point you may note a growing resistance, craving what is familiar and comfortable. This feeling may subside over time, or it may not. At the end of the journey, home feels familiar, but somehow you are changed by the experience. You begin reflecting with fresh insight on what you might always have taken for granted. This characterizes a cross-cultural indaba experience, whether across the world or in the midst of differences not far from home.

Powerful journeys occur when you engage with people who differ from you in what you might believe or value or in how you live. Such encounters can be challenging, sometimes painful, but they also can bring moments of grace when there is a mutual feeling of being heard and accepted across the differences. In such moments, you may feel a special kinship with those you otherwise might not meet or seek out. As personal bonds form, you and the people you meet may come to understand each other in a different way—not necessarily agreeing, but realizing that differences need not destroy relationships. This type of journey is what *indaba* is about.

Indaba comes from Zulu culture, but the concept underlying it, as a way of communal listening and conflict transformation, is shared by cultures across the world. The cultures from which such listening processes come are different from those formed out of Western intellectual tradition and European Enlightenment ideals. In the West, individual freedom, conscience, and autonomy are prized values. At times, these compete with claims made by others in a community or in wider society. In other types of cultures, members may have an identity that is deeply intertwined with their community, and personal autonomy may be constrained by a strong responsibility and accountability to it.

This conflict in cultural values characterizes a part of what the Anglican Communion found itself entering as it began to shift from a Western colonial form of Christianity grounded in the Church of England to an expression of Christianity that breathes through many different cultures across the world. As a result, autonomy and tolerance, as well as interdependence and responsibility, have been at the heart of the varied struggles across the Communion. These came to a head at the threshold of the twenty-first century.

ANGLICAN IDENTITY AND THE COMMUNION

More than forty churches serving 165 countries and eighty-five million members make up the Anglican Communion. Each church has its own autonomous governing body. Their relationship to one another is much like close relatives in an extended family. The family may have shared customs and a tradition that provides a common identity among its members, but the relatives have their own immediate families where authority relations and customs often differ. Therefore, decisions that Anglican Communion councils or bodies make are given serious consideration by the member churches (also called *provinces*), but each decides whether it will support them. The archbishop of Canterbury is considered the spiritual leader of the Communion but has no direct authority over any of the member churches other than the Church of England.

Anglicans share similarities in identity and practice with both Catholics and Protestants. As a denominational tradition, Anglicanism has given rise to a number of Protestant movements and denominations, such as Puritanism, Congregationalism, and Methodism. Yet like Roman Catholicism, Anglicanism is understood by its churches around the world as sharing in a common catholic tradition with direct roots to the apostolic era. Over the centuries, Anglican churches have developed a wide range of internal religious expressions from evangelical to catholic, which has resulted in varied viewpoints on matters of faith that at times have severely strained relationships. These differing expressions have added further complexity across the range of cultures that constitute the Anglican Communion.

The Anglican Communion, in its leadership and ethos, historically has been dominated by older white male bishops from Britain, North America, Australia, and New Zealand. This began to change in the 1960s through movements for political independence across Africa, along with a fresh vision of mission relationships based on mutual responsibility and interdependence.[1] These shifts brought new leaders into the Communion who were raised in the cultures they represented and who offered different visions and understandings of what faith and life together might mean. Their growing visibility and voices have added an increasingly diverse cultural vibrancy to the Communion. Female bishops from several provinces and continents, as well as female clergy and lay leaders, have become part of this growing diversity.

As a result, a common journey together no longer could mean

---

[1] Ian Douglas, "The Exigency of Times and Occasions," 27–28.

an agreeable stroll through the English or North American countryside, so to speak. Over the last three decades, that journey has grown increasingly surprising, frequently tumultuous, profoundly educational, occasionally painful, and for many, ultimately gratifying. As the Anglican Communion's global leadership and mission become characterized more and more by mutuality, this new type of journey will not end where it began.

The Anglican Communion and *Indaba*

Indaba was brought into the Anglican Communion at a time of strong tension and bitterness that had arisen from growing disagreement over how Scripture and tradition should be understood and how faith ought to be lived out. These differences were linked to the rising global multicultural diversity in Anglican leadership and a huge growth in Anglican churches over the last several decades across Africa and parts of Asia and Latin America.

Historically, as colonial Anglicanism extended its spread across continents and cultures, tensions had begun to grow over whether Anglicanism should be strictly a colonial church or be allowed to express aspects of the indigenous cultures. By the mid-1860s, a crisis had developed in Cape Town between two bishops who held very different views on this matter,[2] and the situation reflected mounting concerns elsewhere across the church. In 1867, the archbishop of Canterbury called bishops across the Anglican churches to meet at London's Lambeth Palace to have an informal conversation about concerns involving the relationship between Anglicanism and indigenous cultures.[3] The meeting was viewed so positively afterward that Lambeth Conferences typically have been held every ten years since.

Over the years, however, Lambeth meetings became agenda-packed affairs, with parliamentary-style debate and

---

2 Also see "South Africa."
3 Stephen Neill, *Anglicanism*, 360–61.

voting on resolutions as the primary means of conversation and coming to a common decision. Even though the decisions have held moral but not legal status for the autonomous member churches, by 1998 the meeting had become so politically charged, in part through the increasing diversity of cultures and theological views, that faithful leaders were accusing one another of faithlessness and intolerance in both religious beliefs and cultural understanding. These tensions threatened to split apart the Communion.

An issue capturing widespread attention may be a symptom of a deeper concern that needs to be addressed, which was the case with the conflicts that surfaced over homosexuality in the Anglican Communion during the 1990s and the next decade. Differences over scriptural interpretation were very real, but much of the conflict ignored the vast social, cultural, and historical contexts that also affected both understandings and the norms surrounding human sexuality. Definitions, for instance, differed sharply across cultures over exactly what was homosexuality. Subtexts of social change, postcolonialism, and Western imperialism also were deeply intertwined with the issue. Other religious denominations whose global memberships have grown in diversity and voices have faced similar conflicts.

A different type of conversation

A design group was appointed to come up with a different way of gathering for the 2008 Lambeth Conference, one that might help bishops from around the world come to a deeper awareness of how different cultural surroundings and perspectives might affect the ways in which they understood various matters. Archbishop of Cape Town Thabo Makgoba, who was part of the group, suggested *indaba* as a process that might help accomplish this need for greater cross-cultural understanding. He had noted several consistencies between *indaba* and how the Apostle Paul had urged that conflict be addressed in the early Christian community of Corinth, which had been strongly conflicted over differences in beliefs and culture.[4] The design group therefore decided to try a form of *indaba* for the Lambeth meeting.

Bishops from around the world gathered each morning in small Bible study groups to read and discuss Scripture. Afterward, they met in larger, forty-member *indaba* groups for a focused conversation on a theme or issue. Each *indaba* group had a scribe who summarized what was discussed each day and contributed those notes to an overall reflections document of all the *indaba* conversations. At the end of the Lambeth meeting, this reflections document noted that many bishops had felt a deeper sense of connectedness across their many differences and a strong desire to continue this type of dialogue into the future.[5] It also noted with sadness that a sizable number of bishops were not present for various reasons, including many who stayed away to protest the presence of bishops from the Episcopal Church because it had an openly gay, partnered bishop, even though he hadn't been invited to the Lambeth meeting.[6]

Indaba after Lambeth

Indaba's overall success at Lambeth brought greater insight into some of the cultural conditions that affect how bishops have understood matters of faith and how that faith is lived out across the various churches and cultures. After Lambeth, many expressed an interest in exploring how *indaba* might be used more widely in the Anglican Communion and also to involve the grassroots of church leadership.

An experimental project was formed to explore how *indaba*

---

[4] Archbishop Makgoba makes analogies between *indaba* and 1 Corinthians 12. See Thabo Makgoba, "An Anglican Microcosm," 68–70.

[5] Reflections Group, "Lambeth Indaba," 4. Also, field observation of media briefings and research interviews (Nesbitt).

[6] The Rt. Rev. Gene Robinson was the only diocesan bishop not invited. Also not invited was the Rt. Rev. Martyn Minns, who had been ordained by the Anglican Church of Nigeria to oversee breakaway Episcopal congregations through the network Convocation of Anglicans in North America (CANA).

might be effective in the everyday lives of the churches. Known as the Continuing Indaba and Mutual Listening Project, it consisted of two basic aspects: Resource Hubs of scholars, developing materials from their own cultural contexts; and Pilot Conversation groups, bringing together a mix of laity and clergy from different dioceses across the Anglican Communion.[7] Funded by a grant through the Satcher Health Leadership Institute of the Morehouse School of Medicine, the three-year pilot project (2009–12) was approved by the Anglican Consultative Council (2009) and evaluated by a research team of scholars. It also was observed by an ecumenical team for reflection on what other denominations might learn from the use of *indaba*.

Building on the Lambeth *indaba* experience, the Pilot Conversations sought to help people learn how to talk about their differences without letting them overcome or destroy their relationships—a skill sorely needed in both religious and secular life. At the project's end, the researchers found that the *indaba* process had improved the ability to listen across differences and had developed deeper cross-cultural understanding. Most important, the groups were able to remain in conversation even when sharp differences over sensitive issues threatened to break them apart. Participants also expressed a desire to continue their relationships after the project ended.

The stories of each Pilot Conversation and what was learned from their experience form the heart of this book. The tensions the groups confronted were similar to those that many people face when challenged by differences in views and culture. Some involved pragmatic issues, such as women's ordination and the role of women in society, sexuality, race and ethnicity, poverty and economic development, and the legacy of colonial history. Others arose out of our basic human condition, such as how one

---

7   An Anglican or Episcopal diocese is a geographic region within a wider church, with self-governance and autonomy in administrative and pastoral matters that don't conflict with the churchwide constitution and canons. A diocesan bishop oversees the diocese and represents it in matters of churchwide deliberation and governance.

moves from perceiving another as *different* toward building a relationship based on mutuality, respect, and caring.

After the Pilot Conversations ended, several dioceses across the Communion saw hope in what *indaba* could accomplish and contributed financial gifts that allowed Continuing Indaba to develop resource materials and offer guidance for those wanting to try *indaba*. A dedicated website was developed to share guidelines, writings from different cultural and theological perspectives, and other resources from the Continuing Indaba project.[8] In 2013, *indaba* became a core process in Archbishop of Canterbury Justin Welby's commitment to reconciliation across the Anglican Communion. The role of *indaba* was to offer an opportunity for a fresh beginning, which sets people on a path to live reconciliation as an ongoing and unending process. What people do with this opportunity is a matter for all.

The practice of *indaba* has continued to grow. Some have used it to build deeper understanding and stronger relationships across diverse geographic, socioeconomic, and cultural differences. Others have looked to it for help with reconciliation and the healing of long-standing, deep wounds and trauma from violence. Occasionally, *indaba* has been brought into large meetings when the participants in a discussion with sharply conflicting views needed to benefit from deep listening to one another in order to understand the varied concerns that underlay the tensions and find a way to move forward together. It also has been used by dioceses and others to build better internal relationships and cohesion across differences.

INDABA POSSIBILITIES AND CHALLENGES

Religious communities have been especially challenged to find constructive ways of handling conflict in their midst. Differing

---

8   Resources are available at https://continuingindaba.org. The site has undergone revision since 2012, but a range of materials remain from the Pilot Conversations and the Resource Hubs. Additional resources and guides are available for those wanting to design and hold *indabas* on their own.

beliefs or practices can be held with sacred fervor. Too often conflict is suppressed, avoided, or arbitrarily resolved rather than addressed in a way that respects differences of viewpoint or understanding. *Indaba* offers a way to transform conflict so that a community can live healthily with internal differences in its midst.

Indaba's use in the Anglican Communion represents a growing awareness of the wisdom that can be found in our diverse cultural treasuries on how to live in mutually respectful relationships. It also suggests a path for people who share a common bond such as a faith tradition to remain in relationship across their differences. In this way, the Anglican Communion serves as a case study for other organizations that have a far-reaching multicultural or global presence.

When concerns are understood more fully from various points of view, the insights that result can expand the possibilities for decision-making and also solutions that take into account a wide range of understandings. This increases the likelihood that points of common ground will emerge and trust will grow. Relationships that are maintained in the midst of conflict can open fresh possibilities for healthy social change and also for cohesion that is built on mutual respect.

Indaba processes have the potential to be useful across differing faiths, where valuing the integrity of differences is important in finding a way to move forward together. It also may be useful in a range of ways where people seek to work together in goodwill across the different contexts and understandings that exist in any community. If we have truly entered into the *indaba* process, it will offer a fresh way to experience faith and community across cultural and other differences.

Challenges to *Indaba*

The story of *indaba* is not without controversy. Before the 2008 Lambeth Conference, some bishops had been wary that *indaba* would be used to pressure them to change their beliefs about homosexuality. Others had thought that simply talking, without resolutions and decision-making, would be a waste of time and resources. Some suggested that the substitution of *indaba* for the traditional parliamentary process was a way to avoid the possibility of a "Global South" block vote on divisive issues.[9] Similarly, *indaba* also was ridiculed as a cowardly way to avoid enforcing conformity to Anglican orthodoxy.[10] Yet either a parliamentary vote or a measure of enforcement would have fractured church relationships within the Anglican Communion, perhaps beyond repair.

When the Continuing Indaba project was announced in 2009, some were suspicious of its motives, since the funding source was located within the United States, even though the grant had no limitations on what might be discussed or what the outcomes might be.[11] Some thought that it might not support conservative interests despite reassurances that no ideological strings were attached. However, bishops who were part of the conservative Global Anglican Future Conference (GAFCON) alliance did participate in Continuing Indaba.[12] Moreover, others who took part ranged across the spectrum in their theological beliefs. Some were strongly opposed to women's ordination. Many held widely contrasting views on homosexuality, social justice, Scripture, worship, and other matters. Their involvement brought both theological and cultural diversity, as well as credibility that the process respected differences in views and culture.

These challenges to *indaba* point to a tension that can arise during an open dialogue on matters of religion. People can hold fast to their religious beliefs, even to the point where they believe theirs is the only true understanding, but they also can be authentically curious about what cultural or other

---

9   Ian T. Douglas, "Equipping for God's Mission," 178.

10   E.g., David W. Virtue, "Lambeth."

11   Matthew Davies, "Listening Process a 'Gift' to Church," 2.

12   The Global Anglican Future Conference, held in 2008, resulted in a declaration stating fourteen points of Anglican orthodoxy that bond Anglican adherents as a movement. See "GAFCON Jerusalem 2008."

conditions have led others to hold such strong differences of view. But when people are unable to sit with others holding different beliefs, unless seeing it as an opportunity to pros-elytize, they likely will distrust *indaba* or any mutual listening process as threatening to their faith or as a waste of time. This poses a significant limitation to *indaba,* which is discussed in chapter 1. It also limits the possibility of communal life together beyond narrow conformity.

Nonetheless, *indaba* as adapted by the Anglican Communion has enhanced the ways people have been able to communicate across differences of culture, faith, and understanding. It has been invaluable for helping give voice to those who historically have been marginalized, especially by dominant Westernized forms of communication. It also has helped people learn about one another at a deeper level, across sometimes vast differences in beliefs and culture. Both similarities and sometimes surprising differences have surfaced in the process. Ultimately, it has helped build relationships across the Communion that are grounded in mutual respect.

THE RESEARCH BEHIND *INDABA!*

The grant for the Continuing Indaba and Mutual Listening Project involved research to discern whether the *indaba* made a difference in building relationships across differences in view-points and culture, as well as where *indaba* possibilities and limitations might lie. Specifically, it evaluated the effective-ness of the design of the *indaba* process in a number of areas:

- keeping sensitive conversation from polar-izing into debate;
- moving participants beyond mutual listening toward a common purpose;
- engaging participants in mission issues that might lead to action;

- ensuring consistency with Anglicanism, or the Anglican Way;[13] and

- determining which aspects might be useful elsewhere, beyond the scope of that project.

The researchers were not involved in designing the project. They also used multiple research methods to accommodate different cultural customs, technologies, and purposes. These involved interviews, field observation, and both online and paper questionnaires. Data gathered in one format either validated data in another or helped the researchers search for deeper meanings when discrepancies arose.

The research team consisted of three social scientists from different disciplines and cultures: the Rev. Canon Dr. Mkunga H. P. Mtingele, a Tanzanian lawyer, executive, and social scientist specializing in leadership and conflict management; Dr. Joanna Sadgrove, a British anthropologist; and the author, an American sociologist. As researchers, our different cultural and disciplinary viewpoints were invaluable for how each of us approached the research and analyzed its findings. At least once we found ourselves in *indaba* as we sorted out different understandings based on our cultural locations.

To share our different research voices and perspectives, each of us has written a narrative of one or more of the Pilot Conversations, with details or insights contributed by the others. Comments from participants have been included anonymously to give the reader a personal sense of the *indaba* journey that was taken. We are keenly aware that our narrative and what we conclude may differ from the perspectives of individual participants, and we caution the reader that any collective story cannot begin to capture the richness, intensity, and diversity of every person's experience. Our aim was simply

---

[13] The Anglican Way has been understood as the interplay of Scripture, tradition, and reason, which are the three primary sources of Anglican authority. As these interact, there is a constant need to discern God's will both in relation to the passage of time and across particular contexts. See *The Virginia Report*, paragraph 3.11.

to present an overview and identify several central tendencies amid the rich variety of viewpoints and experiences.

The research findings included in this book cluster around areas of broad interest to readers, especially what might be useful for learning from the Pilot Conversation journeys and for adapting *indaba* to other contexts. These findings are set forth in the case studies and in chapter 7. Further details and findings are summarized in the appendix. Several of the Pilot Conversation stories also have been told from a somewhat different perspective in *Living Reconciliation* (2014), a book and study guide by Phil Groves and Angharad Parry Jones, the Continuing Indaba project management and administrative team. Other accounts by participants have been published in news media and online, including the Continuing Indaba website and Facebook page. Taken together, all provide varied and interesting perspectives on a shared experience.

Other parts of the book draw on additional research conducted by the author, including the 1988, 1998, and 2008 Lambeth Conferences and the 2013 Women's Indaba (cosponsored by Anglican Women's Empowerment and the Anglican Communion Office). Findings on other *indabas* were gathered through personal interviews and correspondence or by Continuing Indaba director Phil Groves. We communicate what has been learned from this research to demonstrate that living with conflict can be both creative and constructive in developing mutually respectful relationships.

CHARTING THE JOURNEY

This book explores how people build relationships and come to care for one another in the midst of differences in viewpoints, cultural and personal backgrounds, age, gender, race, ethnicity, and other ways people are often grouped or defined. The journey also shows how conflict can be transformed into a worthwhile experience. As communities become increasingly diverse, it becomes all the more important to have an intentional way to help people come to know and respect one another for their differences as well as their commonalities.

Throughout the book, we characterize *indaba* as both a journey and an adventure. The notion of *journey* illustrates that *indaba* is a process rather than an end in itself. This type of journey involves leaving comfortable assumptions behind and stepping into the cultural context of others who may have very different habits, expectations, and assumptions. Adventure reveals those aspects of *indaba* that bring to our awareness new and sometimes surprising insights. Occasionally it challenges how we think about the world and about others. The notion of *adventure* therefore suggests that the experience will be unusual, involve risk, and lead to unexpected and perhaps transformative outcomes.

Chapter 1 tells the story of how *indaba* came into the Anglican Communion and the possibilities that unfolded. It emphasizes that *indaba* is a form of community engagement based on a relationship of mutuality, which differs from many Western understandings of community and practices of listening, dialogue, and decision-making. It also discusses *indaba* as a process of conflict transformation, in which differences remain but no longer block relationships. As a process of mutual listening that strives to develop reciprocal respect across differences, *indaba* also has been used to explore mutual-mission relationships, which differ from the traditional donor-recipient mission approach that has characterized the colonial and modern eras. The challenges and limitations of adapting *indaba* across cultures are also discussed.

Chapter 2 describes the Continuing Indaba and Mutual Listening Project and what it sought to accomplish. It explains how *indaba* was adapted for use across cultures, the dioceses that took part, and how the teams of participants proceeded. The various steps of the journey are sketched out as a conceptual map for the case narratives that follow. The hopes of both the participants and their bishops are expressed at the outset of this journey, based on initial survey and interview data. Chapters 3 through 6 tell the stories of the four Pilot Conversation *indaba* journeys. Each gives rise to a different narrative, based on the varying cultures and concerns of the dioceses and the teams that participated. Although the bishops had planned specific themes to guide the Encounters and Conversation, other themes emerged over the course of each journey, providing vital subtexts that sometimes became central to the *indabas* and their outcomes.

Chapter 3 describes the journey of teams from Derby, England; Mumbai; and New York. It is a story of participants from three parts of the world expanding their limits of understanding, struggling with cultural stress, and finding renewed faith and mission as they encountered one another's cultures, puzzled, wept, recognized differences, and forged personal bonds and commitments. It points to how people seek and find patches of common ground in the midst of sometimes vast cultural and economic differences. It also offers important lessons about the challenges of engaging across differences in culture, language, hierarchy, and dominance and about ways of responding to stress that sometimes create barriers between people.

Teams from Toronto, Hong Kong, and Jamaica discover a sense of sibling relationship in their diverse histories of colonialism in chapter 4. They draw on their own internal cultural histories and adapt them to create new ways of having conversation when they realize that not everyone is participating. It is a story of how participants work on ways to soften the sizable differences of power and status among them so that everyone has an opportunity to be heard and respected, and how they struggle to stay together as family might do when strong differences in beliefs and understanding emerge over sexuality, particularly homosexuality. Despite the pain and struggle to listen, hear, and accept what holds this group in communion, they reaffirm this Anglican family relationship as they learn about and come to understand one another's differing contexts. The three distinct cultural voices work together to create the type of genuine encounter that is at the heart of *indaba*.

How teams from three different African cultures build relationships with one another despite their strong differences in beliefs, worship practices, expectations, and very different cultural histories provides the focus for chapter 5. The teams—from Ho, Ghana; Mbeere, Kenya; and Saldanha Bay, South Africa—learn how culture influences their different understandings of leadership and how faith is lived out. The chapter also tells a story of deep personal pain felt by those on both sides of conflict and how mutual respect for one another can emerge through *indaba* processes without forcing a change of beliefs. A core issue around which the story emerges is the differing roles of women in the life of these three Anglican churches. A key emphasis involves how reconciliation can occur on different levels while team members maintain differences in beliefs and practice.

Chapter 6 offers a unique glimpse at how *indaba* challenges the way that cross-cultural mission partnerships have operated in the past and how it opens up new possibilities for the future. Because the teams—from El Camino Real, California, USA; Gloucester, England; and Western Tanganyika, Tanzania—had formed a partnership before the *indaba* journey, their experience shows how *indaba* can both challenge and deepen existing cross-cultural relationships. Embedded in this account, which is told through the lens of technology and economic disparity, is a story of women discovering and supporting one another across vastly different cultural contexts. It also involves the struggle to cope with various cultural understandings of time, mission, and sexuality, and to find a way to remain together across their differences.

From the four Pilot Conversation journeys, chapter 7 discusses insights and research findings in four key areas: mutual listening, understanding differences and transforming conflict, building relationships, and becoming aware of mutuality of mission. *Indaba* moments, when participants moved into a special space of deep listening, understanding, and strengthened relationship, are analyzed in relation to what characterized them and what is necessary to help reproduce them. The practical aspects of listening and conversing through the use of *indaba* are discussed, along with a number of elements that contributed to *indaba* working well across the different contexts. Special concerns about adapting *indaba* for use in Western cultures are also noted. Additional details on the research and its findings are set forth in the appendix.

Chapter 8 offers examples of how *indaba* and similar processes have been adapted in other ways across the Anglican Communion. These include diocesan *indabas*, the use of the process in diocesan and church governance, and *indabas* among distinct groups such as youth and young adults or those based on race and ethnicity, gender, or sexuality. Some processes have sought to soften and transform conflicts. Others have focused on getting to know and understand one another across cultural or geographic differences. Yet others have sought to build cohesion, a sense of mission, mutual learning, peace, and reconciliation. A discussion of the first Anglican women's *indaba* shows how it can build relationships among women working together across vast cultural and socioeconomic differences.

Chapter 9 looks at the value of *indaba* for helping the Anglican Communion strengthen the ways in which members understand their relationships with one another as part of a diverse, multicultural organization grounded in a shared faith tradition. It also discusses a shift from the need for complete agreement of beliefs and practices to understanding and valuing one another more deeply across human differences. The relationship between *indaba* and Archbishop Justin Welby's commitment to reconciliation is emphasized as the culmination of the *indaba* journey as it is applied in the Communion. The book concludes with further uses and possibilities for *indaba* and similar processes in building global relationships and transforming conflict across communities of faith and beyond.

MAKING THE *INDABA* JOURNEY POSSIBLE

As with any adventure, many were involved in preparing the way for those who actually took part in the *indaba* journey. Foremost is former Archbishop of Canterbury Rowan Williams, who envisioned the need for a Lambeth Conference that would differ from the Lambeth meetings that had preceded it, who took the risk to venture in a new and transformative direction, and whose support for the Continuing Indaba and Mutual Listening Project opened the way for *indaba* to take root locally around the world.

Indaba could not have been possible without Archbishop of Cape Town Thabo Makgoba offering it as a means of gathering and discussing important matters in a different way at Lambeth, similar to conflict processes set forth in the New Testament. All the bishops who took part in that Lambeth meeting and who willingly engaged in the modified *indabas*, who shared their thoughts and suggestions about it afterward, and who were willing to consider trying a form of *indaba* again, some with their own dioceses, have given invaluable gifts that go toward helping others see the many ways in which *indaba* can produce creative pathways forward.

The Rev. Canon Dr. Phil Groves, who oversaw the Anglican Communion's listening process and the use of *indaba*, has worked tirelessly to provide insight and commitment to carry the *indaba* experience forward. Together with the Rev. Canon Flora Winfield, Secretary for Anglican Relations, they helped make possible the Continuing Indaba and Mutual Listening Project. Special gratitude is extended to the Anglican Consultative Council (ACC 14) that authorized the Continuing Indaba (CI) project and affirmed the ongoing use of *indaba* in the Anglican Communion, and to the generous grant that made the CI project possible, administered through the Satcher Health Leadership Institute of the Morehouse School of Medicine.

Dr. Cecelia Clegg, of the University of Edinburgh, brought insights from her experience in working with the peace process in Northern Ireland to the design and facilitation of the Continuing Indaba project. Also vitally important has been the international Reference Group of Anglican leaders in guiding the development of Continuing Indaba, the cross-cultural facilitators who guided the teams in many hours of deeply reflective conversations, and the dedicated commitment of the project administrator, Angharad Parry Jones. Research colleagues, the Rev. Canon Dr. Mkunga H. P. Mtingele and Dr. Joanna Sadgrove, contributed invaluably to the research design, field research, and cross-cultural analyses. Together we stepped into the challenging terrain of multicultural evaluation. Our varied skills, perspectives, and locations made this research possible.

With their dedication and enthusiasm, the teams of clergy and laity from dioceses around the world who planned and hosted encounters in their home locations, traveled to one another's homes and cultures, reflected on their experiences, and entered into sometimes tense and often rewarding *indaba* conversations have helped further the *indaba* journey across the Anglican Communion. The willingness of all participants in the Continuing Indaba project to be interviewed, observed, and asked to fill out survey questionnaires from the start to end of the journey have provided an invaluable overview of the project and the insights that have resulted. *Indaba!* shares those experiences anonymously for others to learn more about the possibilities that an *indaba* journey may hold.

Especially important has been Archbishop of Canterbury Justin Welby's recognition of *indaba* as a focus for reconciliation as he took office, as well as his enthusiasm that *indaba* and the process of honest conversation it represents must continue to be part of the life, mission, and work of the Anglican Communion. His continuing commitment and the affirmations by the Anglican Consultative Council (ACC 15 and ACC 16), as well as the outcomes of the many other *indabas* that have been held since 2012, have been vital to sharing the Anglican Communion's *indaba* story and continuing the process of multicultural and global transformation.

Indaba as an Anglican Communion Adventure

~~~

WHEN YOU COME TO THE END OF A ROAD, your life is about to change. This saying illustrates a major shift that the Anglican Communion made at the dawn of the twenty-first century when it set aside its common Western forms of decision-making and invited *indaba* into its midst. The signposts of this coming change had been clear for at least three decades, especially as bishops from across the world came together for the Lambeth Conferences.

Bishops at the 1988 Lambeth Conference had remarked on the growing cultural diversity of its participants. About fifty African bishops had met as a region for the first time and put together a platform setting forth their concerns. They spoke at that meeting with a message that economically, politically,

1

and theologically challenged those from the West.[1] Discussions over the ordination of female bishops were called out as a "first world" concern, one that was trivial in relation to the pressing issues of apartheid, poverty, and polygamy that faced their own societies.[2] Out of that meeting came a resolution encouraging bishops to seek dialogue with those whose views differed, in the hope that deeper cross-cultural understanding might emerge. A process of consultation also was encouraged on matters that threatened the Communion's unity.[3]

Both the cultural and theological diversity of bishops at the next Lambeth Conference (1998) and the politics and tensions surrounding that meeting made it clear that the familiar Western format of study papers, resolutions, parliamentary debate, and voting was poorly equipped to express the mind of an increasingly diverse Anglican Communion. Political networks and coalitions that crisscrossed churches and continents were becoming commonplace. The issue that coalesced these networks was the place of homosexual persons in the churches, although other complex matters lay just under the surface, such as authority, autonomy, and imperialism. Along with the passage of Resolution I.10, which set forth a traditional heterosexual understanding of marriage and human sexuality, another call was made for a listening process, in this case to hear the voices and experience of homosexual persons who had not been part of the discussions.[4] The road of "business as usual" at Lambeth had ended. Lambeth's future and that of the Anglican Communion itself were at stake.

When Archbishop of Cape Town Thabo Makgoba offered *indaba* from Zulu culture as a possible format and way forward for the 2008 Lambeth Conference, he sought to put forth another way of having sensitive conversations, one that might help the bishops hear and understand a little better some of

---

1 "Africans Critical of Western Policies," 1, 3.
2 See Paula D. Nesbitt, "The Future of Religious Pluralism and Social Policy," 248.
3 "Resolution 1."
4 "Section I.10."

the cultural and contextual differences that affected both their beliefs and how they understood others' concerns. Through mutual listening, they also might be able to explore points of common ground. This new direction would present its own adventures, challenges, and transformative insights.

INDABA: ANOTHER WAY OF GATHERING

Indaba in Zulu culture is a way of gathering the community together for a serious discussion. The word does not translate neatly into English, partly because of the different cultural contexts out of which these two languages arise. In an *indaba,* members of a community meet for the specific purpose of listening to others' views about a concern facing the community.[5] Everyone gathered is encouraged to speak, which helps the community understand the matter from a variety of viewpoints. As a concern becomes more fully understood, the community is better able to identify those places where common ground may exist, despite differences that remain, and to find a way forward together.[6]

In its traditional Zulu context, *indaba* isn't an explicitly religious process. Yet Archbishop Makgoba believed that it could be applied to religious matters when he suggested it for the Lambeth meeting. As he pointed out:

> [A concern in Zulu culture] might be stock theft
> [or] poor service delivery, but in the case of the
> Anglican Communion it might be questions
> related to the way we handle the Bible, sexuality,
> post colonialism, autonomy concerns and our
> many missional challenges.[7]

Indabas are expected to have outcomes. Some may lead to a practical decision. Others may sort out the underlying

---

[5] In different contexts where *indaba* or similar formats are used, not everyone in the community is necessarily included, as will be explained later in the chapter.

[6] Admin. "Essence of Indaba."

[7] Ibid.

meanings and seek deeper understanding of differences or clear tensions away in order to maintain good relationships and improve cohesion in a community. They also may offer advice, build relationships, seek reconciliation, or strengthen commitment to a shared purpose. Because *indaba* depends on listening and considering all views and what might give rise to them, an outcome may be unexpected and sometimes quite creative.

Other cultures have practices that share similarities with *indaba*, such as the *baraza*, a Kiswahili word for a comparable form of communal discussion in parts of Kenya and Tanzania;[8] *padare* among the Shona of Zimbabwe; and *imbizo* or *lekgotla* in other Southern African cultures.[9] *Indaba* also shares some common features of practices such as sacred circles among Canadian First Nations or Indigenous cultures and talking circles of other North American tribal peoples. Similarities between *indaba* and *addaa* in Bengal and *manji* in Punjab (India) also have been noted.[10] The *Loya Jirga* ("great council") in Afghan tradition brings together tribal elders and other leaders to deliberate and offer advice as a communal process as well.[11]

Indaba as Community Engagement

Community holds different meanings across cultures. In the West, its meanings can range from one's residence in a geographic location or one's civic participation to a group having a shared interest, background, identity, or other characteristic

---

[8] A *baraza* is a village or communal meeting involving not only the leaders but also those with least status in the community. John Mark Odour, "Exploring the Baraza Model for Conflict Resolution," 84, 87–88.

[9] *Imbizo* in Xhosa involves a traditional meeting called by the head of the community to listen to news or concerns of the community and for discussion. See Ebenezer Ntlali, "Indaba," 53; Janet Trisk, "Indaba and Power," 73; "Continuing Indaba: What Is Indaba."

[10] Sushma Ramswami, "Under the Banyan Tree," 121–22.

[11] A *Loya Jirga* can be considered as both a process and an event that seeks broad and equitable participation among Afghan people. "The Emergency Loya Jirga Process."

that sets it apart from others. Our English word *community* comes from the Latin roots *com-*, meaning "together with," and *mūnis*, "ready to serve."[12] From these roots also come diverse words such as *ministry* and *communication*. The concepts underlying these words all express relationship and mutuality through both serving and being served.

In some Westernized cultures, this relational notion of community has eroded over the last several decades.[13] Individuals with a high degree of mobility often move in and out of communities and relationships based on shared interests. As a result, it is relatively easy to leave rather than to remain and struggle to live with differences and conflict. Although leaving may reduce feelings of tension, it also robs people of needed skills to develop and maintain cohesion in both their faith and civic communities, as well as in wider society. Moreover, it can lead to isolated thinking and a breakdown of the ability to live together in complex societal and global relationships.

In small towns, villages, and rural areas, or in some cultural groups, community tends to remain more homogenous. It may be strongly identified with a particular place, or perhaps an ethnic, tribal, clan, or other network system of family and kin relationships. In some African cultures, the community provides its members with both identity and agency that arise from a sense of common belonging. This interdependent relationship can be expressed in the saying "A hand does not scratch its own back."[14]

Within Chinese cultural traditions, interdependent relationships are expressed through family networks, symbolized by the family name preceding one's given name.[15] In these contexts, a person's identity and actions are deeply rooted in the larger group, which makes leaving or disidentification a far

---

[12] Walter W. Skeat, *A Concise Etymological Dictionary of the English Language*, 102.

[13] For an American context, see Robert Putnam, *Bowling Alone*; Robert N. Bellah et al., *Habits of the Heart*.

[14] Translation from the Swahili *mkono mmoja haujikuni mgongoni* in D. A. Masolo, *Self and Community in a Changing World*, 241. Also see 142, 250.

[15] Frankie Lee, "'He' Theology," 143.

more serious decision than what is typical in more Westernized contexts.[16] Consequently, many Chinese, African, and other communities that highly value interdependence put more effort into lessening tensions that surround conflicts. The task at hand becomes one of holding people together as an integral part of the community despite the differences and conflicts that remain.

Indaba as a form of community engagement comes out of a particular cultural context where both the community and its members have a strong mutual identity and commitment. It assumes that everyone belongs and that differences can be worked out even if not resolved. Paradoxically, *indaba* offers a way to bring both of these perspectives—contemporary Western and communal tradition—into conversation. Each can learn about the other's cultural understandings of community that inform differing views and actions on given issues.

As such, *indaba* calls participants from Western cultures to reflect more deeply on the value of remaining in community, especially when strong differences and tensions arise, and to search for mutually acceptable outcomes. It also asks those from communal cultures to hear earnestly the differing cultural contexts of others who value being in relationship despite views or practices that produce tension. This type of mutual interaction can create a fresh understanding of catholicity,[17] of living in unity amid diversity, which suggests a postimperial way of building relationships across the world in the twenty-first century.

Indaba as a Challenge to Western Ways

Communal processes such as *indaba* put priority on hearing different viewpoints and maintaining relationships as a key part

---

[16] In Western societies, members of upper-class families have tended to maintain a more cohesive family identity, considering the implications of their actions on the family's reputation as well as its resources.

[17] Mark Chapman elaborates on how interactive pluralism forms a different model of catholicity in his introduction to *Christ and Culture*, 12–13.

of any decision. These differ from the parliamentary debate and majority-rule decision-making typically used in Western cultures and in many of their religious as well as secular organizations. Parliamentary decision-making can be very efficient in large communities, organizations, and societies, especially where a solution is needed quickly. But in Western debate, where an argument favors one position over others, often by critiquing the weaknesses of competing views, a competitive relationship between views emerges. This typically results in a win-loss outcome, especially when decision-making is finalized by a majority vote. Moreover, the debate and voting easily can become politicized, with negotiation little more than trading concessions among competing groups. When the process hardens into adversarial relations, it inhibits the likelihood of exploring and finding any common ground.

Parliamentary processes also have perpetuated elitism among ruling groups, which historically have been dominated by Caucasian men in Western colonial and postcolonial societies. Participants highly skilled in public rhetoric and debate have held an advantage over others not as eloquent or fluent in those discursive forms or perhaps in the language being used. Many historically have relied on relationships with ruling elites to have their concerns represented, which have perpetuated relationships of dependency on others' dominance and power. At its extreme, parliamentary debate and its outcomes have become a performance and its context a stage or theater that is both a contested and managed site for attention and political actions, such as what occurred at the 1998 Lambeth Conference.[18]

Archbishop Thabo Makgoba, when he put forth the idea of *indaba*, had warned that the Anglican Communion's heavy reliance on parliamentary debate could "feed destructive attitudes of competitiveness, dominance and power, over and against one another, that then run through our common

---

18 Paula Nesbitt, "Covenant or Conflict at Canterbury."

life."[19] This reliance also encouraged the growth of polarization through its system of *for* and *against* position-taking. In contrast, African decision-making typically has been based on consensus, where any majority vote would need further consultation with the community, especially with those who had dissented, as a way to maintain unity.[20]

As a legacy of colonialism, Western societies have given little credibility to cultural and social traditions rooted outside of Europe and Europeanized countries. Those whose cultures had been suppressed under colonialism also resultantly have tended to disvalue important aspects of their own traditions.[21] The pull of Westernized society has reinforced this tendency. At risk is the loss of historical understanding and perspectives for addressing conflict from a wide variety of cultures. *Indaba* being brought into the Anglican Communion has symbolized the value of other cultural ways of addressing concerns alongside those commonly used in the West.

The Challenge of Differing Worldviews

Our assumptions, beliefs, experiences, language, culture, and personal background all help us make sense of the world from a certain standpoint. These tend to form a *worldview* that offers a basic interpretive framework as we encounter new situations, ideas, or concerns. We think and speak from particular contexts. The way we ask questions or have conversations comes out of these contexts. Different worldviews can give rise to conflicting expectations that create both bewilderment and tension in cross-cultural conversation. Common Western practices of adversarial debate and critique are viewed negatively in some cultures as a way to shame others or cause them to lose face. In Chinese tradition, for example, the notion of

---

[19] Makgoba, "Anglican Microcosm," 66–67. Also see Thabo Makgoba, "Addressing Anglican Differences."

[20] Vinay Samuel and Christopher Sugden, *Lambeth*, 147.

[21] Lucas Nandih Shamala, "Approaches to Peacemaking in Africa," 14.

face (*Mientze*) extends to one's family reputation and status,[22] so that the loss of face is a serious matter involving more than just the individual. Critique must always be made in a way that maintains an ethos of mutual respect and harmonious relationship.

Reactions across the world to the Westernizing influences of globalization have shown that the values some hold—such as individuality, tolerance, or equality—are not necessarily understood by others in the same way. Even the meaning of life itself can vary. For instance, the African concept of *ubuntu* expresses life as a seamless continuity, from ancestors to unborn descendants, from humanity to the simplest forms of life and to all matter. Personhood is understood as inter-dependence with one another, expressed in the saying "Each person is because the other person is."[23] *Ubuntu* as a way of life through shared identity promotes an ethos of respect and equal treatment, although these concepts are perceived some-what differently than in the West. In another example from Chinese traditional culture, Frankie Lee writes:

> When one's emphasis is on human relation and
> the responsibility of every person to promote
> harmony, and less on the rights of individuals,
> people will then be more willing to forbear one
> another, and to engage open dialogue. This
> is a different way of thinking, in opposition
> to modern Western stress on the individual,
> "rights" and "equality."[24]

As a result, to impose Western understandings of individual autonomy can be understood as pressing an imperialistic

---

22 Lee, "'He' Theology," 137–38.

23 P. T. Mtuze, *Introduction to Xhosa Culture,* 108. Lucas Nandih Shamala has written extensively on *obuntu* among the Abaluya of Western Kenya as an ethos that promotes peacemaking. See Shamala, "Approaches to Peacemaking in Africa," 13–23. Also see Michael Battle, *Ubuntu.*

24 Lee, "'He' Theology," 148.

worldview on other societies, one that in the past has torn apart the fabric of other cultures and their worldviews.

A conflict in worldviews emerged as Anglicanism spread across Britain's nineteenth-century colonial empire. The problems that arose from colonial beliefs in the primacy of British culture and how it should be expressed through the church led to the first Lambeth Conference of Bishops in 1867. Worldviews also collided more than a century later at the 1988 Lambeth Conference. One of many clashes at that meeting arose as bishops sought to pass an emergency resolution to address the role of violence in South Africa and Northern Ireland. Both Archbishops Desmond Tutu and Robin Eames spoke passionately from their own social contexts, one emerging out of frustration with apartheid and the other out of distress over the bombings that had terrorized communities for decades. The clash between sanctioning and condemning the use of violence resulted in the emergence of a statement that sought to mediate between these contexts.[25]

The *indaba* process of the 2008 Lambeth Conference was well suited to help bishops understand the different worldviews that underlay many of the conflicts tearing at the fabric of the Anglican Communion. A North American bishop admitted to understanding, for the first time, an African bishop's concern over his advocacy for sexual-orientation equality. Because they both were part of the Communion, this relationship meant to the people in the African bishop's culture that whatever the North American bishop said or did was just as if his African counterpart had said or done it as well; he would be held personally accountable for the actions of the other bishop. This conversation made clear the assumptions, challenges, and moral limits of autonomy when trying to maintain relationships across worldviews.[26] It also presented a challenge to the Western understanding of tolerance, often seen

---

25 Michael Marshall, *Church at the Crossroads*, 152–54.
26 Field research at the 2008 Lambeth Conference (Nesbitt).

as a solution of minimal harm, which is based on a particular understanding of relationships and boundaries that isn't necessarily the same in other cultures.

INDABA AND CONFLICT

Conflict is a part of human life. It brings different ideas and views to the surface, which can lead to deeper understanding of a situation. It also can be a creative means of learning and growth and an opportunity to deepen relationships. Sammy Githuku notes that in some traditional African cultures, conflict is an aspect of spirituality.[27] Belief in the sacredness of life influences the importance not only of addressing a conflict but also of seeking reconciliation when a conflict has arisen. Lee points out that in traditional Chinese cultures, differing viewpoints are sought in order to understand why a disagreement or conflict has occurred, since the ultimate goal is *he*, or "harmony," and implies that reconciliation will be necessary in order to attain it.[28] In both of these contexts, reconciliation involves seeking to understand the varied concerns and finding a way to move forward together.

Too often the fault lines of conflict are picked up and emphasized without exploring the deep roots that are enmeshed in a range of other issues. This is especially so when conflicts extend across cultures. Differences of worldview, prejudice, and misunderstanding can intensify the concerns already present. Sometimes the means of addressing conflict have relied on top-down authority to control and limit differences. This can suppress a deeper exploration that trustful questioning and conversation among varying viewpoints might stimulate. If one understands the concept of authority to focus on the guidance and growth of others in their belief and faith

---

[27] Sammy Githuku, "Conflict and African Spirituality," 108.

[28] Lee, "'He' Theology,'" 134.

understanding rather than to control or limit it,[29] the implications are clear: conflict can be a constructive opportunity to learn about other perspectives and ultimately to gain wisdom, without escalation to hostility or violence. *Indaba* offers a process to help achieve that.

Indaba as Conflict Transformation

Conflict transformation focuses on building deeper understanding that allows participants to remain in relationship, even though disagreements may linger. According to John Paul Lederach, conflict transformation simultaneously addresses the immediate content of the conflict, the long-standing patterns and differing contexts that surround it, and the relationships of those involved.[30] The aim is not to try to resolve conflict by forcing one solution on everyone, but to find a collaborative solution that can be accepted by all. This involves shifting the structure of participants' relationships in a direction that they feel is mutually respectful and just. The primary process for achieving this is through facilitated dialogue or conversation.[31]

Indaba, as used in the Anglican Communion, is not intended to provide an immediate solution to a conflict or to favor one position over another. As a process of conflict transformation, *indaba* brings to the surface the differences of view within a group or community. Through listening and asking questions to understand the various cultural and other contexts that surround those differences, participants often come to see the conflict in a different way. They may continue to hold their own

---

29 Authority is based on the Latin root (*auctor*) meaning "one who causes to grow," *Auctor* comes from the verb a*ugere,* meaning "to increase." Skeat, *Concise Etymological Dictionary*, 32. Also see the *Online Etymological Dictionary*, s.v. "authority," http://www.etymonline.com/index.php?allowed_in_frame=0&search=a uthority&searchmode=none, and s.v. "author," http://www.etymonline.com/index. php?term=author&allowed_in_frame=0.

30 John Paul Lederach, *The Little Book of Conflict Transformation*, 10–22.

31 Although some point to differences between dialogue and conversation, the terms are used interchangeably in *Indaba!* because of the underlying process of mutual listening and respect.

beliefs, but they try to understand the integrity of the culture, faith, or experience that undergirds others' beliefs. The understanding that the *indaba* process evokes can help break down polarizing stereotypes and build mutual respect that becomes part of discerning a path forward together.

Transforming Conflict in the Anglican Communion

As the issue of homosexuality emerged in the Anglican Communion at the end of the twentieth century, it became a lightning rod for a range of long-standing conflicts on the legacy of colonialism, the imposition of Western values and norms, and for some North Americans and others, a frustration with progressive changes in their churches.[32] Global networks and coalitions linked those who shared similar positions on this issue, despite their differing cultural contexts that influenced how homosexuality was defined or understood or what other issues the concern represented. The issue was sometimes cast as a conflict between the Global North and the Global South, but this dichotomy overlooked the differences that existed within each of these two spheres and only served to confound the complexity of the differing concerns across cultures.[33] For many, authority of Scripture was an overarching symbol that allowed these varying understandings and concerns to coexist under the surface of an issue that had bonded them. For those on the other side, sexual orientation inclusivity was justified through a deep commitment to social and spiritual justice.

Many bishops arrived at the 2008 Lambeth Conference with a sizable amount of wariness and distrust. Most had not been at the 1998 Lambeth meeting, but they had heard about its animosity. They also had experienced the bitter and polarized

---

[32] James E. Solheim, *Diversity of Disunity?*, 196–209; Nesbitt, "Future of Religious Pluralism."

[33] See Samuel and Sugden, *Lambeth*, 4–19.

relationships that followed. Several felt that a meeting based on *indaba*—simply listening to different views and conversing together—would be a waste of time and money. Positions on key issues such as homosexuality seemed to be all too clear. Some could not see the point of participating if nothing would be voted on.

For conflict transformation to occur, participants would first need to become acquainted with one another in a more balanced way, so that they might learn more about their differing cultural contexts and explore where common ground might exist. Those designing the *indaba* process added some structural steps so that participants wouldn't simply retreat into old ways of speaking about the conflict:

- An optional hospitality week was offered by dioceses in the United Kingdom so that visiting bishops could encounter and learn about faith and mission in another cultural setting.

- A meditative retreat led by Archbishop of Canterbury Rowan Williams opened the conference.

- In a daily small-group Bible study based on the Gospel of John, participants reflected on a common passage from the vantage of their own personal understanding and experiences.

- A daily thematic agenda began with celebrating common ground and Anglican identity and then moved on to evangelism, social justice, serving together, safeguarding creation, and Christian witness in a multifaith world. These themes were followed by more sensitive topics such as the abuse of power and human sexuality.[34]

---

[34] "Official Programme & Event Guide."

This structure helped widen the experience so that the *indaba* groups might be a place to listen and learn in a fresh way. Some *indaba* groups, however, felt frustrated that they were not quickly launching into the divisive sexuality issue. A few decided to set their own agendas, based on the interests of participants. Others found that the different themes helped them learn a bit about each other's perspectives on a range of topics, as well as to build trust before the more difficult conversations later in the meeting.[35]

The daily Bible study groups, which met just before the *indabas*, were prized for the conversations they brought forth. The small size of those groups, each with eight bishops, offered an intimacy not possible in the larger, forty-bishop *indaba* groups. Five Bible study groups then came together to form an *indaba* group, and their growing relationships and mutual trust spilled into the *indaba* in ways that helped increase communication and understanding.[36]

By the second week of Lambeth, the mutual respect among the bishops that had emerged, from both the Bible study groups and the *indabas*, also deepened their mutual understanding.[37] Some bishops admittedly were less positive about their *indaba* group experience, citing its large size, insufficient time for conversation, poor facilitation, or the imposition of a daily thematic structure.[38] Yet at the end of the conference, the collected reflections document from the *indabas* stated:

> There has been a wonderful spirit of dialogue
> and we want that to continue beyond the
> Conference by every means possible—"the indaba
> must go on," as one group expressed it. For many
> of us have discovered more fully why we need
> one another and the joy of being committed to

---

35   Field research, 2008 Lambeth Conference (Nesbitt).

36   On-site interviews, 2008 Lambeth Conference (Nesbitt).

37   Clive Handford, "Celebrating Common Ground," 53.

38   On-site interviews (Nesbitt). Also see Reflections Group, "Lambeth Indaba."

one another. At a time when many in our global
society are seeking just the sort of international
community that we already have, we would be
foolish to let such a gift fall apart.[39]

A number of bishops commented that although they had not
changed their minds, they had come away with a greater
appreciation and understanding of the complexities surrounding their differences. Most hadn't expected that *indaba*
would resolve the deep conflicts, but they were transformed in
a way that caused many to return home more willing to try to
stay together as a Communion. Some bishops also had developed relationships across provinces that would result in new
cross-cultural mission experiences.[40]

INDABA: ANOTHER WAY OF LISTENING

Selective listening, as part of our human condition, allows
us to hear what we need from an array of voices and sounds,
while ignoring the rest. Some may listen *only* to gain what they
want to know. Others may listen on several levels—beyond the
words spoken, to the emotions and the surrounding context of
what is being said, in order to understand more fully what the
speaker intends. Conflict transformation depends on this mul-
tilevel way of listening.

In Western cultures, critical listening styles are highly
valued: one listens to identify strengths and weaknesses in
another's argument. Here, the focus of listening is on the
relative value or merit of what is being said. In other cultures, listening may occur as a means of paying respect, of
recognizing the speaker's personhood in the community, or

---

[39] Reflections Group, "Lambeth Indaba," 4.

[40] For instance, one of the Continuing Indaba pilot conversations would be built
on a mission relationship among three diocesan bishops that had arisen out of the
Lambeth Conference.

of building and maintaining relationships. In a culturally diverse group, these may all occur at once, which leads to different assumptions about how people understand what has been said. Effective listening is influenced by other factors as well, including differences in vocabulary, dialect, language, culture, knowledge, or experience, as well as the perceived prestige of the speaker.

Listening is a core aspect of *indaba*. Each person listens to understand a viewpoint or situation and any circumstances surrounding it from the position of the speaker. The listening needs to be open-minded, without evaluating or critiquing what is being said, particularly if the listener may hold a differing view. Questions may be asked in order to understand more fully, but they are not intended to provoke an argument or criticize a speaker's viewpoint. Through this process, *indaba* participants engage in both mutual listening and mutual learning about the complexity of a concern from many angles.[41]

According to Archbishop Makgoba, a concern facing the Anglican Communion has been that too little careful mutual listening has occurred.[42] As a result, there has been little real understanding of one another, which has led to both insensitivity and misunderstandings that have threatened the viability of the Communion. The ability to listen beyond what one expects, or what makes one comfortable, is vital to deeper understanding and the development of wisdom. The mutual understanding that develops helps build relationships of mutual trust.

Listening and the Problem of Inequality

Mutual listening processes such as *indaba* have assumed an equality of each voice being valued and respected within a group. However, differences in traits such as age, gender,

---

[41] Another way of translating the Zulu word *indaba* has been "respectful engagement." Mark Chapman et al., editors' preface to *Christ and Culture*, xviii.

[42] Makgoba, "Addressing Anglican Differences."

race, ethnicity, family status, education, and experience, as well as the varying ability to use a shared language with the same vocabulary or proficiency, often result in disparities that affect not only who is more likely to speak but also how a voice is heard or respected by others. Traditional *indabas* within Southern African communal cultures, for instance, typically limited participation to male members of the community as a way of controlling differences. Women were excluded, as were uncircumcised men in those communities where circumcision signified full membership.[43] Here, it is important to keep in mind cultural differences in how societies are organized, as well as how the concepts of equality and equity have been differently understood. Even Westernized understandings of equality historically have excluded those who weren't male and of European racial and cultural descent.

When *indaba* was adapted for the 2008 Lambeth Conference, only bishops participated, which meant that they shared a similar status in church authority and collegiality. Some status differences existed in the type of office the bishops held (archbishop, diocesan bishop, assisting bishop, and so forth), the size and economic situation of their diocese, their gender, fluency in English, and other aspects. However, the shared bond of episcopal authority created a level of cohesion necessary for mutual listening to be able to occur.[44]

Radical equality across all differences is profoundly difficult to achieve. It also assumes a Westernized understanding of equality that may differ from that of other cultural contexts. In some cultures, to express views that differ from a person of higher status can be considered disrespectful. Although participants from Western cultures may have less concern over

---

[43] Trisk, "Indaba and Power," 73; also see Douglas, "Equipping for God's Mission," 172. Male circumcision was considered a rite of passage into full membership in the community, which served as a basis for inclusion. Women's views presumably were represented through the men who participated in the *indaba*.

[44] *Indaba* groups at the 2008 Lambeth Conference varied in their effectiveness. Some bishops felt that cultural status differences affected others' ability to hear them; they also felt that sincere efforts were being made to try to listen and understand. Field research and interviews, 2008 Lambeth Conference (Nesbitt).

expressing personal differences of view, hierarchal and other status differences still affect the extent to which some may speak or remain silent. For example, religious leaders may dominate a group conversation, unaware that younger or less experienced members are silent.[45] A discussion also can be framed in a way that limits or excludes some participants, even if unintentionally. These disparities become even more far-reaching in cross-cultural listening, where differences in cultural customs, language, and values such as hierarchy can lead to misunderstanding and disappointed expectations regarding the candor or equality of participation expressed in the group.

Silence, for instance, often is understood in Western culture as meaning that others agree with what has been said, as evident when parliamentary processes are used. Yet living histories of marginalization and oppression have given silence a different meaning for many, where expressing different views would not be heard or could result in further subjugation. Moreover, the meaning of silence varies by culture. Agreement cannot be assumed. If the dominant voices continue speaking while others are silent, assuming that others have nothing further to add, then mutual listening has not occurred.

Some inequalities that inhibit mutual listening can be offset. The emergence of equality, when defined as mutual respect, depends on participants who hold a dominant status being able to listen and regard the thoughts of others as having equal worth. A common practice is for high-status members to signal that differing views are truly welcome. This creates a Durkheimian boundary of sacred space where all hold equality in the moment, although they will reassume status or role differences outside the gathering.[46] Other practices involve reframing a conversation in a way that makes it easier for more members to share their views, using various methods such as mutual invitation or speaking in turn, and exercising deep

---

45 Field research on the Continuing Indaba and Mutual Listening Project (Nesbitt). See also Phil Groves and Angharad Parry Jones, *Living Reconciliation*.

46 Emile Durkheim, *The Elementary Forms of the Religious Life*, chapter 1.

listening to make space for others to speak at their own pace. The use of small groups based on shared characteristics, with each later giving a brief summary to the overall group, offers another helpful way of mutual listening, especially where some may feel inhibited about speaking to the overall group or where the topic is sensitive. To listen openly and fully not only creates deeper understanding and mutual respect but also strengthens the ties that bind relationships together.

INDABA AND MISSION

Nowhere has the need for transformative relationships been more critical than in how mission has been carried out. Mission traditionally has been understood as a geographic and numerical spread of a faith, moving outward from a core or home location. Since religion always is lived out through a particular culture, when it spreads to other locations it transmits certain values from its host or donor culture. Mission therefore becomes a delicate balance between sharing a religion's core meanings and imposing on others one's own cultural understandings and norms regarding how it should be lived out.

Christianity in its early years developed a wide diversity in how it was embraced across different cultures. But this raised questions over Christian identity that the emerging church needed to face. Would Christianity remain closely tied to fulfilling Jewish law, or was the core of Christianity's message truly adaptable to other peoples and cultures? Great tension arose among early church leaders over whether obedience to Jewish law was theologically required, as well as whether Jewish Christians should hold higher status than other converts to Christianity. Strong cross pressures were applied so that relations of mutuality and tolerance of differences might exist across varying cultural contexts in which the Christian communities were developing.

Centralized control within Christianity developed over the

early centuries, eroding many of the varieties of Christian expression as leaders struggled over what was authoritative or heretical to Christian faith and practice. In Western Christianity, mission became permeated with imperial and colonial aims. For both Catholic and Protestant missionaries, the gospel was nuanced in ways familiar to their own European and North American cultures, which resulted in imposing moral values and worship styles based on those cultural understandings. The Anglican Church was exported to support British colonial projects, but it also was shared through evangelism, and Anglican evangelists and their counterparts in other Protestant denominations often mirrored the types of dominant-subordinate relationships that colonialism had fostered. This not only disvalued other cultures but also often made religious motives into agents of imperialism and hegemony.[47]

Postcolonial views of mission have challenged this center-to-periphery model, relying instead on relations of mutuality. Mission needs to be grounded in interdependence and mutual responsibility.[48] Mutual mission is postcolonial in its assumption that all have something to give or teach and all have something to learn from one another. Both parties must be donors and also must be recipients. Any exchange of financial resources must be secondary to the purpose of the mission partnership and must be accompanied by a clear mutual awareness of what the other partner offers that also is of value.[49] The empowerment that arises when former recipients realize they have something of value to offer their partners not only helps lessen the disparity in power relations that a one-way flow of economic resources creates but also forms the conditions for mutual mission to thrive. Although it may not be possible to

---

[47] Wendy Fletcher, "Living Church after the Fall," 161.

[48] A growing movement toward mutuality in mission relations within Anglicanism, following World War II, led to the 1963 Anglican Congress (Toronto) document, *Mutual Responsibility and Interdependence in the Body of Christ*, which broke ground for Partners in Mission and other mission efforts modelled on mutuality in relationships. David E. Sumner, *The Episcopal Church's History 1948–1985*, 163–64; *Proceedings of the Anglican Congress, Toronto, 1963*, 118.

[49] Phil Groves, *Global Partnerships for Local Mission*, 18–19.

dismantle the historical interplay of colonial influences within worldwide Anglicanism, choices can be made to focus on aspects within Anglican tradition that are grounded in mutual respect and affirmation. These can be helpful in transforming relationships across cultures. As Christopher Duraisingh understands this postcolonial vision, global Anglicanism must become multicultural and multivocal, with each voice having an opportunity to speak and be given serious consideration.[50]

Indaba as Mutual Mission

The hope for *indaba* at the 2008 Lambeth Conference was based on an understanding of mission rooted in mutuality: the reconciliation of all humanity and creation into relationship with God and one another through Jesus Christ.[51] Unity in the church was perceived as the Body of Christ, valuing diversity in its midst and in its various expressions. Leaders hoped that *indaba* might create a widespread shift in the understanding of mission from a traditional donor-recipient model to one of mutuality that would both equip bishops for mutual involvement and generate mutual respect across cultures.

The shift to mutual mission was rooted in a deeper change that was necessary: an identity for the Anglican Communion that affirmed cultural diversity rather than perpetuated colonial hegemony. It was hoped that *Indaba* would bring about an authentic conversation about Anglican identity and what that meant in a multicultural Communion. The richness of differing worldviews that *indaba* provided could offer opportunities for mutual learning, deepening relationships, and developing respect that might make this conversation possible. In this way, the Lambeth experiment with *indaba* might open a fresh path forward for a transformation in the Anglican Communion's self-understanding.

---

[50] Christopher Duraisingh, "Toward a Postcolonial Re-visioning of the Church's Faith, Witness, and Communion," 347.

[51] Douglas, "Equipping for God's Mission," 168.

ADAPTING *INDABA* ACROSS CULTURES

Taking one cultural practice and applying it to another culture is quite common, but it can be both challenging and controversial. From one viewpoint, the use of *indaba* elsewhere may be just part of a wider process of cultural diffusion. Ideas and practices have been borrowed and adapted across cultures throughout history—through travel and migration, political conquest and colonialism, economic trade, religious mission, and other means of communication.

From another viewpoint, practices such as *indaba* come out of specific cultural understandings. To export them to other cultures, as if they were a commodity, not only misrepresents a practice but also robs a culture of a distinctive feature of its identity. Cultural co-optation, where a dominant culture adapts practices to its interests, often without regard for the host culture and the context from which the practice emerged, has been sharply criticized.[52]

Janet Trisk warns about uncritically using *indaba* outside its traditional village context, since it could be distorted as a way of deliberately excluding voices and perpetuating patriarchal power.[53] Also, when *indaba* is adapted for use in cross-cultural situations, the sense of individualism and indifference among some from Western cultures can create sizable tension with those whose cultures are deeply rooted in the importance of maintaining relationships. This can play out through differing expectations over how candidly and autonomously participants will speak.

In adapting *indaba* across cultures, there is a risk of changing it in a way that is unrecognizable or subverts its original purpose. Archbishop Makgoba, when introducing *indaba* to the Anglican Communion, addressed this concern by writing:

---

[52] George E. Tinker, *Missionary Conquest*, 121–22.
[53] Trisk, "Indaba and Power," 73.

> *Indaba* is not about trying to make everyone
> into Amazulu, nor about transplanting elements
> from one culture into a completely foreign and
> inappropriate context. I also know that *indaba*
> is far from perfect—it is not always conducted
> inclusively, and it can be abused by leaders intent
> on getting their own way.[54]

Makgoba created a bridge between *indaba*'s traditional context and its use in the Communion by making point-by-point comparisons to similarities in New Testament Scripture in 1 Corinthians 12 regarding how Christians are to live and act together when their differences arouse concern or provoke conflict.

As Archbishop Makgoba worked with the group adapting *indaba* for the 2008 Lambeth Conference, the parliamentary process of previous Lambeth meetings was set aside, and *indaba*'s use paid respect to a culture that had been marginalized through colonialism and Western imperialism. As Jonathan Draper writes:

> There is a nice irony that the first Lambeth
> Conference was called, in part, to decide whether
> or not the Bishop of Natal, John Colenso, had
> gone too far in accommodating Zulu culture
> and the fact that the most recent Lambeth
> Conference met in Indaba groups—a Zulu form
> of meeting.[55]

The risk in adapting *indaba* was that changes made to accommodate both the Lambeth meeting's aims and Western cultural sensibilities could distort it to the point that it might not be useful. Several African bishops had commented in interviews during the Lambeth meeting that the process used was

---

54   Makgoba, "Anglican Microcosm," 68.
55   Jonathan Draper, "Continuing Indaba," 16.

"not *indaba*."[56] In a traditional *indaba*, participants might know each other well and would share both language and culture. The conversation would be directed toward finding a shared way forward as a specific outcome. In the Lambeth *indaba*, few bishops knew one another, nor did they know much about the others' cultural contexts. The sessions were too short, and the daily themes were problematic for some. Relationships and trust needed to be built before decisions and outcomes might be possible. Nonetheless, the African bishops that were interviewed also commented that the Lambeth *indaba* was better than what had been used at previous meetings. It provided an opportunity to speak and be heard, to explain and to learn, and to build relationships that otherwise might not have occurred.

The Limits of *Indaba*

Indaba fits well with a postcolonial ethos of mutual respect and mission, but there are limits to how effectively it can be adapted across cultural differences. A Western assumption of gathering people together for *indaba*, expecting that they will participate as autonomous individuals in the conversation, is bound to collide with other cultural worldviews. Cultural differences in communication styles, in what is appropriate to discuss and with whom; differences in language fluency; disparities in status or dominance—all can test the limits of an *indaba*'s effectiveness across cultures.

Another concern over the cross-cultural use of *indaba* involves the exposure of participants to different understandings and realities that may prompt dissatisfaction with their own culture's norms and way of life. Vast socioeconomic differences, varying customs for gender roles, the availability of consumer goods, and other disparities have raised concerns over the corrupting influence of Westernization on other cultures. Others have countered that protections can lead to a condescending paternalism. When participants show respect for

---

56 Brief interviews conducted during unstructured time following the daily *indabas* at the 2008 Lambeth Conference (Nesbitt).

each other's differences, recognizing both the value and limitations of their varying cultural contexts, they can help rebalance such concerns, as occurred during one of the Continuing Indaba Pilot Conversations (see chapter 6).

When *indaba* is used in a cross-cultural setting, people from all the participating cultures need to be involved in planning. If the leadership is dominated by Western understandings and worldviews, those from other cultures may feel coerced into difficult conversations on topics not ordinarily discussed with strangers or forced to participate in other ways that offend their customs and practices. Moreover, planning must include participants directly affected by a concern so that the participants hear all sides. When the Lambeth Design Group adapted *indaba*, members from the West were in the minority. Although the Lambeth *indabas* included only bishops invited to the meeting, a variety of workshops and parallel events offered opportunities to converse with Bishop Gene Robinson, who had been excluded from the meeting, and other Anglicans who were openly gay, as well as to listen to transgender people, persecuted Christians across the world, youth, Pentecostal and Roman Catholic guests, and others.

Indaba also needs sizable amounts of time to find common ground and a pathway forward. It is neither a quick nor easy way to make decisions, especially with a large group. From a Western perspective, *indaba* represents a long-term investment in building relationships and mutual understanding. These are necessary for the kind of trust to emerge that will increase candor and respect for differences. As the Lambeth *indabas* showed, an *indaba* with virtual strangers is possible, provided that the aims are limited, such as mutual listening and understanding, which must first be in place before the group can move further. Over time, greater communal engagement and commitment can emerge, and then mutually agreed-upon decisions become more easily achieved.

Indaba and similar processes depend on relationships of authenticity and mutual respect among participants. Where participants hold different levels of status in a group, those with higher or dominant status must take steps to create space for others to participate equally in the conversation. Dominant voices can be unaware of how easily they take over a discussion or they aren't hearing everyone, which erodes the ethos necessary for *indaba* conversation. Also, when participants hold perspectives that limit their willingness to listen openly to others, when they try to convert others to their viewpoint, or when they hold private motives that run against the goodwill of the *indaba*, they disrupt the trust built within the group and the prospect of authentic conversation. Other limitations arise when people speak as a performance or with a desire to impress others with their knowledge. *Indaba* processes depend on personal authenticity and respect for mutual trust to develop.

In sum, *indaba* is successful across cultures only insofar as the leaders and participants are prepared to exhibit sensitivity toward other cultural understandings and relationships, which can help them reflect on the assumptions they bring to the conversation, listen openly, and encourage one another to speak. An *indaba* must create a safe and accessible space for all present to be heard and respected as companions on a shared journey. *Indaba* is at its best in situations where differences of view or understanding exist, where the need to find a solution that respects different perspectives is important, and where time can be invested in the process. In some cases, an *indaba* or other type of mutual listening can work alongside more pragmatic forms of decision-making, so long as the group is not expected to reach a decision before all are ready to do so. Above all, the requirement that all voices with a stake in an issue or concern are included and heard must be taken seriously.

THE JOURNEY FORWARD

At the start of this century, the Anglican Communion faced a dead end on the road of Western imperialism, and a growing diversity of views had arisen over which path was the right one for it to take. *Indaba* offered a way forward, one that could bring that diversity into conversation and help build authentic multicultural relationships across vast differences of geography and understanding. Where the *indaba* path is chosen and followed, cohesion results and common ground can be cultivated along the way. This provides a trustworthy foundation for a fresh road on which to travel together on a shared journey of mission and ministry.

This next phase of the journey is not without many continuing challenges, including the use of *indaba*. The next several chapters share the stories of the Pilot Conversations that followed the Lambeth Conference, as well as how *indaba* helped build relationships and transform a number of conflicts. Altogether, the introduction of *indaba* has helped the Anglican Communion move into a different future. In this way, it has come to be a symbol of a shift that recognizes life with one another has changed in a more interdependent and global way.

~2~

Preparing for the Journey

The Continuing Indaba Project

~~~

AS THE BISHOPS JOURNEYED HOME from Canterbury after the 2008 Lambeth Conference, a haunting question remained. Would the *indaba* experience at Lambeth have any lasting effect on the Anglican Communion? After listening to one another at Lambeth, some bishops had begun to understand some of the cultural differences that influenced the issues and tensions they faced. The ability to learn about one another's cultures was a powerful aid in helping them begin to understand the differences of view and mission priorities. Cultural boundaries were breached in a way that helped mutual respect and trust develop.

During Lambeth, some bishops had privately met with U.S. Episcopal Bishop Gene Robinson, the only diocesan bishop who hadn't been invited, to try to understand his viewpoint as the only openly gay partnered bishop in the Anglican Communion, despite their disagreement on the matter of homosexuality. Bishop Robinson was in Canterbury during the conference. Another bishop spoke of a colleague, opposed to homosexuality, who had contacted him about developing a partnership for AIDS education. Three bishops from different continents, holding conflicting views on several topics, vowed to continue their conversation begun at Lambeth and formed a partnership to get to know one another better and share mission. Common ground—in compassion and in the need for education and shared mission—allowed these bishops to imagine how they might work together despite their differences of view.

In all, bishops who held differing views were being heard and understood in a fresh way. They may not have changed their positions, but they had begun to be more understanding and respectful of their differences. In this manner, *indaba* had come to symbolize a shift in heart if not in belief. The possibility existed for them to venture forward together as companions who strongly differed, rather than as adversaries. But what was necessary for the journey to continue?

FROM *INDABA* TO CONTINUING INDABA

During the autumn after the Lambeth Conference, an enthusiasm to continue *indaba* opened a window to explore how it might be used more widely in the Anglican Communion. Many wanted laity and clergy also to participate. In the wake of the Lambeth Conference, a group had been appointed to make recommendations. Its report emphasized that a listening process needed to continue across the Communion.[1] In response, the Rev. Canon Phil Groves, who had overseen the *indaba* process

---

[1] Windsor Continuation Group, "Report to the Archbishop of Canterbury," 5–6.

at Lambeth, and the Rev. Canon Flora Winfield, secretary for Anglican relations, proposed a project to help extend *indaba* more widely. It became known as Continuing Indaba.[2]

A key hope for Continuing Indaba was to help mutual listening and conversation continue on issues that were dividing the Communion. Although human sexuality was a core issue for most churches, Continuing Indaba recognized that the topic needed to arise and be discussed in relation to the cultural frameworks and concerns of those who were in conversation together. For some, other issues might be more urgent or pressing: polygamy, women's ordination, youth, or perhaps the church's public voice on social justice. A conversation also needed to include those who were directly affected by any concern being discussed. If homosexuality was discussed, for example, then the conversation must include gay and lesbian persons.

Continuing Indaba was brought to life in the months that followed. Known as the Continuing Indaba and Mutual Listening Project, it put people at the grassroots into conversation with one another across the Communion. It was based on a research proposal to develop both theoretical and practical models for cross-cultural use and was funded through Morehouse School of Medicine's Satcher Health Leadership Institute.[3] In May 2009, the Anglican Consultative Council, which had used an *indaba* format at its meeting in Jamaica,[4] formally approved it. Since this type of process had never been tried, it would be evaluated for how well it met its proposed aims: faithfulness to Anglicanism, effectiveness in enabling mutual mission, and replicability in other situations across the Anglican Communion.[5]

---

2 Groves had overseen the listening process through the Anglican Communion Office. Winfield was part of Archbishop of Canterbury Rowan Williams's leadership group at Lambeth Palace. The archbishop supported the Continuing Indaba project.

3 "Continuing Indaba and Mutual Listening in the Anglican Communion." At the time the proposal was submitted, the Satcher Health Leadership Institute was named the Satcher Center for Excellence in Sexual Health.

4 Trisk, "Indaba and Power," 73.

5 See "The Continuing Indaba and Mutual Listening Project."

CONTINUING INDABA
AND MUTUAL LISTENING PROJECT

Two objectives guided the project, known simply as Continuing Indaba. First, the conversations needed to create an ethos where mutual listening and understanding could occur. This meant that debates and other competitive behavior, as well as pressure to conform to a particular viewpoint, needed to be avoided. To keep these from arising, no immediate decisions would be made on sensitive issues. Second, the conversations needed to cultivate a sense of equality across differences of culture, language, viewpoint, age, gender, race, ethnicity, and other attributes. Additionally, it was hoped that the cross-cultural relationships developed in Continuing Indaba might contribute to mutual mission both locally and globally.[6]

A test of Continuing Indaba's success would be whether participants could remain in conversation across their differences once their deepest concerns and conflicting views were brought up in conversation, and also whether they could continue to work together with mutual respect without trying to convert others to their viewpoint. Ultimately, if successful, *indaba* might help strengthen commitments to one another across the Communion.

One of the first steps was to gather a Reference Group of advisors who would offer impartial advice as the project began to take shape. The Rt. Rev. David Chillingworth, primus of the Scottish Episcopal Church, headed the Reference Group. Phil Groves and Flora Winfield, who represented the Anglican Communion Office and Lambeth Palace, oversaw development of the project.

Since little had been written on *indaba*, resources needed to be developed as a way to help people understand its use in the Anglican Communion. Theologians and church leaders met at Resource Hub consultations that were held in Africa, Hong

---

6   Draper, "Continuing Indaba," 22.

Kong, India, the West Indies, the United States, and England. They were to focus on ways that people seek to sort out conflicts or communicate in different cultures. They also were to consider how *indaba* might be adapted in a way that was compatible with both Anglican faith and its differing cultural contexts.[7] Many of these resources were gathered into a book, *Creating Space*,[8] which would be provided to participants in the Continuing Indaba conversation journeys.

The next step involved putting together a workable format. Just as bishops had been invited to stay for a week in one of the United Kingdom dioceses to experience local Anglican life and mission before the 2008 Lambeth Conference began,[9] Continuing Indaba would have participants encountering one another's cultures before the formal *indaba* conversations. Cecelia Clegg, who had worked with a Northern Ireland process where Catholics and Protestants experienced one another's daily life and saw the conflict from the other's context, was the *indaba* project's design and facilitation consultant.[10] Continuing Indaba would create an ambitious global exchange of understanding, with teams visiting one another's home cultures to begin to understand how issues facing their churches might have both similarities and significant differences.

A Cross-Cultural *Indaba* Design

In traditional *indabas*, since participants would share a culture and likely know each other, conversations typically involved differences of viewpoint rather than worldview. For a cross-cultural *indaba*, participants would need to have a personal awareness of one another's cultural contexts, which would help them understand how an issue or concern might affect

---

7 "Continuing Indaba: Celebrating a Journey," 8.

8 Phil Groves and Jonathan Draper, *Creating Space*.

9 Douglas, "Equipping for God's Mission," 172.

10 Dr. Clegg was convenor of theology and ethics, School of Divinity, University of Edinburgh and is now retired. See Cecelia Clegg, "Between Embrace and Exclusion," 140–53.

each other in very different ways. Embedded in the *indaba* design were encounters with one another's dioceses and cultures, along with formal *indaba* conversations that would depend on relationships built among participants and possibly might translate into mutual support for one another's missions beyond the end of the project.

The *indaba* participants would be part of a Pilot Conversation group that consisted of eight-person teams from three dioceses in different parts of the Anglican Communion. Within each Pilot Conversation, the teams could explore whatever they shared in common and where they differed, without pressure to agree or make decisions. They would begin their relationship with a planning meeting for their bishops, followed by team visits to one another's cultures, called Encounters (fig. 2.1).

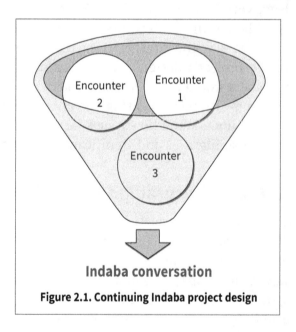

Indaba conversation

Figure 2.1. Continuing Indaba project design

Each Encounter was designed as a brief cultural immersion that would introduce the visiting participants to everyday life in the host's culture, with the hope that questions might arise over how their differing cultures affect their various worldviews and viewpoints. Encounters could vary depending on what the host team thought might best help the guests understand the culture and mission of the diocese. The role of the Encounter was to create the space for guests to have an authentic experience of *otherness*, where they might feel keenly aware of different cultural norms and activities, in order to help them reflect on how a shared concern might be understood from another vantage point. All diocesan teams would serve as both hosts and guests.

The Encounters, lasting about one week in length, had three phases. The *Welcome phase* offered an orientation to the diocese, its mission priorities, and the surrounding culture where its mission was carried out. In the *Diverse Activities phase*, participants would experience the everyday life of the diocese, which might include visits to schools, sheltered workshops, local parishes, and other sites that might help visitors understand both the diocese and its surrounding culture. In the *Closure and Departure phase*, the diocesan teams would meet separately to reflect on their experiences and identify questions they would like to ask each other. The teams then would meet in a facilitated session to share their questions and reflections. This was not to be a formal *indaba* conversation, but rather an opportunity to come to understand one another better in preparation for the formal conversation.

Ideally, guests were to stay in the homes of the host team or others in the host diocese, although in several dioceses this was not feasible because of the vast geographic distance between where host participants lived or the tight living quarters common in that community or region. Sometimes guests and often hosts would stay together in retreat centers, hotels, or other facilities. In that case, they lost some opportunity for intimate conversations with local families, but they did gain time to talk informally together about their experiences.

The Encounters were to avoid simply showing visitors a good time, showing only the most positive aspects of the diocese, or showing projects that needed funding with the hope that teams would return home to raise money. These would not accomplish the Encounter purpose and could reinforce traditional donor-recipient mission relations and notions of inequality.

Between Encounters, participants were to reflect on their experiences and note their thoughts and reflections in private journals. It was hoped that the three teams would grow in relationship with one another across the three Encounters in ways that would build understanding and trust.

Holding the indaba conversation

At the end of the Encounters, the three teams met at a neutral location for a three-day formal *indaba* conversation hosted by the Continuing Indaba staff. A pair of facilitators experienced in cross-cultural dialogue would help the teams create a sense of safe space and encourage them to ask questions or speak what was on their minds and hearts. The facilitators' role was to help keep the conversation moving in an open and constructive direction, without trying to stifle conflict or force a resolution.[11] They would design and adjust the format of each *indaba* to help participants engage as fully as possible.

Unlike a traditional *indaba*, here the goal was not to come to a decision. Instead, the *indaba* offered an opening for earnest conversation, with the hope that a continuing relationship among the teams might allow further conversations to occur. The objectives were to take participants to an uncomfortable place in the journey of their relationship and to help them find ways of listening and speaking with each other about the differences that had emerged.[12] This would require openness to hear what made one uncomfortable, self-discipline to speak only for oneself, courage to stay with the process, and perseverance when the path appeared most difficult. It also would take faith.

---

[11] Most of the facilitators had taken part in a preparatory workshop before the start of the conversations.

[12] Cecelia Clegg, "Instructions for Final Conversation."

The *indaba* conversations typically opened with a brief orientation by the Continuing Indaba project management about what to expect. Evaluators and ecumenical observers were introduced. Participants were able to decide where and when they could be observed and when recordings and note-taking were to be suspended.[13] The facilitators typically then invited each participant to share something from home that they were bringing to the conversation and explain what it represented. In turn, as participants discussed their objects, they placed them at the center of the large circle around which they were sitting.[14] They were then invited to express the hopes and concerns they brought to the conversation. The next task would be to decide on the norms and boundaries that would help them feel safe in the conversation. This step often took longer than expected, as concerns were raised over power and marginalization that needed to be worked out. Teams who had just come from their third Encounter also needed time to reflect on their experience before moving ahead into the *indaba* conversation.

"What shall we talk about?" was a persistent question across the *indaba* conversations. Participants didn't feel that there were too few topics, but that many topics could lead in both interesting and yet difficult directions. They spent a lengthy time on deciding those topics. In some cases, the process would become an *indaba* itself. Varying customs as to what was appropriate to speak about publicly or to share with new colleagues added to the hesitancies.

Each day of *indaba* conversation was framed by worship and Bible study, much as it had been at the 2008 Lambeth Conference. At Lambeth, a form of *Lectio Divina* introduced by the Southern African delegation had been used; this was adapted by Continuing Indaba. The format made reflection on

---

[13] For the purpose of the research project, a pair of evaluators and sometimes an ecumenical observer watched the *indaba* from behind the participant circle. *Indaba* project staff from the Anglican Communion Office (ACO) were present to serve as a resource to the group but did not participate in conversations unless certain information was needed.

[14] Articles could be removed when the group wasn't present, and then returned to the circle when the group reconvened.

Scripture both vividly descriptive and personal. Participants would name a word in the passage that caught their attention. After the passage was read a second and sometimes third time, and they again named a word that stirred them, participants in turn might describe where the passage touched their life or what was God calling them to do or be. In some cases, this process also included a dialogue where others might ask questions to understand more fully the context of what they were hearing. As with Lambeth, the biblical reflection sometimes seamlessly spilled into the *indaba* conversation that followed and often helped make it easier to have sensitive, meaningful discussions.

During the conversation plenaries, everyone sat in a large circle, directing their questions and thoughts toward the center, rather than to specific individuals. These plenaries allowed everyone to hear what was said. They were interspersed with several small group *indabas* where more intimate conversations could take place. Key points made in the small groups were then shared with the entire group.

At the end of the third day, as the facilitators began a process of summary and closure to help the group end the *indaba* part of their journey, participants were asked to express something they would like to say to the group. Uttering good-byes to others often was difficult, accompanied by hopes to stay in touch online or through Facebook. Occasionally future meetings were planned, although primarily as individuals or as small groups.

Facilitating the indaba

In large groups with lively discussions, the voices speaking quickly and loudly are often the ones that are heard. Those who feel that their comments are more important or worthwhile may interrupt or talk over others, sometimes unaware of what they are doing. As a result, many valuable insights are unheard, especially from those who feel marginalized from the conversation. Such patterns do not represent an *indaba* approach to conversation. Thus it is necessary to have a leader, or facilitator, who does not participate in the conversation in the same way as others. This person can observe when a conversation is becoming dominated by a few voices, or when others are not speaking, and can shift the way that the conversation is unfolding so that everyone has an opportunity to be heard and understood.

Indaba facilitators need special skills that give them the ability to understand various dynamics that might arise when cross-cultural groups are in conversation or other forms of diversity are present that could result in skewed conversation patterns of dominance and marginality. They need to be sensitive to different cultural understandings and behaviors, such as body language and the role of silence, that could be misunderstood by others. Often their experience of being "the other" in various social or cultural circumstances helps increase awareness of what is needed to have authentic conversation across sizable differences of status and other traits, including what may be helpful for those feeling marginalized to be able to participate fully. They also need to be sensitive to when participants are feeling anxiety.[15]

Cross-cultural groups ideally should be cofacilitated by facilitators from different cultural backgrounds and perspectives. Cofacilitation is helpful to any group. Each facilitator may observe and hear what is happening somewhat differently, and thus cofacilitation allows for greater awareness of cultural differences that may be present. Sometimes participants may identify more with one facilitator or the other. With the facilitators working together, they keep participants more fully engaged and also can demonstrate how differences can work together, modeling cross-cultural understanding and collaboration for the group. Moreover, they bring different skills and methods to the facilitation process.[16]

Cross-cultural facilitation also helps avoid the use of a

15 "Distinctive Facilitation."
16 Ibid.

Western facilitation process that focuses on practical outcomes and action plans, which often doesn't take into account differences of culture and worldview that must first be understood. Additionally, cross-cultural groups need to be facilitated at a slower pace, so that people listening and speaking in a different language from the one they normally use have time to think about what they are hearing and form what they want to say.[17]

Facilitators typically join a group of participants who have already built relationships, and they must quickly come to understand those relationships while guiding the group process. They also need to be aware that their facilitation will affect the group and be sensitive to the questions and practices they use. Ideally, they should seek to help all participants feel comfortable and encouraged to share their thoughts, often by selecting the most appropriate tools, methods, or facilitation styles.[18] Not all facilitation methods fit well with *indaba*. For instance, goal-oriented styles that seek efficiency or narrowly focus on surface issues tend to overlook deeper concerns that need to be allowed to surface. Other styles or tactics may be appropriate for some groups and their cultural contexts but not for others. Since cultural differences influence what is understood as appropriate facilitation, as well as the challenges of diversity within the groups, training in both cross-cultural conversation and cross-cultural facilitation is vital for *indaba*.

For *indaba* and other processes that seek to build relationships among participants across differences, the issues that arise can be complex and heavily nuanced. Breaking down into small groups—dyads, triads, or groups based on constituency or shared interest—can be especially helpful in creating a setting where everyone can speak and build trust. They are especially good for those who are speaking in a language they don't use daily, to share stories, to talk about sensitive

---

[17] Ibid.
[18] Ibid.

concerns, and where mutual listening occurs in a more intimate setting. Plenaries, in which the entire group meets, are ideal for sharing themes, suggestions, or brief summaries while protecting the intimacy or confidentiality of what may have been said in the small groups. Plenaries also are important to ensure that everyone hears the same information or concern when rumors or difficult situations arise.[19]

For Encounters, facilitators were to create a safe space for the participants to share their reflections, ask one another searching questions about their missions, and help them identify areas of unease or conflict. In situations where anger or conflict was arising, the facilitators needed to help participants respond in a positive way without forcing a resolution. They also had to keep the group focused when necessary and manage the time allotted for the group reflection. Facilitators were to avoid expressing their own ideas about the topics under discussion or directing participants on what to think.[20] This was true for the *indaba* conversation as well.

Selecting the participants

A number of bishops wanted to have their dioceses be part of the cross-cultural Continuing Indaba experience. However, forming the right triad of dioceses for each Pilot Conversation was a sizable challenge. It was necessary that each Pilot Conversation be distinct in some manner so that different ways of using *indaba* might be tested. If a diocese had a relationship with one or more other dioceses that were interested in taking part, that would weigh in their favor.

There were other criteria for selection as well. A diocese had to be able to clearly express its mission and live it out, including a mission that involved vulnerable, marginalized, or excluded peoples. The dioceses also needed to differ in significant ways, such as in size, culture, mission, beliefs, worship

---

19   Ibid.
20   "Guidelines for Local Facilitators of Encounters."

style, or issues they faced. The dioceses should be on solid footing, with stable leadership; ideally, bishops would have a few years' experience. Additionally, *indaba* should represent some form of challenge or risk for a diocese taking part. Finally, a diocese needed to be able to fit within the timetable for the project, since grant funding depended on its completion by a fixed date. This last criterion proved to be the most difficult.

In the end, four Pilot Conversation groups were able to meet the criteria (table 2.1). Three of the Pilot Conversations combined dioceses from both Northern and Southern Hemispheres. The fourth Pilot Conversation took place entirely within Africa and explored how well the *indaba* process might work across diverse African cultures and Anglican churches. The tight timeline was not feasible for a fifth pilot conversation, which would have been among Spanish-speaking dioceses.

Table 2.1. Pilot Conversations in the Continuing Indaba Project, by Diocese and Church (or Province)

Pilot Conversation 1	New York *(Episcopal Church)*	Derby *(Church of England)*	Mumbai *(Church of North India)*
Pilot Conversation 2	Toronto *(Anglican Church of Canada)*	Hong Kong Sheng Kung Hui[a] *(Province)*	Jamaica and the Cayman Islands *(Province of the West Indies)*
Pilot Conversation 3	Saldanha Bay *(Anglican Church of Southern Africa)*	Ho *(Ghana) (Province of West Africa)*	Mbeere *(Anglican Church of Kenya)*
Pilot Conversation 4	Western Tanganyika *(Anglican Church of Tanzania)*	El Camino Real *(Episcopal Church)*	Gloucester *(Church of England)*

[a]Hong Kong Sheng Kung Hui had province-wide participation.

Within each Pilot Conversation, the three dioceses varied widely in geography, in theological views, and in other ways. Some participants brought strong evangelical roots; others were deeply Anglo-Catholic in their religious understanding and expression. One Pilot Conversation consisted of a diocese with a female bishop, a diocese opposed to women's ordination, and a diocese with female priests in a church that didn't allow female bishops. Another conversation included openly gay clergy and those who opposed homosexuality. Some participating churches also were members of the Global Anglican Future Conference (GAFCON).

The dioceses in each Pilot Conversation also varied in their acquaintance with one another. Those in Pilot Conversation 4 (see table 2.1) had begun to work together in partnership following the 2008 Lambeth Conference. The dioceses in Pilot Conversation 1 had some relationship with one of the other dioceses but not both. In the other two Pilot Conversations, the dioceses were interested in taking part but unfamiliar with one another. Hong Kong Sheng Kung Hui, in Pilot Conversation 2, actually consisted of the entire province (church) and drew participants from its four dioceses; for sake of brevity, it will be referred to as a diocese or a diocesan team in the discussion of the Pilot Conversation.

Gathering the leaders

The bishops who served as convenors for their diocesan teams met with one another in 2010 to consider the topics that would frame their Pilot Conversations.[21] The purpose of their gathering was to learn more about the other dioceses and their missions, including the challenges that arose in carrying them out. The bishops had chosen to become involved with the project for varying reasons. A common theme was their feeling that the outcome of the 2008 Lambeth Conference had made it important to continue *indaba*. As one bishop noted, "I came back from the Lambeth Conference transformed. It didn't change my convictions, but it did change my attitudes."[22]

Most bishops hoped that Continuing Indaba might strengthen the Anglican Communion, allowing people to speak openly about their differences, yet with love. They also looked forward to *indaba* offering them "a different paradigm of how to be

---

21 Because of scheduling conflicts, more than one convenors' meeting was held.

22 Interviews of all bishops were conducted on-site, between sessions, or afterward via Skype.

together," in the words of one bishop, where they could feel more comfortable with diversity without letting disagreements destroy their relationships. As another emphasized, "The Communion is held together with relationships, not by Instruments of the Communion. Relationships make a difference."[23]

Personally, most of the bishops hoped to learn aspects that might enrich their own ministries and to gain a better understanding of the Anglican Communion. They expected to have their own thinking challenged, particularly by hearing different interpretations of Scripture, learning from others' differences, and having their understanding broadened around mission concerns. As one bishop commented:

> We can learn a lot. I hope to learn from how my brothers and sisters are doing mission work and the strengths and weaknesses of their ways of doing things. . . . We can learn what challenges others face and how they try to solve these. This will help us understand how to be a witness to the gospel in the face of these challenges.

Another bishop reflected, "Learning from others is a challenge as it reminds me my position is not the only one in the Communion or the world. And it is not infallible." Several expressed the hope that their experiences might help further overall unity despite their differences. As one noted:

> I hope that we will discover and be able to celebrate our common humanity. We will continue to find that we are a Communion and a Community. To use the African Ubuntu philosophy, we become persons because of other persons.

Overall, they hoped that *indaba* might offer a means for reconciliation to the wider Communion.

---

[23] All quotations in this section are from interviews by the project evaluators Mkunga Mtingele and Joanna Sadgrove.

The agenda for the convenors meeting was structured in a Western format, with steps and sessions organized by allotted time. As the convenors began their meeting, it was assumed that each bishop's introduction would be a one- or two-minute summary before they moved on to the purpose of their gathering. The bishops, however, described their dioceses with deep affection and pride, offering extensive detail and insights into their histories, their experiences, and themselves.[24] This created a conflict over the use of time. The facilitator, setting aside the time frame, let the stories unfold, aware that a much deeper acquaintance and understanding were necessary for the *indaba* journey on which they were embarking. This tension between the process of *indaba* and its adaptation to a Western framework would recur throughout the Pilot Conversations.

Setting the indaba agendas

As the convenors met with their Pilot Conversation partners, they were asked to frame what they wanted the Encounters to focus on. Their hopes about what might come out of the Pilot Conversation centered on learning about their differences and how to find common ground that might help them to work together. Other hopes included learning how other dioceses engaged in mission, becoming more open and knowledgeable about other cultures, exploring other views and learning from one another, giving others an accurate view of the diocese, having others understand where they stood, and breaking down the "us" and "them" dualities, as well as that their dioceses might learn more about being part of a wider Communion and have a role to play in it.

Although the emphasis of the Encounters was to be on mission, many bishops felt that they should not avoid topics of real concern that lay outside their mission priorities if the *indaba* was to be useful. As a result, the agendas began to combine both mission and shared concerns. Some bishops wanted to be

---

24 Evaluator comments from the 2010 Continuing Indaba Convenor Consultations.

active participants in the Encounters and the formal *indaba* conversation; their reasoning was that the bishops' presence would cause participants to feel that the *indaba* was more valuable. If the bishops found it helpful, *indaba* more likely would be shared or used within their dioceses. Another reason was the need to know what was occurring, because the bishops ultimately were responsible to the dioceses. But their participation also created a challenge in how to neutralize the differences in status and power, since participants might speak less freely and openly with their bishop present. The bishops also were unaware, as the conversations unfolded, of the amount of influence they held on others.

Other bishops felt they couldn't personally commit the amount of time needed, so they chose a trusted team leader who would keep them informed. Each team had a leader or coordinator who served as the link person between the diocese and the Anglican Communion Office. The link person also worked with the convenor to put together the Encounter that each diocese would host and often was involved in selecting and preparing team members. At the end of 2010, the link persons came together for a training session where they met their counterparts in the Pilot Conversation groups to plan and discuss how the Encounters might unfold.

Forming the teams

A passage from a welcoming letter to participants captures what Continuing Indaba hoped they would achieve on their team adventure:

> We ask you be eager to see the world around you
> as others see it, and to help others see the world
> as you see it. We hope the journey you are on
> will enable you to be more effective in mission in
> your own context.[25]

---

[25] Letter to participants in Continuing Indaba from Phil Groves, 2011.

Participation was to be a spiritual journey, involving prayer and trust in God and in one another. It required a commitment to step into areas that would feel uncomfortable and openness to other people with different worldviews.

Each team needed to represent the diversity of its diocese on the key concerns it wanted to address, which meant that diversity for one team might differ from that for another. For some dioceses, racial, ethnic, or multicultural diversity was very important. For a few, diversity in sexual orientation was central. As a result, teams from every diocese included both ordained and lay members, men and women, younger and older members. Some also included members of minority races or ethnicities, or gay or lesbian members, in those locations where these were part of the diversity of diocese. In some countries, homosexuality was illegal, so formally including openly gay or lesbian participants represented an unsuitable level of risk and potential harm. Instead, space would be made in their Encounters for a listening session that included gay and lesbian people in the local community.

Participants needed to be able to listen carefully and uncritically, be sensitive to cultural differences, and have some experience in collaborative teamwork and cross-cultural interaction. Practically, they had to understand and speak English, or the common language used for the conversation. They also would be required to spend about a month in travel. Taken together, these last requirements limited the diversity of those who could participate.

Preparing the participants

The adventure of a journey often begins before one leaves home. This was true of the *indaba* journeys. Participants were expected to be introduced to the practices of listening, hospitality, inclusion, and other matters, as well as to be prepared for cultural shock where vast differences in environment might cause disorientation. The link persons were to distribute copies of *Creating Space*, the collection of materials relating to *indaba* gathered from the Resource Hubs, for team members to read and discuss.[26] Participants also were to record their thoughts throughout the *indaba* journey in a private journal or diary. Nearly all members participated in team training before they set forth. However, the quality and extent of the training varied widely.

Participants came to the *indaba* experience from a variety of backgrounds and interests, according to a survey questionnaire they filled out at the beginning of their journey. Many were deeply involved in church life, in their congregations and dioceses, and a few had done mission work in the Anglican Communion. Some had sizable cross-cultural experience, while others did not. Most were knowledgeable about their diocese, its mission, and the concerns it faced and knew some or all of the other members on their team. But about half knew very little about the other dioceses in their Pilot Conversation.

Interested, hopeful, enthusiastic, curious, and *adaptable* were the words that participants most often selected to characterize their feeling about the journey ahead, according to the survey. Many felt that being part of this *indaba* experience would deepen their faith along the way. Some hoped that it might help them become more open-minded and broaden their understanding of God and of one another. Concerns centered on anxiety over offending others and the inability to express oneself in a way that would be heard as intended. Others wanted to resist their temptation to talk too much or to be judgmental.

Participants most frequently hoped to learn more about others and the varying cultures and contexts in which they live out their faith, as well as how those might shape their views on various issues. Many also hoped to gain practical insights on mission and ministry. Some were interested in exploring possible ways that *indaba* might be useful in their home dioceses, such as learning how other dioceses approach similar situations and challenges. More than three out of four felt that their own way of thinking would be somewhat to strongly challenged, particularly by differences in viewpoints and culture.

---

26 Groves and Draper, *Creating Space.*

At the end of the project, participants were expected to share their experience after returning to their dioceses and communities. It was hoped that what they learned might inspire fresh mission activity or deepen what already was taking place.

THE START OF THE JOURNEY

Continuing Indaba would become a vessel for four separate Pilot Conversation adventures, each bringing together three diocesan teams from across great distances to encounter one another, to learn, to question, and to build relationships along the way. They would visit one another's dioceses, encounter their cultures and mission activities, and then travel to a new location for a facilitated *indaba* conversation. It was hoped that they would listen and discuss their experiences and insights in a fresh way, with deepened understanding and mutual respect.

The Pilot Conversation journeys would take between six and nine months to complete. The planning and development that made the journey possible took more than two years. As an experimental project, it did not have a well-worn map to follow. The itinerary was constructed ahead of time, but many details were adjusted as the project and its participants moved along; this led to frustrations, although the teams willingly adjusted in the spirit of the adventure.

The Continuing Indaba project had envisioned that the same participants would journey together throughout the process. For the most part, they did. However, a few members traveled only partway and were replaced by new participants. In some cases, unforeseen circumstances caused a change of plans.[27] At times, these changes affected the level of cross-cultural understanding and the depth of group relationships. Fortunately, a core of participants journeying across all Encounters provided stability to the experience, helped new

---

[27] In other situations, a clash between the purpose of the project and the convenors' desire to bring in new participants partway meant that relationships and trust needed to be freshly built at different points.

participants gain understanding, and kept the changes from impairing the overall journey.

The next four chapters introduce the Pilot Conversations and their unique contexts. Figure 2.2 depicts the Pilot Conversations' travel routes, numbered in the order by which they began their journeys (see table 2.1). Each offered a different kind of journey with its own adventures, insights, and story to share. The adventures vary in style and emphasis. Each story is told through the voice of the researcher who followed that Pilot Conversation most closely on its journey.

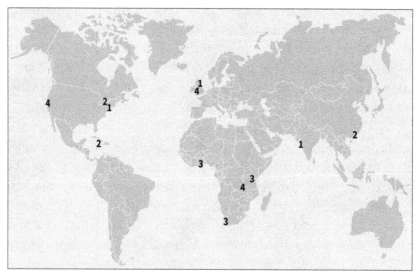

Figure 2.2. Journey of the Four Continuing Indaba Pilot Conversations
Adapted from Hellerick (Own work) [CC BY-SA 3.0 (http://creativecommons.org/licenses/by-sa/3.0)]. via Wikimedia Commons

~ **3** ~

Touching
Ground Zero

The Search for Common Ground in
New York, Derby, and Mumbai

~~~

NEW YORK AND MUMBAI EXCITE THE IMAGINATION with all the diversity and hustle that a metropolis has to offer. Both are cultural nerve centers for national energy and vitality; both have vast socioeconomic differences in their midst; and both share a legacy as former British colonies. Derby, England, the apex of the triangle, is a small city richly steeped in tradition and hard work. Joined together for a Pilot Conversation, these three regions offer an intriguing contrast in geography and history. They also represent an adventure into cross-cultural understanding and mission.

So began this first Pilot Conversation, bringing people together from cultures where the differences felt both as slight and vast as one could imagine. What participants shared was a deep faith, enriched by their bond as members of the Anglican Communion. This bond would provide vital common ground when nearly all else felt shaken.

The bishops (convenors) had set three common priorities to explore in their differing Anglican contexts:

- how they engaged with pluralism and public witness;
- how they addressed social justice; and
- how they equipped and encouraged leaders for mission.

Like a map, these priorities would guide the teams through their three Encounters, although other issues would surface along the way. The bishops also agreed that the purpose of the Encounter visits for participants would be fivefold: to increase awareness of the local culture and how Anglican faith is expressed in that context, to listen and share reflections, to allow concerns to be raised, to respect differences, and to later apply what they learned to their own dioceses.[1]

All three teams were well balanced between laity and clergy, and each included one or more ordained women. Although each team had a young adult, the team members averaged around fifty years of age. The age gap at times would result in feelings of alienation among the three young adults, but it also nurtured a felt connection among them across the different cultures.

About half of the participants believed they held a different perspective from others on their team, according to a survey at the start of their journey.[2] Their reasons for participating

---

[1] Convenors meeting, Woking, England, July 2010.

[2] Data from the initial participant survey were gathered before or at the first Encounter.

also varied. Some wanted to travel and expand their horizons. Others wanted to meet people who "do things differently" and to "gain new ideas." Yet others wanted a deeper understanding of mission and of ways to find common ground. One, from a racial/ethnic minority group, wanted to represent the presence of that voice.

The teams varied in other ways. One team included its convenor, a diocesan bishop, as a member.[3] Another was led by an archdeacon who had a supervisory role over some of the participants. The third team was led by a laywoman who depended on the cooperation and engagement of teammates for support. These internal status differences at times would create tension, either because of the restraint that some felt in expressing themselves or in team commitment and cohesion. The teams' first Encounter would begin in New York.

ENCOUNTERING NEW YORK

New York is a cross section of cultural and religious diversity, home to twenty-two million people in the metropolitan area. Culturally, it takes pride in self-motivation and hard work, which undergirds the fast-paced lifestyle that many either thrive on or endure. This is supported by the myth of New Yorkers rising from immigrant poverty to a self-made fortune for future generations, even if for many it will not come true. The fall of the World Trade Center's twin towers on September 11, 2001, catalyzed a fresh tenderness within the city's culture that softened its abrasive reputation.

Anglican tradition has been rooted in New York since the seventeenth century. The diocese was one of the original nine to form the Episcopal Church following the Revolutionary War. Although the Episcopal Church is a descendant of the Church

---

[3] Originally, the Indian team was made up of participants from both Mumbai and Delhi dioceses. The bishops and members of both of these dioceses took part in the first Encounter. Delhi, however, was unable to continue in the Pilot Conversation, so additional members from Mumbai joined the team for the remainder of the journey.

of England,[4] expressions of Anglicanism vary widely amid New York's congregations of African American, Caribbean American, Latin American, Asian American, European American, and other ethnic communities, as well as those striving to be fully multicultural. New York also is the home of the Episcopal Church Center, General Theological Seminary, and other key church organizations and agencies, making the diocese central to the arteries that course through the heart of the church's 1.9 million members.

The Diocese of New York embraces not only New York City but also surrounding counties, bringing together urban, suburban, and semirural congregations and lifestyles. Beyond the tall steeple of Trinity Church Wall Street are numerous small congregations, many poor in resources but rich in mission spirit, struggling to keep their doors open so that work with the surrounding neighborhoods can continue. In the midst of this rich core of church life and mission, it can be easy not to know one's neighbors or understand the challenges they face—in the parish next door, across town, or across county lines. This has challenged the diocese's cohesion and focus, and it underlies New York's approach to mission.

First Steps toward Common Ground

As flights landed on Monday, May 9, 2011, participants from India, England, and New York met one another for the first time. For several, this would be their first journey to New York. The visiting teams stayed in a retreat house on the city's Upper East Side for most of the weeklong Encounter, while New York team members commuted during the day. Morning and evening worship would frame most of the daylong activities.

---

4 Following the Revolutionary War, Anglicans in the United States could not have bishops ordained by the Church of England, since it is a state church. Instead, the first U.S. bishops were ordained by the Scottish Episcopal Church, which is independent of government. The United States also chose to designate its church as Episcopal instead of Anglican. All three autonomous churches are part of the Anglican Communion, a more recent entity that recognizes a shared common theological and ecclesial tradition.

The Encounter began on Tuesday with lunch at Holy Apostles Soup Kitchen, feeding more than twelve hundred homeless persons daily, followed by a walk along the High Line and a subway ride uptown for an orientation to the diocese and its mission activities. Following Evening Prayer next door in the Cathedral of St. John the Divine, team members dined and had conversation with the dean. In reflecting on the day, some visitors were amazed at the size of New York's homeless population, as well as the programs that feed and clothe them. They also wondered whether dependency was being perpetuated by feeding the homeless without taking steps for social change. One had observed little interaction between donors and recipients beyond the delivery of food or services and questioned if this was typical. Another was surprised by the tension that American religious leaders expressed, in wanting to take bold steps that risk controversy and also might offend the very donors on which the church depends.

On Wednesday, the teams visited the Bronx Zoo, where they shared reflections as they strolled past the animal exhibits. Later they visited St. Ann's after-school program, where the children were given bilingual attention and tutoring, and the teams learned about the needs of children from families that work long days. Several were moved by the children and also the personal care they received.

Thursday morning, the teams stood at Ground Zero, site of the 2001 attack on the World Trade Center. The memorial hadn't yet been built, and a deep hole still scarred the cityscape. Members of the New York team were visibly shaken. Some reflected with tears on where they had been when the towers came down and what it had meant to them and to the city. For the Indian team, Ground Zero brought back memories of the 2008 Mumbai terrorist attacks. British participants, trying to understand the raw emotion that Ground Zero evoked, reflected on the decades of violence over Northern Ireland in their country.[5] One noted that on this common ground of vio-

---

5 Another account of the encounter with Ground Zero can be found in Groves and Jones, *Living Reconciliation*, 54–56.

lence, they could understand better the depth of each other's suffering and remember how people came together when crisis arose in their own contexts. Leaving Ground Zero, the teams visited a neighborhood center at Trinity Church Wall Street, and then rode the Staten Island ferry to see a church senior housing development there. That evening after dinner, about ten participants strolled to a nearby pub to continue their conversations.

On Friday, small groups journeyed to different parts of the diocese—Kingston, Middletown, White Plains, and Poughkeepsie—to understand the types of ministries and outreach programs taking place in more rural areas. Visits included a gathering with Latino youth to learn about their lives as young immigrants, a migrant worker program, a meals delivery program for those with HIV and AIDS, a food pantry, a quilt program, a women's shelter, and a monastery where the brothers take the Mass to the streets and work with homeless ministries. A small group of participants reflected on the day, feeling that it had brought a real encounter with the church—the *people* of the diocese. One New York participant admitted to not having known until that day what ministries other parishes nearby were doing. Families in these communities hosted participants for the weekend.

Hosts and their guests reunited in the cathedral on Saturday to celebrate Catherine Roskam's fifteenth anniversary as a bishop in the diocese and to learn about the historical struggle for women's ordination in the Episcopal Church. A group of *indaba* participants was invited to join the opening procession. As they came up the aisle, they saw a cluster of *indaba* participants in the pews, reached over, and pulled them into their midst. This spontaneous act symbolized a growing shared identity and commitment to one another.

The Encounter concluded on Monday as everyone gathered to reflect on their experience.[6] Some of the British visitors

---

6 A New York participant with a work obligation was present via teleconference for part of the time.

were surprised at how different from their expectations the people and culture of New York turned out to be, particularly in the strong individualism, the prominence of racial issues, the sizable poverty and homelessness, and the warm hospitality. One had felt deeply disturbed when visiting a food pantry, realizing the amount of hunger that existed in the city. Another observed that in England, such programs might find cultural resistance, as people there tend to refuse charity. Several remarked on the faith, hope, and vitality in the diocese, as well as the diversity of belief. "I had assumed that all were liberal; it isn't like that," noted one. "Churches are as different as at home." Another admitted to having spent much of the weekend in culture shock, trying to absorb all that had been experienced.

Several Indian participants felt their perceptions of Americans had changed. The feeding programs had surprised them, and some wondered if they were having any impact. Another was intrigued by how social concerns were integrated with the churches and how faith and action were joined. New York members were startled at the different understandings of common words such as *pluralism*. They also spoke of a felt burden to represent the American people and to correct misperceptions and stereotypes. Many keenly felt the tug of work and home responsibilities during the Encounter, unable to participate fully.

Participants were asked to share the difficulties they encountered. Some struggled over sexual orientation inclusivity. One described how shaken he was when he saw two men hugging, and then was even more surprised by his thought that their deep care for one another was what mattered. He admitted to needing to grapple with this issue. A few thought that their views were seen by others as "behind the times" rather than respected as different. Overall, however, many felt their beliefs weren't changed, but that something else had shifted. Several commented on the power of shared worship. Sensitive concerns emerged in their reflection session, although more time and trust would be needed before an *indaba* conversation would be possible. First steps in finding common ground had been taken.

DISCOVERING DERBY

Derbyshire, a county near the center of England, embraces a variety of small and midsize towns mingled with rural countryside and forests. The city of Derby has only about 250,000 residents, although 1.5 million people live in the metropolitan area. Derby is considered the birthplace of the industrial revolution, the first mill having opened here in 1717. Although the economy has broadened, manufacturing is still vital to the area. Some districts in the north also have a long mining history. Long-term unemployment and the lack of economic opportunities still afflict the region following the closure of the coal mines in the 1990s.[7]

As a state church, symbolized by the monarchy as its titular head, the Church of England has both a self-understanding that emphasizes serving the common good and distinct responsibilities. It can act as an advocate for social justice but has limited autonomy in what can be done without government involvement. The Derby Diocese covers all of Derbyshire, having some three hundred churches of varying sizes, as well as school, hospital, and prison ministries. As with much of England, the diocese is concerned about how to induce people to participate in church. Other priorities involve the need for increased stewardship, social justice, and reshaping the church to fit with contemporary needs.

Since 2000, the Derbyshire area has grown in racial diversity by about 20 percent.[8] A small, growing Muslim population has brought pluralism and the public expression of faith

---

[7] Bolsover District Council, "Employment Topic Paper," 5.

[8] Kirsty Green, "Fall in Christians, Increase in Muslims as Census Figures Reveal Religion Shift."

to the fore. The diocese also has an ecumenical partnership with Baptist, Methodist, and United Reformed churches, seeking to counter the inward focus of many local congregations. Together they've formed a regional ecumenical partnership with the Church of North India.[9] The Pilot Conversation offered a way to develop and deepen the diocese's relationship with Indian Christians.

Exploration of Anglican Bedrock

The teams reunited in Derbyshire on Monday, October 3. Some of the Derby team were concerned that their own Encounter wouldn't be as spectacular as the New York Encounter, but they were reminded that the purpose was to experience daily life and understand the church in British culture. After a late-afternoon orientation and dinner, participants either rested or walked to a lecture on Muslim-Christian relations at the cathedral. Worship would open and close each day together.

The next day began with a visit to Derby City Center to learn about the church's engagement with civic and secular society. The bishop met with the team members and discussed pluralism and public space. This was followed by a conversation with the dean of the cathedral on its involvement with the wider society.

On Wednesday, the teams visited a university and multifaith center to explore what Anglican chaplaincy meant in a pluralistic context. They then ventured to Normanton, an ancient village now part of Darby's inner city that richly expresses its local ethnic and multifaith diversity. Mosques, Sikh *gardwaras*, and Hindu temples mingle with Anglican, Catholic, free Protestant, and house churches, some serving the Polish, Serbian, Ukrainian, and other ethnic groups that have settled in the area. This and similar transitional areas, affordable to immigrants, also have been sites of human trafficking and prostitution. At a local parish, the group heard about Restore,

---

9   "The Derbyshire Churches in Partnership with the Church of North India."

a project to help those who have been involved in sex work, and other ministry activities in the Normanton area. After dinner, they met in small groups to reflect on the experience.

Thursday brought direct encounter with English tradition and culture. A visit to a Church of England school was followed by a tour and lunch at Locko Park estate, built at the site of a thirteenth-century hospital for lepers.[10] There they were briefed on the English patronage system and the distinctive role that the Church of England plays as an established church. The teams then journeyed into the countryside to meet a local patron at his estate, followed by Evening Prayer and supper at Thorpe Church, the parish he supports, where they learned about more rural ministry in the diocese.

On Friday, they met to learn about the relationship of the diocese in supporting clergy and laity in mission work. One New York participant later noted that the Encounter had caused him to reflect on what the differing ways of paying clergy salaries might mean for both freedom in and difficulties of engaging in mission. Clergy in the Church of England are paid by the diocese, but in New York they typically are hired and paid by the parish, which affects the extent and type of mission they undertake. Congregations in areas where the need for mission outreach is greatest often have few resources for paid clergy and programs, yet wealthier congregations sometimes resist focusing on outreach efforts. That evening, participants met the families who would host them for the weekend.

The teams and their hosts reunited on Saturday, attending a playback theater and evening feast at St. Werbergh's in Spondon. One member of the Derby team, familiar with the dramatic method of playback, worked with the actors while participants shared their experiences from the New York and Derby Encounters. Participants then watched actors reproduce the scenarios. Some later remarked that the playback theater had helped them explore their feelings about the Encounters and had brought fresh insights. It also strengthened ties with

---

10 "History of Locko Park and Hall."

one another as they became aware of the others' differing perceptions of what had happened. They spent the next day with their hosts, learning about English family life.

As the participants reunited on Monday, they visited Danesmoor to hear about Sanctum, a Fresh Expressions ministry and a social space for an alternative young adult subculture.[11] Derby, site of a large annual heavy-metal event, draws young adults from across the country. Afterward, the teams journeyed to Holmewood, a former coal-mining village, to learn about the 1980s miners' strike and the impact that the mine closure had on the community, as part of the Encounter's focus on social justice. There they heard largely negative impressions of the church from former miners, but also about fresh attempts being made to reconnect the church and the community.

That evening, some participants visited the Church on the Bus, which moved around the city of Chesterfield offering food, hot drinks, clothing, and counseling to the homeless community there. Other participants ventured to the Gates, a chapel and café bar run by the Order of the Black Sheep, a Christian community affiliated with the Church of England for those on the margins of both church and society. The Gates offered worship, Bible study and reflection, community family time, mentoring, and other activities or services.

The teams' final day opened with a facilitated conversation to explore what they had encountered during their time together. In reflecting on the Derby experience, one participant later noted that it had made him think about his own church with fresh understanding. Others, too, felt that it had helped them value their shared religious heritage as common ground in the Anglican Communion, which bonded them despite their differences. In all, the second Encounter had moved the teams beyond politeness, into deeper relationship and trust with one another.

---

[11] "Sanctum." Fresh Expressions is an ecumenical program focusing on exploring nontraditional forms of church to reach individuals and groups not part of traditional church communities. For more information, see https://www.freshexpressions.org.uk/.

VISITING MUMBAI AND BEYOND

The city of Mumbai offers a spectacular diversity of Western and traditional lifestyles, bolstered by its growth as an international filmmaking, finance, and technology center. With twenty-three million people in the metropolitan area, the city's extremes in wealth and poverty are highly visible as limousines, motor scooters, and oxcarts mix uncomfortably in traffic-filled streets. Mumbai's name—derived from Mumbadevi, the goddess of the fishermen originally living on the islands that made up the area[12]—was officially changed from Bombay in 1995 to remove a vestige of colonial rule and strengthen local (Marathi) identity and culture.[13] Mumbai historically was an important hub for the Indian independence movement.

The contemporary rise of Hindu nationalism has brought religion to the forefront in a region of remarkable religious and cultural diversity. About two-thirds of Mumbai's population identifies as Hindu, 17 percent as Muslim, and 4 percent as Christian.[14] The Church of North India (CNI), formed in 1970, unites Anglican and several mainline Protestant denominations to work together in shared Christian mission.[15] Sensitive issues and topics typically require CNI oversight, which makes it easier for the church to balance its diverse traditions and perspectives and also helps maintain public unity in a society where religious tensions have risen sharply over the years.

The CNI's Diocese of Mumbai, with seventy thousand members, carries out a wide range of ministries. With an Anglican polity of bishops, a presbytery, and a strong emphasis on laity, the congregations vary in liturgy and beliefs within the broad

---

[12] In the nineteenth century, the islands were transformed geographically into a single island. "Bombay: History of a City."

[13] Christopher Beam, "Mumbai?"

[14] Other religious minorities include Jainism, Parsism, Sikhism, and Judaism. "Mumbai," *New World Encyclopedia*.

[15] The other Protestant constituent denominations are Congregational, Presbyterian, Methodist, Baptist, Brethren, and Disciples of Christ.

tenets and unity of the church. Many focus on helping those at risk or in poverty, offering education and skills training for low-income youth and missionary work in remote areas. Public advocacy on matters of social justice is difficult, as it can trigger an increase in religious tension, persecution, and violence.

Common Ground amid Cultural Differences

We walked the New York road; we walked the Derby road; now we walk the Indian road with Christ. Look for Christ in people. It may look different.

This advice was offered to the visiting teams as they began their Mumbai Encounter on Thursday, January 5. All participants stayed together at the YMCA in central Mumbai, across the street from a Muslim *madrasa*, in a neighborhood where homeless families rolled out blankets on the sidewalk at night, one tethering its goat to a fence. A welcome shawl was placed over each visitor's shoulders by the host team, a local scholar briefed them on aspects of Indian society, and the bishop oriented them to the diocese. Participants then walked to a nearby social services center that taught occupational skills to young women and men from low-income backgrounds, visiting classes on tailoring and fashion design, computer skills, hand painting, and crafts.

On Friday morning, the teams visited a home for poor, elderly widows and talked informally with them. Some widows spoke English, and the Mumbai team translated for others. Next, the participants visited a high school and junior college,[16] where students greeted the teams with chrysanthemum garlands and dances from the local cultures. The school's biggest challenge was to persuade parents in lower-income areas to

---

16 The school was founded by the United Church of Christ, now part of the Church of North India, and is open to students of any religious or secular background.

let the students continue their education beyond grade ten, a time when many start work. After lunch, the teams visited a traditional Anglican school and also a former colonial church that now houses both Anglican and Jewish congregations in a demographically changing neighborhood. The day concluded with a visit to a shelter for orphaned girls (or those whose mothers are unable to care for them). Reflecting later, visitors remarked on having watched residents in the widows' home and at the shelter voluntarily helping with cooking or caregiving, which differed from the strict caregiver-client model in New York and Derby. Another remarked on seeing a beggar give money to a little boy. One asked the Mumbai team, "How do you keep doing this? The weight of needs is huge." A Mumbai member replied, "People give from their pockets," noting their generosity.

As a preface to the theme of *social justice*, on Saturday the teams visited Mani Bhavan, home to Mohandas Gandhi during his political activity in Bombay and where he was arrested in 1932. They also visited Wilson College, one of India's earliest colleges, which opened as a school for girls at a time when women weren't allowed to be educated.

On Sunday, small groups visited churches in Mumbai and surroundings, worshiping in Tamil, Marathi, or English. One group traveled to a poor village where a Tamil church was located. As the minister led the group members through the streets to the church, they were greeted with garlands, fireworks, and drums. Everyone removed their shoes before entering the church, where men sat on one side, women on the other; chairs for visitors were placed near the front. After worship, local women and men gathered around the visitors, talking through translators and taking pictures together.

The next day, two minibuses took participants to the Palghar region, about fifty miles north of Mumbai. Sunlight glistened on a river where women were washing clothes as the buses entered a village, on their way to visit a school and orphanage run by the Church of North India. Some of the students were children of missionaries working in dangerous areas where families weren't safe. The bishop pointed out that the missionaries and schools were at the heart of the diocese. The visitors watched students perform dances from local cultures and do Warli painting, a local tribal art form more than forty-five hundred years old.

On Tuesday, the group traveled to a church in the Dhahanu region, where missionaries to the tribal areas were meeting. The male and female missionaries greeted the visitors, handing them freshly cut coconuts from which to sip the refreshing juice after a long bus journey. Through a local interpreter, they spoke of the physical danger of being a Christian in those areas. Many tribal villages lived in fear of upper-caste landowners, for whom Christianity's rejection of the caste system threatened their power. Missionaries risked their lives for their work. They asked the visitors for their blessing, and one by one the group members held each missionary's hands and blessed them. A festive lunch awaited, although the missionaries would eat later so that there would be enough food for the guests. On the return to Mumbai, the participants spoke very little. Many were feeling saturated by the powerful encounter and the cumulative effect of the journey.

Wednesday brought a medical emergency for a participant, and the morning's events were put on hold as team members milled about and prayed, anxious to hear news. The group returned to the theme of social justice that afternoon, visiting a shelter for girls rescued from sex trafficking who were trying to rebuild their lives. It also visited a drop-in center for sexual minorities in an unmarked industrial building and heard from some about the discrimination and violence they experienced in Mumbai.[17] The bishop clarified that the visit was not an endorsement of sexual diversity, but that the topic was important for many visiting participants and might help them understand what sexually marginalized people

---

[17] Sexual minorities include those who are gay, lesbian, bisexual, and transgendered.

experience in Mumbai. An evening boat ride on the bay offered a reflective end to the Encounter.

The group flew to Bangalore the next day and took mini-buses to an ecumenical retreat center.[18] The tropical grounds and walking paths offered a peaceful environment for digesting the experiences and stresses of the week, as participants sought to regain focus for the *indaba* conversation that would begin the following day. The Encounter had affected each of them differently. Some were energized; others were experiencing cultural shock. A few were having difficulty with unfamiliar foods, while others felt their patience decreasing and irritability growing as cultural differences overwhelmed their coping skills. Several had disregarded the Encounter program to instead go souvenir shopping or had made evening pilgrimages across town to the Four Seasons Hotel's rooftop bar as a means of coping with the dissonance they felt. Fragile group cohesion also had frayed as the stress increased. Several on the Mumbai team, however, felt that the Encounter had strengthened their relationships and increased a sense of commitment within their diocese. They also felt humbled by seeing so much being done in their own diocese.

PARTICIPATING IN THE *INDABA* CONVERSATION

On Saturday, January 14, the *indaba* conversation opened with worship and a brief welcome. Two facilitators, from Botswana and Canada, invited the group to express their hopes and concerns. Common hopes were for honesty in conversation and mutual respect. These also would become key norms for their *indaba*. The major concern was that participants would simply return home and resume their daily lives, and nothing useful would come out of the *indaba* experience.

---

[18] The teammate who had suffered a medical emergency arrived later and was cared for separately at the retreat center. The group offered constant expressions of care, support, and prayers.

Participants met in small groups that afternoon to reflect on their Mumbai Encounter. The most common impression was amazement at the hard work and dedication of the Mumbai diocese to its mission, and also how it respected the different local cultures. Several described having felt Christ's presence in a variety of situations—in the young women healing from sex trafficking; in the new missionaries' singing and staying firm in the face of violence; in visiting the drop-in center for sexual minorities; and in worshiping in Marathi at an Indian team member's church, without understanding the language yet comprehending what mattered. Several noted that the Encounter had challenged them to think freshly about their understanding of Christ, the role of evangelism and mission, and how to respond in the midst of human need. Others talked about how important relationships were to learning. As one remarked, "Knowing one another's history, and how and why you are different, makes a big difference."

The second *indaba* day opened with a sense of great fatigue. Many participants had exhausted their mental and emotional resources. The facilitators invited them to reflect on what *indaba* meant to them by sharing a symbol. One by one, they placed symbols at the center of the circle of team members and explained them. These symbols and what they represented included the following:

- a drawing of an arrow—from the starting point to the future
- reference to a picture of a laughing Christ in the chapel—the importance of laughter
- travel bag from the New York Encounter—their journey together
- battered camera—feeling of being cracked open yet still able to work
- a piece of chocolate—missing comforts from home

- drawing of a question mark—*indaba* is about questions; it is a privilege to be able to ask so many
- wristwatch—the time God has given; it should be utilized properly
- shawl—to help one stay warm when feeling cold, both inside and outside
- flower—the relationships of caring and sharing that help the team members bloom
- bracelet—reminder that *indaba* was the result of the *Windsor Report*,[19] an ironic blessing.

The facilitators then synthesized common themes that had arisen from the previous day's discussion, which the group decided would become the topics for their three *indaba* conversations:

- How can we build genuine mutual understanding on the issue of the ordination of women and the church?
- How can we build genuine mutual understanding on the issue of homosexuality and the church?
- How can the church be a catalyst for social change?

The *indabas* would take place in small groups consisting of two members randomly selected from each diocesan team. Before the groups began, the facilitators noted that two kinds of "why" questions typically are asked: questions that invite a person to open up and share more, and those that tend to be judgmental. Team members should avoid the latter.

---

[19] The *Windsor Report*, resulting from the 1998 Lambeth Conference, recommended more formalized organizational relationships by posing the development of an Anglican Covenant as a way to recognize and enforce doctrinal and organizational authority; it also recommended a listening process. Lambeth Commission on Communion, *The Windsor Report 2004*.

The ordination of women had emerged as a surprising theme. All three diocesan teams had one or more ordained women. However, the Western teams struggled with the lack of more female clergy in the Mumbai diocese, while Indian members noted that cultural acceptance and the church's vulnerability in that society were also crucial to consider, and that change was slowly coming. The topic also may have served as a proxy issue for emotional frustration or cultural shock, or as a way to bond in the absence of other ties. It proved to be a strident test for *indaba* conversation.

After the first *indaba* conversation, everyone met together to share what had occurred within their group. Some were surprised to find that both common ground and mutual respect had emerged. Others struggled to find a way to engage everyone and to move to a place of deep mutual listening and understanding. One small group confessed to having tackled all three topics in one session, and its members weren't satisfied with the result. In another group, much of the conversation had focused more on why *more* women weren't ordained than on seeking a deeper understanding of the differing cultural contexts. As emotions began to rise, the discussion had grown more superficial. Several participants admitted that it was hard to hear views that conflicted with their own. As one said, "We were consistent with our past practices, talking past each other, regardless of our underlying thoughts." One group that had consisted of all women was surprised at the diversity in their midst, yet they also valued the safety and sisterhood that an all-women group had brought.

Sexual orientation was a divisive topic within teams and, culturally, across teams. Yet most groups struggled with it more effectively during the afternoon *indaba*. The facilitators visited groups that had difficulties. One enthusiastically welcomed the help; the members of another group preferred to try harder themselves. Afterward, as everyone came together to reflect in a large plenary group, a participant noted that people had put themselves in places that were uncomfortable and had stayed there, adding, "I felt we were in *indaba*." In that group, members had shared personal struggles on the topic, from their own faith and cultural viewpoint, and they wondered openly, asking questions about each other's contexts and phrasing their thoughts in a way that invited others to join in. In another group, a comment had been made that was deeply upsetting, affecting the group's ability to have *indaba*. Some had thought it was intentional, although other evidence suggested it could have arisen out of misunderstanding.[20] The all-women group acknowledged that they were able to share around human sexuality in a way that would have been difficult with men present, and they were surprised how the cultures of all three teams were struggling with similar issues.

The last day opened with a third *indaba*. In one group, participants had difficulty with the broad topic of social justice. Awkward silence followed each comment, until one person mentioned a tension between what she believed was called for as a follower of Christ and what the church as an institution could actually say or do. Another pondered over the dilemma of how to move people toward places where they aren't comfortable, but not to where the pushback becomes too great. Conversations bounced comparatively among the three cultural contexts as Western participants made efforts to ask about Indian culture and how social change was approached in their context.

At the final session, participants shared what they were taking with them from the *indaba* experience. One remarked, "I learned interconnectedness: if you pull one thread, everything else bunches up. . . . My actions affect others, and that cuts both ways." Another added, "I have more questions now than ever before. I feel there are ways we can be supportive to each other." And from another, "I found the meaning of Christ again." Participants also expressed feelings of being taken

---

20 Based on comments in other contexts, this situation could have been a matter of language or understanding that needed further exploration and conversation. The group did not have a facilitator.

apart, gratitude for a relationship that would last, a desire to return to the familiar, and having come a long way from the first Encounter. Having seen one another with fresh eyes, the team members had difficulty saying good-bye.

In the end, nearly two-thirds had felt that the *indaba* conversation was very meaningful, according to survey data. As one commented, "Our discussions became more honest and tough, but we worked through." Many felt they were in the midst of changing their thinking, although not necessarily their beliefs. They had found commonalities across their diversity. They felt in different places but on the same overall journey. As one summed up:

> This experience has given a face to the Anglican
> Communion. . . . We are the Anglican family. Do
> we stay or go is not the question. . . . We don't
> have to travel the same path to reach the same
> destination. I'm hopeful.

Another added, "The journey will continue, each of us going to different places; but we will meet each other along the way."

PIECING TOGETHER COMMON GROUND

The teams had struggled through their differences by searching for common ground. At Ground Zero, they found this common ground by reflecting on their own cultural experiences of terrorist violence. In Derby, several were struck by the importance of their shared religious heritage tying them together as an extended family. In Mumbai, the cultural conflicts that Westerners experienced were softened and transformed by respect as they reflected with amazement at all that the diocese, its missionaries, and ministries were accomplishing.

After participants returned home, worldviews formed connecting lines like points on a triangle. Some stayed in touch, while others let the experience work quietly within. Several participants mentioned in survey comments or interviews having had a spiritual awakening or feeling freshly committed to a new way of engaging in church, as well as awareness of societal differences. Some of the Mumbai team members came away with closer working relationships and deeper cross-cultural understandings. A Derby team member experienced a significant deepening of faith, which eventually led to ordination. A year later, two New York team members designed an *indaba* for their diocese. The journey had brought them to a somewhat different place than where they had begun.

FACING CHALLENGES
TO COMMON GROUND

This Pilot Conversation faced some of the greatest challenges to forming common ground across their differences. Strong advocates of their positions had the most difficulty in trying to listen openly and ask questions that didn't imply blame or stem from the need to change others. Additionally, some participants were on a deep personal journey that in some ways conflicted with the shared group journey. Two of the diocesan teams lacked internal cohesion. Weak internal ties led to individual relationships with members of other teams instead of strengthening team relationships. Final survey results, however, showed that weak team cohesion did not hinder the strong enthusiasm for *indaba*, which all found to be a meaningful experience, or reduce the impact members felt it had made on their lives.

Without cohesion, how could relationships deepen and shared identity grow? Cross-cultural solidarity became particularly strong among the women, partly because of interest expressed by Indian women in learning about the other women's contexts and the women's willingness to talk deeply and personally in ways that didn't occur in mixed-gender groups. The Indian men appeared open to more cross-cultural conversations, but those didn't occur as often. This may suggest gender differences in how cross-cultural engagement and cohesion are built. Gender also may be influenced by status and power, particularly in the willingness to make oneself vulnerable in a way that allows serious engagement to occur.

Another challenge involved cross-cultural shock. The quietness of Indian participants in New York became understandable to the American and British teams once they had visited Mumbai, where they experienced how silence can be a means of coping with cultural stress and difficulty in understanding their surroundings. Some participants disengaged as a way of coping with their experience. For others, criticism and occasionally conflict may have been an outward expression of internal stress. The tendency for Western team members to build easy conversational bonds and socialize frequently with one another could be as much a reaction to cultural stress as an expression of status and dominance. One interviewee noted that coping with cultural differences was very hard work, especially trying not to dominate by reverting to Western norms. Similar to the shopping side trips and Western hotel visits by several British and American team members, in New York the two highest-status Indian team members had engaged in different treatment, such as riding in taxis while others took the subway or a bus, or not attending some Encounter activities. Such actions, while understandable as a response to cultural stress, perpetuated differences within the group and accentuated patterns of privilege and dominance, and they also inhibited the development of mutual mission across cultures.

Despite these challenges, participants' enthusiasm at the end of the Pilot Conversation journey was unmistakable. Most participants had thought that the formal *indaba* conversations had the strongest influence on their entire journey, according to the final survey. They also felt that the Encounters had helped them develop cross-cultural awareness that opened a door to finding genuine common ground and allowing the *indaba* conversation to be effective. As an interviewee noted,

"We have moved some—we are able to talk about our differences in more complexity. In New York, we were barely able to have that conversation."

Personal reflection sessions based on Scripture, using a form of *Lectio Divina*, provided a tool for finding common ground and to offset differences in culture, power, and worldview. Subjective reflections were shared and heard. The Derby Encounter's playback theater also provided an external mirror where participants could hear stories and concerns, allowing them to consider shared situations and quandaries from other standpoints, gain fresh insights, laugh a bit, and share their emotions, while softening their differences.

The ability to listen to others also steadily improved from the first Encounter to the end of the *indaba* conversation.[21] As a Derby participant wrote several months later:

> The *indaba* process has made me a much more
> empathetic listener. Making others confident
> in expressing their deeply held ideas and
> responsible for their prayerful discussions are
> elements that I actively encourage whenever I
> lead meetings.[22]

A majority strongly felt that they had become more comfortable talking with others who held views different from their own, according to the data. They also felt that their thinking had been challenged by the *indaba* process. More than half claimed that *both* their understanding and views had been affected; another third thought their understanding had been affected even though their views remained the same. Several commented that they had a better understanding of others in the Anglican Communion, including a fresh awareness of the importance of knowing one another.

---

[21] All had thought that Continuing Indaba had been somewhat to very effective in developing mutual listening. The final survey asked for an evaluation of each Encounter and the *indaba* conversation. The post-Encounter questionnaire also gathered an assessment. These were cross-validated by field observation.

[22] Admin, "A Teacher Reflects . . . Telling the Indaba Story" (boldface in original).

As this Pilot Conversation illustrated, walking away from conflict and uneasiness can be tempting. Yet the group stayed together in the midst of their difficulties and struggled to hear different and sometimes painful differences in worldviews—across cultures and occasionally within their own teams. This struggle, somewhat like their experience during the visit to Ground Zero, was emotionally exhausting and at times defied understanding; yet it enhanced the common ground of mutual respect, on which trust could be built. They would return home and continue *indaba* in fresh ways.

~ **4** ~

Siblings in a Global Family

Toronto, Hong Kong Sheng Kung Hui, and Jamaica and the Cayman Islands

—Joanna Sadgrove

~~~

TORONTO, HONG KONG, AND JAMAICA comprise perhaps the most diverse geographic and cultural Pilot Conversation triad. Christianity in each location has distinct philosophical, historical, linguistic, and cultural influences shaping its expression and development. Each location has occupied a different position in relation to the power structures of colonialism and within the Anglican Communion, as articulated by participants at various points on their *indaba* journeys. The intersections of these diverse experiences generated intense discussion about identity, power and marginality, which illuminated how the history of people in one location can inform new ways of thinking about similar issues in another location with a different history. Together these three teams explored and discovered both common roots and vast differences of history and culture that shaped their growth.

When the convenors met together in 2010 to identify the common themes for their Pilot Conversation, they decided to set them within an overarching theme of *reconciliation*. By this, they wanted to focus on how to engage one another across their social diversities so that the energy generated by any conflict could be directed ultimately toward reconciliation. Within this framework, specific themes were chosen to be addressed in the Encounters:

- *Youth alienation*: Consider how to extend a message that speaks to where young people actually are, rather than where the church assumes them to be.

- *Cultural and religious differences about homosexuality*: Explore the diverse views held by examining the differing cultures and social circumstances that have shaped them.

- *Social justice*: Discuss what social justice might mean in different social and cultural contexts, and also whether there is a relationship between social justice and evangelism.

Convenors were aware of the discomfort that a conversation on differences over homosexuality might generate. They also recognized the potential divisiveness of other issues such as socioeconomic disparity, identity, and racism. These themes would be addressed in different ways at each Encounter. Conversations would not be held without those most intimately affected by a given topic being present and participating in the discussion. Some team members were selected to ensure diversity of experience was fully represented.

THE TEAMS

Each diocesan team consisted of eight people, with good representation across the categories of age, gender, and clergy or lay status. The teams also differed in several ways. Although all had a male majority, the women on the Toronto team—a bishop, a priest, and a lay leader—provided a good balance in conversation and interactions. The Jamaican team had a female priest and two laywomen, but their five male teammates included two bishops and a prominent lay leader whose voices contributed powerfully to the conversations. The two female Hong Kong team members tended to be less vocal than their six male teammates, but their insights were critical in shifting the nature of the conversation on several occasions. By the end of the Pilot Conversation, interactions would be more gender balanced.

The average age of the Toronto team was older, although the team did contain some young adults. The Jamaican team reflected a similar age profile. When combined with a much younger Hong Kong team, which had only one member over age sixty at the outset, strong interaction among the younger members across the three teams helped balance the overall age bias.

Participants had varying reasons for joining their teams. These included an interest in *indaba*; a desire to help the church, to travel, or to be part of a meaningful if difficult conversation; and the feeling that they couldn't say no to the invitation.[1] Their most common hopes were to become better listeners, to hear and understand other viewpoints, to find commonalities across their different cultural settings, and to come to see challenges as opportunities.[2]

---

[1] Coevaluator field notes (Nesbitt). In their opening session at the Ocho Rios *indaba* conversation, the Continuing Indaba project manager asked team members why they had agreed to participate.

[2] Responses to a questionnaire at the start of the Encounters.

Everyone on the Jamaican and Toronto teams made the entire journey from the first Encounter to the final *indaba* conversation. Two members of the Hong Kong team could not make the last Encounter and *indaba* conversation, and a new team member was added who was already known by all the participants because she had been actively involved in hosting the Hong Kong team's Encounter.

ENCOUNTER IN TORONTO

Toronto, Canada's major financial and business center, is arguably the country's most cosmopolitan city. Its nearly three million people speak more than 140 languages and dialects. About half of Toronto's population was born outside of Canada. Thirty percent speak a language at home other than the two official languages, English and French.[3] Toronto also is home to the largest population of Canada's First Nations people.

Toronto's cultural diversity is evident in its varied faith expressions. Slightly over half the population identifies as Christian, with Roman Catholic being the largest single denomination. About a quarter of the population identifies with other faith traditions, primarily Muslim, Hindu, Jewish, Buddhist, and Sikh. The remaining quarter of the population doesn't practice or identify with any religion.[4]

The Anglican Diocese of Toronto is the largest diocese of the Anglican Church of Canada, which has its headquarters in Toronto. Besides the urban center, the diocese includes a significant rural area that extends over sixteen thousand square miles. It encompasses a range of worship styles but is broadly traditional and recognizably Anglican in its liturgy, traditional hymnal, and Book of Common Prayer. Having more than two hundred congregations,[5] the diocese is responsible for a

---

3 "Diversity."
4 "Toronto Backgrounder."
5 "Profile of the Diocese."

number of social welfare ministries, including feeding programs for the homeless.

The Anglican Church's relationship with the First Nations people was a major influence on the Toronto team's thinking and informed their understanding of how historical roots and responsibilities relate to oppression and abuse in the present. The team communicated a strongly inclusive ethos, particularly in relation to women and same-sex blessings.

On Tuesday, May 31, 2011, all three diocesan teams met for the first time in Toronto. The Encounter program had four basic elements:

- introductory presentations;
- visits to diocesan ministries;
- weekend hosting by Toronto team members and others; and
- group discussion in plenaries and in diocesan teams.

For much of the Encounter, participants would stay at a convent. Sharing accommodations would allow them to socialize informally at the end of each day, and spontaneous conversations would help them get to know one another and build relationships. Worship framed their week together.

The presentations included an opening introduction to the nation of Canada, the Anglican Church of Canada, and the Diocese of Toronto. An emphasis was placed on the church's public apology to the First Nations people, acknowledging wrongs that the church had committed through its historical operation of residential schools. Other presentations focused on the mission themes for the Pilot Conversation, including youth and the topic of homosexuality. For the latter, outside speakers offered differing perspectives on the ordination of noncelibate gay and lesbian individuals.

Visits to social justice ministries included feeding programs for the homeless, a church program supporting those in poverty or who were unemployed, and a church-run drop-in center for female sex workers. Team members also visited other outreach projects focusing on the Encounter themes: a church-run restaurant operated and staffed by people with disabilities, and a church in Toronto's poorest area that served as a daytime drop-in center for homeless persons, offering basic medical and social services, a food bank, and a counseling center. Hong Kong team members later mentioned a notable visit to a Toronto landmark, where they were surprised at how the tourists blended in with the city's diverse multiracial and ethnic population. As one commented in a church article on the Encounter, "What a picture of harmony in diversity!"[6]

Over the weekend, Jamaican and Hong Kong team members stayed in the homes of Toronto participants or with members of their congregations. These home stays allowed small clusters of participants to interact and in most cases to meet and socialize with friends of their hosts, which introduced them to a wider social circle of Canadians. The closeness evolving out of these early shared experiences, the intimate conversations, and the relationships that developed within the context of the daily and parish life of the Toronto team were, for some, sustained to the end of the *indaba* conversation.

Throughout the course of the Encounter, participants discussed the presentations and their experiences together. The first formal dialogue, on the topic of social justice, took place on the third evening. The next day, the Encounter discussion focused on youth ministry and the challenge of attracting youth to church. The third conversation, on homosexuality, occurred on the eighth day, with outside speakers sharing how they had been in conversation for two decades while maintaining their differences of view on the topic.[7]

Early plenary discussions generated concerns that a few voices dominated the conversations while others remained

---

6 "Indaba in Toronto," 8–9.

7 Ibid., 9–10.

silent. The use of a "talking stick" was introduced by Canadian team members, a method used in some First Nations communal conversations, where only the person holding the stick is allowed to speak. This helped the group create a different pattern of dialogue and allowed more voices to be heard. However, patterns still emerged where certain (generally male and authoritative) voices spoke for longer periods of time than others. Some of the female participants would regularly pass on their opportunity to speak when the talking stick came to them. Nevertheless, it helped the group develop a more effective way of communicating and hearing different views.

"Learning how to listen to each other was difficult," commented one participant on a post-Encounter questionnaire. Another Toronto team member mentioned having learned through *indaba* how the Canadian Indigenous People's Sacred Circle could be helpful in improving the inclusivity of group interactions by using the talking stick. That the group was able to *learn* collaboratively how to develop its communication was extremely important for group cohesion and confidence at this early stage. Many of the visitors were profoundly challenged by some of the styles of engagement and the differences of view in this first Encounter. Yet visiting participants also reflected that despite tensions over the issues, it was evident that the church's mission continued to carry out the core message of the Gospel.

ENCOUNTER WITH HONG KONG

The second Encounter was held in Hong Kong. Hong Kong Sheng Kung Hui (SKH) is a young province in the Anglican Communion, founded in 1998, following the 1997 handover of the British colony of Hong Kong to the People's Republic of China.[8] The political agreement made Hong Kong a special administrative region for the next fifty years. This format is

---

8 *Sheng Kung Hui* means Holy Catholic Church. "Hong Kong Sheng Kung Hui."

often referred to as "one country, two systems,"[9] acknowledging Hong Kong's national affiliation yet relative independence in various areas, including religion.

The Anglican Church (SKH) includes three dioceses and the missionary area of Macao. Like its predecessor during the period of British colonization, the Anglican Church has schools and congregations serving both Chinese and English-speaking populations, although today the primary language of worship is Cantonese except in areas with many English-speaking expatriates. The overall worship style is "broad church," flexibly adapting to cultural differences. A new Chinese hymnal retains Anglican hymnody but also includes many Chinese compositions and lyrics. With the influx of immigrants from mainland China in the 1960s, the church also offers social services programs along with its focus on education and evangelism.[10]

Both Hong Kong and the Anglican Church (SKH) are in a state of transition as they negotiate their identities between British and Chinese historical and cultural influences. The influence of Confucianism on Anglicanism has inflected Christianity here with a particularly pragmatic orientation that looks to building for the future. It also has led to an emphasis on action as a direct outcome of listening and dialogue. Culturally, the Chinese emphasis on harmony, which presumes that difference is a basic condition and that the challenge is to keep differences in relationship so that coherence results, was illustrated in many ways during the Encounter. It also provided a foundational understanding for *indaba*.

Participants stayed together in the Mariners' Club (the Mission to Seafarers) in Kowloon, which normally accommodates seafaring workers from around the world. Because of Hong Kong's dense population, homes were unable to accommodate visitors during the Encounter. Some participants expressed disappointment, reflecting on the importance of sharing domestic space for understanding another cultural

---

9 "Hong Kong."

10 "Hong Kong Sheng Kung Hui"; *10th Anniversary of the Province of Hong Kong Sheng Kung Hui*, 28–29.

context. But the compact family apartments in high-rise towers, visible in nearly every direction, offered ample evidence of the lack of space.[11]

On Friday, September 23, 2011, the Encounter opened with worship in Cantonese. Visiting participants recognized the shared Anglican liturgy and its emotional and ritual language despite not understanding the words. For the opening session, the talking stick used in Toronto was culturally adapted to a "talking gong" passed around the circle and struck by each participant before speaking. As a response to some of the dynamics generated by the plenary conversations in Toronto, much of the dialogue would take place in small groups arranged in advance by the Hong Kong team with thought to creating a balance among the different voices. The groups were named "Honesty," "Respect," "Trust," and "Humility." Local facilitators helped with much of the small-group conversation. This enabled some of the quieter voices to be drawn out. Worship and small-group Bible study, which all teams felt had been lacking in Toronto, framed the Encounter.

Archbishop Paul Kwong, primate of Hong Kong Sheng Kung Hui, oriented the group to the church and the region, including its historical and current context and prospects for the future. At least a day was dedicated to each Encounter theme, including family and youth, leadership development, caring for the poor, and the church's voice in the public sphere.

Youth was the focus on Saturday, when the teams visited a congregation with an active youth ministry that emphasized building young Anglican identity. The Anglican Church (SHK) had held a youth *indaba* during the summer, using the themes from the Pilot Conversation. A group of young people shared their reflections on that *indaba* and then modeled a brief *indaba* on youth and alienation for the visiting teams. Afterward, everyone met together in small groups to learn more about young people's concerns, such as the challenge

---

[11] The descriptive content of this Encounter is based on field notes from a coevaluator who observed it (Nesbitt).

of time pressures and parental expectations that affect the youths' ability to participate.

On Monday, the group visited the island of Macao, site of the World War II ministry of the Rev. Florence Li Tim Oi, the first ordained woman in the Anglican Communion. Team members toured an Anglican school, ranging from kindergarten through secondary education and offering adult classes in the evenings. They also visited a family and youth social services center and strolled streets steeped with Portuguese colonial history.

Social service and justice was the theme of Tuesday's visit to St. James Settlement, established at the back of a Taoist temple in 1949 as a Christian club to serve refugees from mainland China. In 2002, the government had invited the settlement to build a new center that integrates different services, including a vocational training center, elderly meal service, day care, and a sheltered workshop for people with mental disabilities. It also serves as the Hong Kong food bank. After touring some of the services, participants heard local speakers representing different views on the role of the church in providing social services and in using its voice for social justice, which could create tension with governmental relationships. Wednesday morning, participants discussed social justice in small group *indabas* and then shared their reflections in a plenary. Several expressed admiration for the creativity in social services programs and the integration of services. They also noted the tensions between working within the system and the call to prophecy.

The group focused on the theme of human sexuality on Wednesday afternoon. As background, the Hong Kong team had provided several papers from different scholarly and religious points of view. The conversation began with panelists from a nondenominational Christian fellowship group that had started as an inclusive welcoming ministry. The panelists noted the conservative cultural expectations of heterosexual marriage and children, and a fear of bringing shame to the family. Despite evidence of societal tolerance, many gay and lesbian individuals are not public about their identities. A visiting participant spontaneously thanked the panelists, acknowledging the risks they had taken in speaking to the group.

On Thursday, a typhoon resulted in all activities being canceled as the city shut down. Confined indoors, participants met in small groups for a conversation on human sexuality, a topic that normally is not part of public discussion in Hong Kong or Jamaica. Afterward, they continued the discussion in a plenary group. During the *indaba*, participants talked from their own hearts, listening to one another's differences and expressing respect for the different cultures, backgrounds, and experiences out of which the differences arose. That evening, as the typhoon subsided, they ventured outdoors for a final dinner together.

The Encounter ended with each diocesan team sharing some of what its members had learned from their experience. The Jamaican team valued the introduction to Hong Kong, which laid a foundation for understanding it better, and was impressed with how the youth viewed themselves as leaders. The Toronto team voiced its respect for Hong Kong as a new region that drew on ancient wisdom, how much and how fast its people work, and how involved people are in their parishes, as well as its appreciation for having learned about the cultural context that affected how issues were addressed. The Hong Kong team said that the presentations had given its members much to think about and valued the deeper sharing and relationships being built.

On Friday morning, as the teams parted ways, they were feeling tension over flight delays and misunderstandings over logistical arrangements. Yet the three teams had mixed together well, partly because they stayed together and partly because of the hosts' detailed attention to making their visitors feel welcome. They also had built on the foundation begun in Toronto.

JAMAICAN ENCOUNTER

Kingston, Jamaica, was the site of the third Encounter. Jamaica has had an Anglican presence since 1664,[12] following British conquest of the island from Spanish control nearly a decade earlier. The legacy of colonialism, West African immigration through slavery and indenture, and numerous rebellions against enslavement and exploitation have been vital and turbulent aspects of Jamaican history that have forged an ethos of independence and pride in Jamaican culture but also have posed considerable challenges around identity. The resultant strength of character has been vital to Jamaica's ability to work through the ordeals it has faced since gaining independence in 1962.

The Anglican Diocese of Jamaica and the Cayman Islands is one of the eight dioceses forming the Anglican Province of the West Indies. In Jamaica, the Anglican Church has about thirty thousand members.[13] Its impact perhaps has been most significant through its ownership of numerous schools, a legacy of the colonial era. In worship, the Book of Common Prayer is very important, yet an African cultural inheritance and religious worldview helps shape Jamaican Christianity, according to several participants on the Jamaican diocesan team. The overall worship style is considered to be "broad church," which incorporates a range of higher and lower church elements, a mix of traditional hymns that are recognizable across the Anglican Communion, and local chant and response settings. Together they produce a lively diversity of worship styles.

The teams gathered in Kingston, Jamaica's capital, on Thursday, February 2, 2012, to begin their third Encounter. Unlike the other Encounters, this time visiting participants stayed with local hosts throughout their visit. Although this made it difficult to socialize with other participants as a group, it did offer the opportunity to learn about Jamaica

---

[12] J. B. Ellis, *The Diocese of Jamaica*, chapter 3.
[13] "Disestablishment of the Church."

and its context from locals outside the Jamaican team. Many participants later reported that this additional perspective on Jamaican life had been helpful. Worship and Bible study framed the Encounter week.

The teams visited several outreach ministries offered by the diocese. These included two church-run homes for school-age girls, a number of church schools, and various church-funded or affiliated social services agencies: health care, a social center for senior citizens, a parenting advice center, and a computer literacy teaching program. A visit to a church in the heart of a downtown Kingston ghetto, where one of the Jamaican team members had grown up, was a powerful experience for the Canadian and Hong Kong participants as they witnessed the extent of material deprivation there and heard of the profound social challenges posed by violence. The team member, who has become a successful businessman, continues to worship there and is heavily involved in outreach work. As in other partnerships where considerable economic disparities exist, teams began to discuss the possibility of supporting ministries at this church through church links, in a traditional donor-recipient form.

Presentations were made about the sociopolitical landscape of Jamaica and the Anglican Church's history on the island. Diocesan Bishop Alfred Reid powerfully described the differences between justice and welfare, illustrating his point by focusing on the relationship between the Global North and the Global South. The North offered Millennium Development Goals while the South was seeking a completely different kind of system.

Other presentations focused on the Encounter themes, including a panel discussion with young Jamaican Christians on issues affecting youth in their society. A presentation on homosexuality involved two speakers who spoke about emotional, biological, and theological aspects of the topic. Both were Anglicans who were prominent in debates over homosexuality in the Jamaican media. One was presented as an expert on the biological aspects of sexuality, posing the notion of sexuality as a spectrum across which many people move during the life course. The other was a priest offering a traditional theological perspective. Participants heard a testimony from a mother who had discovered that her son was gay. Both the presentations and the group plenary sessions used the talking stick method so that everyone would have an opportunity to ask questions and share their thoughts. A full day was set aside for this discussion. Many members of the Toronto team noted the risk that the Jamaican team was taking by even engaging in a conversation about same-sex relationships.

At the end of Encounter, the teams traveled together to the northern coast of Jamaica, where the formal *indaba* conversation would take place. The day was broken up with a visit to Dolphin Cove, where participants were able to swim with dolphins if they wished. As a bridge between the Encounter and the *indaba* conversation, the day of fun and relaxation worked well. The energy was convivial and friendly, and the group was confident. One participant later wrote on the closing questionnaire, "The final encounter was in particular meaningful, trust has already been built and we have somehow become close friends. This creates the environment in which we can be open to talk frankly."

FINAL CONVERSATION

The formal *indaba* conversation took place in Ocho Rios, a three-hour drive from Kingston. Had funding been available, it would have taken place on another island, such as Cuba. The travel day helped the teams transition from the Encounter to a different type of *indaba*. But handing over the hospitality to the project management (and the Anglican Communion Office) was challenging for the Jamaican team, who still felt a responsibility to the visitors in their country. This became especially troubling when logistical problems arose at the meeting site, which embarrassed the Jamaican team leaders even though they had not been responsible for arrangements. Another tension arose with the *indaba* schedule when the Jamaican team leaders felt it would be insulting if the Continuing Indaba teams didn't attend the Sunday morning service at a nearby church.[14] This was brought into the *indaba* for discussion, and participants supported a decision to shorten the schedule so they could attend.

On Friday evening, February 10, the formal conversation began with an orientation session that included meeting the facilitators from South Africa and Ireland, who would help the group enter into several difficult conversations. Saturday involved the group setting norms for their *indaba* and identifying topics they wanted to discuss. They agreed on five broad themes for *indaba* discussion:

- authority of Scripture;
- the Anglican Communion;
- social justice;
- homosexuality; and
- youth.

Team members also shared their hopes for the conversation, often expressing a desire for deeper listening and insight, as well as to move beyond politeness.[15] Anxieties were also expressed.

Throughout the conversation, the facilitators used a number of different group configurations to increase the possibility of everybody's voice being heard. Besides diocesan groups, these included constituency groups—bishops and link persons, youth, men, women, and clergy. Participants who overlapped two or more groups could choose the group to join. In another

---

14 There was a historical reason for this concern, but it would not have arisen if the conversation site had been outside the diocese.

15 Field observation notes (Sadgrove).

configuration, groups of three functioned as dyads, with one person speaking to another for a length of time, while a third member observed. The conversations were briefly summarized and shared in the plenary session that followed, although not everything said in small groups would be shared. This was particularly so for the women's group and the diocesan groups.

Social justice, the first topic discussed, had different meanings and expressions across the three cultures. There also were differing considerations, such as the role of the church in working with governmental agencies, and varying cultural contexts. Advocacy in one culture was done publicly, yet in another it was achieved privately through informal connections. Summaries from the small-group social justice *indabas* were shared in plenary. One saw the role of the church as a voice for the poor. Another saw its role as partnering with secular agencies. Another affirmed the need for both equality and equity but grappled with the dilemma of how to bring this about. Yet another struggled with how much the church could do because of its institutional position and dependence on donor contributions. A common theme running throughout the conversation was that the church needs to go beyond acts of mercy. Education was a helpful potential step.[16]

The next topic was authority of Scripture. Participants were asked to reflect in small groups on how they use Scripture to inform their views and what value it holds in helping their discernment. Cultural differences surfaced as to why this was a topic of discussion, even though all valued Scripture. For some, the tensions surrounding Scripture were palpable. Others acknowledged that there were differences in how authority was understood. Most agreed that they had needed more time to be able to understand others' views in greater depth. Although Bible study and discussion had been part of the Encounters, some had felt that differences of interpretation and understanding had not received enough attention. All three groups

---

[16] The description in this section also draws on coevaluator field notes (Nesbitt and Sadgrove).

expressed appreciation for having engaged with the under-lying theme of scriptural interpretation; this was especially so for the Jamaican team.

On Monday, their final day together, the group focused on the topic of sexuality. Participants formed three-person groups consisting of one person from each team who had not yet engaged with one another. A speaker and listener were to face each other, with the third person observing and time-keeping. The listener and observer were to set aside their own positions and try to understand as deeply as possible why the person speaking felt as he or she did. This was followed by a short period of silence, while the listener reflected on personal feelings at the moment and formulated a question to ask the speaker. The speaker could choose to answer it or not. The three members would swap roles until all had spoken, listened, and observed. After a brief plenary where the group reflected on the depth of the sharing that had occurred, they were asked to merge their triad with another triad to form a six-person group and discuss two questions: How have they managed to retain their relationships in the *indaba* process, given the range of views on this topic? And what have they learned that could help preserve the unity of the wider church when there are sincerely held opposing views on homosexuality?

As participants returned to the plenary, they appeared to be in a good mood. Their final topic would be youth alienation. They returned to their six-person groups and reflected on what fresh perspectives they had gained on tackling youth alien-ation in their own setting. Afterward, one person from each of the four groups sat at the center of a circle and shared their reflections, with participants gathered around. These included an observation that youth alienation was common to all their churches, but expressed in differing ways and having different causes. Making personal connections, building relationships, and listening to youth and young adults were seen as impor-tant, as well as honesty, authenticity, and offering leadership skills and experience. An open discussion followed.

On their final afternoon, several participants urged the importance of using *indaba* and other descriptive processes in the wider church and Communion, especially where parliamentary procedure makes it difficult for some to enter into the discussion. One commented that this kind of *indaba*, with an accent on listening and meaningful conversation, will help hold them together as a Communion. Another added that in *indaba*, he had felt that the three dioceses were different yet equal, with no suggestion that one was better than another.

Despite some frustrations, the group did not openly express conflict. Some were critical of having small groups, but several whose voices were not often heard in the plenaries defended them. One said that it gave an opportunity to reflect and speak in ways that they would not do publicly. The facilitators kept the participants focused and engaged in moving the conversation, which helped stave off potential challenges. In the end, several of the Hong Kong and other participants valued the formal *indaba* conversation as a way to summarize their overall experience and learning across the three Encounters and to deepen their understanding.

NARRATIVES AND THEMES

Both the cultural composition of this Pilot Conversation and the combination of participants with differing voices and personalities helped good relationships and dialogue develop. There were many moments where mutual listening occurred across sometimes profound and painful differences. Colonialism became a metanarrative for the group, enabling it to recognize both similarities and differences across cultures. The group acknowledged that their national histories were all shaped by a third power—British colonialism—and recited and represented sharply varying historical experiences of it.

The colonial narrative had emerged at the first Encounter during a plenary conversation when the teams began to reflect on the similarities and differences of their colonial histories as a way of seeking common ground. Both Jamaica and Toronto members tended to look backward historically for their understandings of national selfhood. For Toronto, an intentionally inclusive selfhood arose out of shame over how First Nations people had been treated. For some Jamaicans, the colonial narrative appeared to bring up tension and anger with those who looked and sounded like former colonizers. These figures became targets for inherited feelings of disorientation and alienation on the part of the Jamaican team. Hong Kong's rather different experience of colonialism both broadened and challenged these identity dynamics. Being future-oriented, Hong Kong teammates expressed some frustration over the others' historical emphasis. For them, colonialism had "turned a fishing village into a global financial center,"[17] and they urged a more pragmatic approach, one that looked to ensuring future success rather than focusing on the pains of the past.

From this narrative emerged the theme of family, which held great cultural importance for the Hong Kong team and also served as a way to listen and maintain relationships despite very different views on the issues the members explored and discussed. The desire to maintain relationships across differences also was embedded in Canadian culture, evident in its political history with French-speaking Quebec.[18]

Another theme that emerged was a sense that not only did each culture differ from the others, but each of these contexts had internal differences as well. Through encounter and conversation, stereotypes were broken down, and participants began to sense a plurality of positions on a number of issues in each location they visited. This also reflected a breaking down of the dichotomy between theology and culture, as some participants began to appreciate how culture and theology tended to interact. Theology might critique culture, but it also was informed by cultural history and experience.[19]

---

[17] Participant interview during the Jamaica Encounter.
[18] Coevaluator interview with a Toronto participant.
[19] Coevaluator field notes (Nesbitt).

The theme of sexuality was very much alive, appearing early during the first Encounter in Toronto. The conversation on lesbian and gay inclusion had been ongoing in the Anglican Church of Canada for more than thirty years. However, as a public conversation, it was new for Jamaica and Hong Kong. This also was complicated by the fact that homosexuality was illegal in Jamaica, and in Hong Kong until 1991, as well as widespread differences in both cultural and theological perspectives. Some Jamaicans heard the Toronto team telling them that they must "catch up" on this issue, and that gay and lesbian inclusion would just be a matter of time. This perception of the need to catch up on the part of the Jamaican team invoked some of the issues and memories around the use of power, including the racialization of power, which had been expressed in their parallel conversation about their national experiences with colonialism. The Hong Kong team provided a moderating presence to the challenges that this tension posed to the relationship between the two other teams.

GROUP DYNAMICS

The Pilot Conversation's group dynamics were at times affected by a number of factors. Besides the average age differences in the teams, Jamaica had two bishops on its team, one serving as the team's convenor, and their positions of authority caused teammates to be reluctant to counter their viewpoints, although differences of view became more openly expressed by the end. The female bishop on the Toronto team was not the convenor or link person. As a member of the team without a dual role, she offered an alternative model of episcopal authority in that her presence on the team did not appear to affect how team members spoke or acted.

Other factors affecting the dynamics of the group included the presence of a member of differing racial and ethnic background on two of the teams. Both of these members helped make easier connections with some of the visiting team members during the Encounter their team hosted. Additionally, one of the Toronto team was a layman in a same-sex marriage, whose presence had a large impact on challenging stereotypes around same-sex relationships that some participants had brought with them into the Pilot Conversation.

Several mechanisms helped the group maintain its relationships across a number of potentially threatening differences. First, each diocesan team generally had good internal relationships based either on friendships that emerged over time or on mutual respect and good humor. Second, the use of silence for two of the teams helped mediate the pace of the conversation. At first the Toronto team members seemed less comfortable with silence than the others and were often quick to speak. The Hong Kong team tended to hold back, taking time to think about the situation before speaking. Although the Jamaican team had a number of confident voices, there also was some withholding, which at times may have helped soften the intensity of disagreement on topics where differences of view were significant, such as sexuality and Scripture. As a third mechanism, humor was often used to mediate tensions as difficult issues arose, and at times it helped members find balance in the midst of their differences. A fourth mechanism was the explicit use of bonding metaphors based on the group's key narrative and themes to remind the members that their differences needn't divide them. These included colonial history, family, community, and harmony.

The metaphor of family, in which people don't have to agree in order to love each other, helped the group affirm their relationships and accept their differences. Participants increasingly referred to this metaphor as the third Encounter moved into the formal *indaba* conversation, when the group was perhaps performing most effectively. Just as extended families typically may have someone who is different in some way, that person is still part of the family even if some don't approve of certain behaviors. The family narrative allowed for recognition of love and relationship without agreement. As one participant commented on the closing questionnaire:

> The encounter has made me more aware that we are part of a larger, global family and like most families we don't all agree but we share common dreams and aspirations.

The family metaphor allowed strong differences to exist within the group while keeping them from seeming too threatening.

Each team was culturally rooted in an innate and experiential understanding that community can and does encompass difference. The challenge of the Pilot Conversation was how to keep differences from tearing the community apart. The perspective and role of Hong Kong strongly influenced the conversation group's ability to hold together through its use and modeling of the harmony metaphor, which by definition implies that differences exist and are kept in a balanced relationship. This understanding of harmony had permeated the Hong Kong Encounter—a harmony that seeks to understand differences and find common ground where accord and peace can emerge.[20] It also had been valuable in softening tensions across the teams' differences.

The closing survey data revealed that the third Encounter had been the most meaningful aspect of the Continuing Indaba process for the majority (75 percent) of respondents.[21] This may have been an outcome of the relationships having been built upon over the previous two Encounters. At the end of their journey, two-thirds had thought that the process had been very effective in developing authentic mutual listening across dioceses, while the others felt it had been somewhat effective. Some had reservations about the value of external facilitators working with an established group, and the facilitators did at times move the conversation into places where loyalty to the family narrative might have resulted in holding back on issues that might prove

---

[20] Lee, "'He' Theology," 133–35.

[21] Response rate to the closing survey was 87 percent.

too dangerous to the stability of the group. Yet external facilitators helped neutralize several established patterns of communication within the group, enabling fresh and deeper conversation to occur and marginalized voices to emerge and be heard.

REFLECTIONS ON THE JOURNEY

This Pilot Conversation group was remarkable in how it developed its own way of communicating on sensitive or difficult issues. The group found and used common narratives to stay in conversation across sometimes vast differences of culture and perspective. By the third Encounter, the holding narrative of *colonialism* had shifted to one of *family*, and the group was marked both by strong relationships among the participants and loyalty to group identity. Throughout the Encounters, the members of this Pilot Conversation had deepened their relationships and ability to communicate. In Jamaica, the strength of relationships had been striking, both on an individual level and as an *indaba* group. All three teams had moved more deeply and reflectively into places of mutual listening and trust.

Overall, considerable enthusiasm for the *indaba* process was expressed, and by the end of the project, it had been adapted for different uses in two of the three participating dioceses. As a participant commented during their journey together, "Our sense of who we are as Anglicans in our various contexts is itself in flux, which makes the needs for continued, ongoing conversation even more important."[22] Several comments afterward indicated the importance of learning to ask questions and listen with an open mind, as well as to understand the role that culture has in shaping differences of perspective.[23] All were valuable to this Pilot Conversation group's ability to journey together.

---

[22] Participant comment from a Reflections statement following the second Encounter.

[23] Evaluator field notes (Sadgrove). Also see "Canada."

Unity in Diversity

A Safari across Differences in Saldanha Bay, Ho, and Mbeere

—Mkunga H. P. Mtingele

~~~

SALDANHA BAY, HO, AND MBEERE are all within the African continent. As Anglican dioceses, they are relatively new. But there are many differences in the culture, history, and geography of the countries where they are located: South Africa, Ghana, and Kenya. This Pilot Conversation found even more differences in how the members of these dioceses worshiped and expressed their Anglican faith, and in the challenges that each team faced as they visited one another's dioceses on their *safari* (a Swahili word meaning "journey" or "trip"). They would find a way forward together in unity while respecting each other's differences, but it would not be easy.

Unlike the other Pilot Conversations, which had dioceses from both the Global North and the Global South, this conversation was able to explore the usefulness of *indaba* for the concerns that churches face within Africa. All three bishops of these dioceses were both the convenors of their groups and active participants in them. The convenors had met together in 2010 and agreed on five mission areas of concern to explore in their Pilot Conversation together:

- land reform, environment, and poverty;
- theological education, formation, and transformation;
- children, youth, and women;
- human sexuality and gender; and
- structure, administration, church leadership, and finance.

These areas would be explored in different ways during the three Encounters that took place in 2011.

Each diocesan group, besides the bishop, included both laity and clergy, men and women, and younger and older adults. The Saldanha Bay team had two parish priests, an ordained scholar, two young adults, and two experienced laity. The Ho team members were mostly laypeople. The group's link person became ordained as a deacon near the end of the Pilot Conversation, bringing the ordained total to three (including the bishop) for the final *indaba* conversation. The Mbeere group had four ordained clergy—two women and two men—in addition to the bishop. At the first Encounter, the other groups' young adult participants observed that there were no young adults on the Mbeere team, and as a result, two were added, both ordained. Mbeere also was the only group with ordained women. Overall, participants were about 60 percent male and 40 percent female.[1] All participants were interviewed at least once during the Pilot Conversation.[2]

---

[1] By the time of the final *indaba* conversation, the composition of all participants was half laity, one-third priests, one-eighth bishops, and one deacon. All statistics in this case study are from participant responses to the questionnaire given at the end of the *indaba* conversation. Its response rate was 100 percent.

[2] The three convenors and link persons were interviewed before the start of the Encounters. Other participants were interviewed one or more times during the Ho and Mbeere Encounters.

At the start of their time together, nearly everyone felt somewhat or very comfortable in cross-cultural conversation even when differences of view were present, according to the initial survey. Participants varied in what they hoped to learn, although many simply wanted to be open to learning from others. They also hoped that others might learn about the cultural and political diversity of their own dioceses, the challenges that their communities face, and the challenges in their mission work.

From the Encounters in other dioceses, they hoped to learn about the differences in culture, beliefs, values, and the ways of "being church" in other communities. They also wanted to know about others' challenges and how they were approached, including the church's work with wider communities. More than half of the participants expected to have their thinking challenged, especially by differences of view and culture.

Listening most often meant being ready to learn from others, according to the survey responses. It also meant taking time to understand others better, including their different views and values, and to respect others across the differences of opinions and cultures. Most participants felt that the *indaba* process would strengthen or increase their faith; two explicitly mentioned it as a journey of faith. But their time together would challenge their ability to listen and understand, including the different ways in which their faith was expressed.

BEGINNING THE *SAFARI*: SALDANHA BAY

The Anglican Diocese of Saldanha Bay, about sixty miles north of Cape Town in the Republic of South Africa, stretches from the rich fields of Malmesbury and the West Coast to the vineyards of Paarl, the urban belt of Belville and Maitland, and areas of the coast where fishing and mining support the economy. It also includes the semidesert regions of Namaqualand North and South.[3] The diocese was separated from the Cape Town diocese in 2005 and is Anglo-Catholic in its worship.

Saldanha Bay has a number of towns along its shore, with a total population of around one hundred thousand people.[4] Saldanha, at the northern edge of the bay, is a major port for shipping ore and has a diverse population. Three primary languages are spoken in the region: Afrikaans (by 70 percent of the people), isiXhosa (20 percent), and English (7 percent). The majority of the population is mixed race or ethnicity (54 percent Colored), which was the background of the diocesan team in this Pilot Conversation. Others are black Africans (about 30 percent), whites (about 14 percent), and Indian/Asians (a little over 1 percent of the population).[5]

On June 28, the teams from Ho (Ghana) and Mbeere (Kenya) arrived in Cape Town. They would begin the formal Encounter the next day at a conference center in Malmesbury. Daily morning and evening worship would be led by members of the different diocesan groups. Daily Bible study also would be important to team building. On the first day, participants were given time to introduce themselves and exchange gifts. Information was shared about the diocese and what would take place in the coming week. During both the first and second days, resource people in the diocese spoke briefly about the mission priorities that had been chosen by the convenors, how each was being addressed in the diocese, and its challenges. Afterward, there was time for questions, open discussion, and small-group reflection.[6]

The next phase of the Encounter, to experience mission in the diocese, began on the second afternoon. To gain understanding of the breadth of this large diocese, participants were

---

3 "The Diocese of Saldanha Bay."

4 "Saldanha Bay Local Municipality (WC014)."

5 "Saldanha," Main Place 163008 from Census 2011. https://census2011. adrianfrith.com/place/163008. Accessed December 29, 2015.

6 Because of the constraint of funds for the project, the author as evaluator could not attend this Encounter and relied on the project administrator for information. At the Ho Encounter, the author was able to interview each participant about their experience at this first Encounter.

divided into four groups, each with two members from each team. These groups were the same as those formed for Bible study. The aim was to meet people in different parts of the diocese in order to learn more about how the mission priorities were being enacted. Each group would spend about five days staying with families in local parishes across different parts of the diocese.

The groups reunited on Tuesday, July 5, for lunch at a parish, and then spent the afternoon in informal recreation, including a visit to Robben Island, a national and world heritage site where former president Nelson Mandela had been imprisoned for eighteen years. That evening, they gathered for a formal dinner at the bishop's house. On the final day of the Encounter, the participants shared their different experiences and reflections. On the post-Encounter questionnaire, several expressed gratitude for the opportunity to have participated. A few commented that it had stirred something new in them or moved them to action.

CONTINUING ON THE *SAFARI* TO HO

Ho is in the southeastern corner of Ghana, between Lake Volta and the Republic of Togo to the East. This is a region of lush vegetation, hills, and some mountains. Ho, the region's capital and largest city, has about one hundred thousand people.[7] The majority of people in this region are involved in subsistence farming, which yields an income of about 40 percent of what a civil servant makes. The low income of the region has a negative impact on youth education, since schooling requires fees that must be paid.[8] Religious belief is strong in the region, which is about 95 percent Christian. Islam and traditional religions make up most of the remainder.[9]

---

7 "City Population."

8 "History of the Diocese."

9 Arnim Langer and Ukoha Ukiwo, "Ethnicity, Religion and the State in Ghana and Nigeria."

The Anglican Church has a small presence compared with the Evangelical Presbyterian Church, which is nationally head-quartered in Ho, and the Roman Catholic Church, which has three dioceses in the Volta region.[10] The Anglican Diocese of Ho is part of the Anglican Province of West Africa. Inaugurated in 2003, the diocese is multinational. It covers the Volta Region of Ghana and extends across the entire Republic of Togo. The diocese is Anglo-Catholic, with a High Church tradition in worship that follows the 1861 Book of Common Prayer. When the bishop was asked to describe his diocese, he said, "It is a forward in faith diocese which strongly holds to the Catholic faith."[11] Because of the rural economy of much of the diocese, the lack of funds has meant that the diocese has no established administrative structures, unlike the other two dioceses in the Pilot Conversation. There is little money for staff or for training clergy. As a result, the bishop's leadership is vital to all that happens in the diocese.

The three teams arrived in Ghana's capital city, Accra, for the second Encounter on Monday, September 5. The next day they traveled to Ho, where they would stay together at a Catholic retreat center during the Encounter. That evening, they had an orientation to the Encounter. Introductions were repeated so that participants could be reacquainted. The pattern of the next three days of the Encounter was structured very much the same way as at Saldanha Bay. Each day began with Eucharist and a homily, followed by Bible study in groups and then presentations on mission priorities. There also was time for diocesan teams to meet together.

In the remainder of the Encounter, participants experienced the life of the church through visits to parishes. They had opportunities to ask questions and have conversations with people in the local churches. They visited the Worawora area in the north on Friday and the banks of the River Volta and the district of Kpando on Saturday. On Sunday, they worshiped at

---

10 "History of the Diocese."
11 Personal interview, 2010.

the Anglican cathedral in Ho and enjoyed an informal after-noon together. A visit on Monday to Keta, on the Ghana coast, included a trip to a historic slave-trading fort and a sea defense project to combat the erosion of the coastal area. After a discussion of the morning's presentations on Tuesday, they traveled to a church in Agbozume, a small town in the south-eastern corner of Ghana, and spent time with the people there. On Wednesday, the teams visited a church in Penyi, near the border of Togo. That afternoon, they held the closing conver-sation for their Encounter. The next morning, they departed for Accra and then home.

Unlike the First Encounter, this time the entire group trav-eled in one minibus and visited the same places together. The bishops in most cases traveled together in a car, which others thought reflected class differences—bishops as a superior class and the rest as ordinaries. Apart from that concern, one par-ticipant said in an interview how important it had been to go together to the same places so that they had the same experi-ences. Since there were no reflection sessions, private one-on-one reflections took place during breaks or after the formal sessions. This sharing enriched each other's understanding.

Throughout their time in the Ho Encounter, the visiting teams experienced differences in food and culture that some-times were challenging. They also encountered a culture that was strongly conservative in its understandings of gender and sexuality. This diocese did not ordain women or recognize their status as clergy, resulting in tension surrounding the two ordained women on the Mbeere team. This tension would con-tinue beyond the Encounter.

MEETING UP IN MBEERE

The Diocese of Mbeere, part of the Anglican Church of Kenya, was created in 1997. It is a rural diocese in the Eastern Province of Kenya, stretching to Mandera in the northeast corner and bordering Somalia and Ethiopia. About 219,000 people live in the region.[12] Despite being rural, the diocese is cosmopolitan, with people from different parts of Kenya. It also serves several different ethnic communities, the majority being Mbeere and Kamba, but also Embu, Kikuyu, and Somalis in the northeast.[13] Subsistence farming is the main economic activity on the semiarid lands. Maize and tobacco are the major crops. In the northeast, people raise livestock, typically cattle, goats, sheep, and camels.

The Diocese of Mbeere serves more than fifty thousand Anglicans and has about fifty priests. It is the only evangelical diocese among the three dioceses in this Pilot Conversation. With about 125 congregations, the diocese also sponsors more than ninety primary and secondary schools, a technical trade school, and a special school for the deaf. Additional projects are supported through partnerships with other groups and organizations; these include child development centers, a lay training center, rental houses overseen by the Mothers Union, a bookshop, and the Mayori Integrated Development Centre, offering training on agriculture and health issues, as well as health services.

Participants from Ho arrived in Nairobi on Sunday, December 4. The Saldanha Bay team arrived the next day. Both groups then traveled from Nairobi and met the Mbeere team on Monday evening. All were present except the Ho link person, who remained at home preparing for his ordination, which would take place on the final day of the Encounter. He would rejoin the group for the formal *indaba* conversation the following week. Because of tight scheduling, the Mbeere Encounter had to be shortened by two days to allow time for the *indaba* conversation.

For the first three nights of the Encounter, the participants were accommodated in a guesthouse in a nearby diocese, since

---

12   Admin, "An Interview with Bishop Moses of Mbeere in Kenya on Continuing Indaba."

13   Information on the diocese is from "Diocese of Mbeere."

the Mbeere diocese had no guest facilities for a large group. During the day, they traveled in four separate small groups to experience different aspects of daily life across the diocese, much as they had done at the Saldanha Bay Encounter.[14] The visits were mainly to churches. The participants met with members of the congregations and others in the local communities, asked questions, and interacted with them.

As in the Ho Encounter, they stayed together as one group at night. This allowed them to listen and share their experiences with each other. At one point, a difference in cultural expectations arose, as members of one of the visiting teams had not expected that they would be asked questions by the local people they met. A mini-*indaba* was held later within the group so that the cultural differences and expectations could be heard and understood, and the tensions were worked out. The next parish visit turned out to be very constructive, and the team was more participatory.

On Saturday, December 10, toward the end of the Mbeere Encounter, a significant event took place. It was a Prayer Day and included a liturgy of repentance. Planned by the diocese, it aimed to reconcile two main clans in the area that had been divided since 1964. This long-standing feud had permeated local politics and caused unrest and violence. Land use in the context of Mbeere was related to these clan divisions and hostilities. The hope was to bring the people of the two clans together, following conversations that used *indaba* with the two groups to think of how the community might be reconciled. At the service, the bishop of the Ho diocese preached and the bishop of the Saldanha Bay diocese spoke about cleansing. One of the participants from the Saldanha Bay diocese gave a moving testimony of how his family had been affected by the apartheid regime, which had led to his mother committing suicide. He had been invited to share his story at the event after telling it to the teams at the Ho Encounter. Overall, the

---

14 This meant that one group was not accompanied by an evaluator, thereby denying the opportunity to observe the group dynamics.

event was both successful and inspiring, and people were very much moved.[15]

Because the Mbeere Encounter had to be shortened, it included only one day that was dedicated to presentations on the key issues and themes, unlike the other Encounters. The Encounter ended on December 11 so that the group could travel the next day to Limuru, where the *indaba* conversation would take place.

HOLDING THE *INDABA* CONVERSATION

The *indaba* conversation began on Tuesday, December 13, 2011, at a conference center next to St. Paul's University, in Limuru. The teams had arrived from Mbeere the previous day. Many were tired and still feeling emotions from the Prayer Day and reconciliation event. Since this was the first of the formal *indaba* conversations, details were still being worked out. The cofacilitators had arrived from Botswana and Australia but did not have a full briefing on the group's experiences or on the conversation itself.

Participants had expected the *indaba* conversation to give them a chance to review their experiences on the Encounters and find consensus on all the key issues, but it initially went in a different direction. The first day was spent on the process that would be used for the *indaba*. Disagreement arose over whether the teams wanted to stay together as a large group, even though some voices were silent, or to meet in small groups for some of the time. Other differences emerged over what they wanted to talk about. This frustrated several participants. Some felt that discussion of the process was a waste of time, as it was not *indaba* and they were impatient for the real business to begin. Phil Groves, Continuing Indaba project manager, rescued the situation by explaining that there had

---

[15] Personal account from field research (Mtingele); Admin, "Interview with Bishop Moses of Mbeere." According to Bishop Moses Masamba Nthuka, the historical enmity has come to an end.

been miscommunication between his office and the facilitators. Participants then relaxed, and the process began to unfold more smoothly. The facilitators also changed some of their wording to be more consistent with the group's experience.[16]

The *indaba* moved well on the next days. *Indaba* conversations took place both in small groups and in plenary sessions. Each day, small groups also held a Bible study. The plenary conversation on women's ordination, on the afternoon of the second day, brought heated discussion. For a few moments, it seemed that the conflict might get the better of the group—that *indaba* wouldn't work, and the group might break up despite all they had invested together. There also was fear that some might have a hidden agenda. This created distrust that added to the tension in the room. At the end of the day, participants spoke about how difficult the conversation had been.

The next morning, they discussed what had happened the previous day, making space for people to speak from their hearts. The differences remained, but something had shifted. The participants spoke of wanting to be one as a group and to allow for their differences. Then they returned to the topic of women's ordination.[17] One participant observed that the discussion of the ordination of women was made easier because of the time they had spent earlier, which had helped deepen relationships and establish trust and mutual understanding. Without time spent in this way, the discussion would have remained at a surface level, in contrast to the deeper conversation they had.

When some had recognized that the group had moved as far as it could go during the *indaba* conversation, someone would ask if the group could take a break. During the breaks, participants reflected, some walked, and some had private conversations. When the group met again, emotions had calmed. If a sensitive topic came up, it brought new insight. Related issues also began to surface, which helped the participants understand their differences better.

---

16 Coevaluators' interview with the facilitators after the formal conversation.
17 Coevaluator field notes (Nesbitt).

Their commitment to one another as a group with a distinct relationship helped them stay with the process until they found a way forward together. In the end, the conversation that actually happened had been difficult and painful at times, but several said that it had been deeper and more honest than they had thought possible.

EXAMINING THE ISSUES
THAT CREATED TENSION

At the *indaba* conversation, there had been two "elephants in the room" creating hesitancy in the discussions: the ordination of women and homosexuality. It was only after these were identified as major concerns that open and meaningful conversation began.

The ordination of women became a major issue of conflict. The tension over it had begun in the first Encounter, at Saldanha Bay, when some participants did not accept the ministry of female clergy. It became worse in the Ho Encounter, when the two female priests were not allowed to exercise their ordained ministry, although they had expected to do so. This adversely affected not only the two female priests but the group as a whole, in that some of the men were in solidarity with them. A male priest from one of the visiting dioceses in the Encounter even declined to take Eucharist in solidarity on this matter.

The tension became so deep that one of the participants publicly declared his intention not to attend the last Encounter, although he later changed his mind. In the last Encounter, the host diocese of Mbeere chose to accommodate those who did not support women's ordination, which diffused some of the tension. A female priest did not celebrate the Eucharist, as it was known that one of the participants would be unlikely to receive Communion from her. The three convenors worked behind the scenes to contain the tension, but the wounds resulting from this conflict were deep for some.

The tension over the ordination of women resurfaced at the Limuru *indaba* conversation. Some who accepted women's ordination wanted to know why it was not acceptable to those who did not. How the comments unfolded made it clear that some wanted to participate in a theological debate. A few others accepted the differences but simply wanted to understand. Those opposed felt that it wasn't the right time for the conversation and chose not to speak about their views. Although the conversation appeared to end without the explanation that had been sought, on the last day the participants were able to talk about the deeper concerns, such as lack of mutual respect surrounding the issue.

There are several possible explanations for this conflict. First, some attributed it to a lack of preparation and understanding of different cultural practices before the Encounters. Second, some participants felt that they were being pushed into accepting the other's position. A related feeling was that the visiting groups had come to teach and dictate instead of being present to learn from the hosts. This increased defensiveness and rigidity. Third, the issue of women's ordination was discussed only in terms of theology, by theologians. It was clear that for some people, the issue was cultural: certain tasks are not culturally acceptable for women to do, serving in the ordained ministry being one of them.[18]

The second issue creating tension was homosexuality, although the disagreement over the issue was not as intense as that over the ordination of women. The three diocesan groups differed on this issue. One group was more flexible in its view of sexuality. Another group was strongly conservative, but it also recognized that homosexuality was a fact of life and was concerned over how homosexuals as human beings were treated. The third group was both very conservative and less tolerant. The group taking the middle road helped mediate between the other two.

---

[18]   The debate was followed by this evaluator in different parishes and in participant interviews.

Although human sexuality had been on the convenors' list of mission issues, it was not directly discussed in the Encounters. The subject did emerge in the parish visits, where questions were asked about it. On one occasion, a visiting bishop explained in response to a question:

> We should not think that homosexuals are
> found only in Europe and USA. They are in our
> pews, homes and communities. We cannot kick
> them out of the church or legislate to kill them.
> What if we find out they are our own sons and
> daughters living in our homes! We have to listen
> to them, understand and love them. The church
> is a house of sinners.[19]

He went on to give the New Testament example of the adulterous woman who was not stoned. Jesus did not judge her, but told her to go and not to sin again. This explanation was echoed by a layperson in one of the parish visits in a diocese strongly opposed to homosexuality, who pointed out that homosexuality was a reality even in that diocese, town, and parish, though officially the church denies its existence. Over the Encounters, the groups continued to hold their different views, but some of the tension and hostility began to soften.

The third area of tension was over the Encounter process itself. This was illustrated in the different cultural understandings arising while making deanery visits in the Mbeere Encounter, where a mini-*indaba* took place so that the differences could be understood and discussed.

Tension also arose over the purpose of the Continuing Indaba project and differing expectations of what the formal conversation should be. According to the project manager, the focus of Continuing Indaba was to create space for whatever the convenors of the Pilot Conversations wanted to discuss. Some participants felt that the project should have handled

---

[19] Comments based on field observation of the visitation (Mtingele).

only the principal issues affecting the worldwide Communion. A participant at the Limuru final conversation commented:

> We avoided the real issues. We were told that it [Continuing Indaba] is about mission, and not homosexuality and the ordination of women. Those against those issues think that the *indaba* process might be a ploy to hide the real issues.

The issue regarding land, the first mission area identified by the convenors, wasn't an issue tearing the Communion apart. The five mission areas included human sexuality and gender, but the bishops chose the priorities to emphasize in their dioceses.

Additionally, the group had wanted a strong leader-led process during the *indaba* conversation, but they did not get it. Instead, the facilitators saw their role as helping and supporting the group as it led its own process.

CONSIDERING GROUP DYNAMICS AND FACILITATION

A number of group dynamics affected what took place in the Encounters and formal *indaba* conversation. The diocesan groups typically took a common stand on certain issues in public, maintaining solidarity, while some members differed privately in their views. For one group, the common good was very important to how it publicly spoke on certain issues. These issues included the ordination of women and homosexuality. Some had a fear of being rejected or seen as traitors by their own group, especially by their bishop. For instance, some participants revealed that it was important in their culture to respect their leader. Therefore, they could not say something in public that they knew was against the leader's view. During an interview, one participant said that his bishop was very cross because of something he had said and had threatened to remove him from the group. Sometimes alliances were in the process of shifting. These dynamics raised questions about how much of what publicly was said actually was owned by the individuals speaking, and what the conversation actually meant.

Another dynamic involved pressure from those with strong voices to stay in one large group and not have small-group meetings. But several who felt that their voices were not being heard did want small groups. In the formal conversation, time was made for constituency groups: men, women, youth, clergy, bishops, and link persons. Some men had joked about having a men's group as well as a women's group. The facilitator said that they needed to figure out what they would talk about, and then speak from the standpoint of men. Later, the men reported back on the issues they had discussed, including men's treatment of women. In the end, the constituency groups brought issues to the whole group that otherwise would not have been raised. They also empowered voices of laywomen and young adults to speak.[20]

In each of the Encounters, a local facilitator was used. Most participants thought the facilitation had been helpful, but a few felt that there had been nothing *indaba* about it. In one Encounter, the facilitator was not aware that it was important for everyone to have a sense of what had taken place in small-group conversations. When the facilitator didn't ask for the content of small-group conversations to be shared with the main group, this was viewed as a lack of transparency and imposition of a "Western process" on them.

The formal *indaba* conversation also had begun with tensions surrounding the facilitation, but the facilitators made adjustments. Later, in an interview, one facilitator said that "there is no generic African culture, but there are things we bear in mind." Her own African background had made it easier to relate to what was happening in the room and help move

---

20 Coevaluator field notes (Nesbitt).

the group along.[21] During the most stressful moments, she summarized comments so that the group could either agree with or reject them and clarify what had been said. This helped them listen in the midst of tension and emotion. At the end, many voiced their appreciation that the facilitation had helped them have a very difficult conversation.

SPEAKING THE TRUTH IN LOVE

Tensions arose in some of the Encounters surrounding hospitality, such as different foods and the types of accommodations. In one Encounter, some complained about the accommodations so conspicuously that a good amount of tension developed. Some members also spoke in their vernacular language, which was known to their own team but not to everyone else. Others complained about these matters privately but did not openly express their discomfort, yet they often were overhead by participants from the hosting diocese.

In another Encounter, a facilitator had to reschedule the program so that time could be allocated for honest speaking; the tension and misunderstandings had to be cleared in order to continue. Despite the time set aside to have conversation about those issues, they still were not openly discussed. By and large, this was about differences in African cultures. Africa is a large continent with very diverse cultures; what they have in common is the importance of maintaining relationships. One cannot openly say something that may be painful or may offend another person. Instead, it should be kept to oneself so that the relationship stays intact.

This raises the question of what "speaking the truth in love" means. In most cases, it is a matter of *how* the truth is communicated to another party. In the case of complaints over hospitality, it would have been better if the concerns had been openly communicated in love. More damage is done when a

---

21   Coevaluator interview notes (Nesbitt).

person hears unofficial complaints. Also, the backbiting that occurred during the Encounters was both unhealthy and against the spirit of *indaba*. In one of the Encounters, the three convenors had acted as a de facto review team on some issues, but not on everything. In both the Ho and Mbeere Encounters, there had been no way for the convenors to review how the previous day had gone and to take action on any issues as they arose. This was unfortunate.

CHANGING PERCEPTIONS AND LEARNING FROM THE *INDABA*

Some participants had felt anxiety that the purpose of *indaba* was to change them. Outside detractors of Continuing Indaba had claimed that it would try to push Western liberal views. This was not true. Another concern over change had to do with how visitors regarded one's local culture and viewed issues that were rooted in particular cultural contexts. One participant spoke his mind on several occasions about his perception that some visiting team members were there to change the diocese. The attitude that visitors held, including private complaints that were overheard, contributed to his concern.

But in *indaba*, change is not about changing one's views. Instead, it is about changing reactions and responses to different views that are expressed by others. It is about being comfortable with differences that may previously have been understood in prejudicial ways. Acknowledging the existence of others with differing views and accepting them is important. But accepting that they do things differently is not the same as agreeing that you will do that too. When people are accepted, despite the differences they have, it becomes easier for them to accept themselves as human beings.

The views or positions of some participants might not have changed on certain issues, but some of the responses to the final questionnaire showed that their understanding had shifted. This is a changed perception that can allow acceptance of differences while continuing to hold the same position. In the end, the group became more respectful of one another. Different views remained, but the participants eventually found a way to walk together that respected those differences.

When the participants were asked how much they had learned from their experience in Continuing Indaba on the closing questionnaire, more than three out of four responded that they had learned a great deal. The others all admitted that they had learned something. All participants were of the view that the project had helped them experience the flavor of the daily life of people from different dioceses and cultures, with more than nine out of ten saying that it had done so very much. Nearly three out of four had discovered new similarities between their diocese and the other two, mostly around the issue of land, but also in youth ministry and youth alienation. They recognized that much needs to be done to involve youth in the ministry and decision-making of the church. Some were concerned that the dioceses had become seed beds where young people would grow but then get transplanted to another church.

Being more open, more tolerant, and listening were related learning areas for participants. They observed that cultural understanding, learning how to listen to different views, and seeking understanding of these views are crucial for the Communion. They also learned to value differences insofar as they could disagree with one another yet still identify as a group. Another point of learning was how cultural differences have affected the values and practices of the church in different locations. As one commented, "I am now aware that being African is not oneness. We are diverse."[22] In one of the Encounters, a participating bishop remarked that he now understands why some bishops take different sides on issues dividing the Anglican Communion.

For some, this was the first time they had been exposed to

---

[22] A response to a question in the final survey after the Limuru *indaba* Conversation.

different traditions within Anglicanism. Some had thought that the Anglican Communion was the same across the world. But as one pointed out, believing Anglicanism is the same the world over "is totally wrong." There are differences; there are diversities across the traditions of the church and doctrines. Some also had misapprehensions as to why two Anglo-Catholic dioceses were paired with an Evangelical diocese, but they came to appreciate each other and the purpose of being together. Several came to appreciate others through the different ways of doing church—worship, celebration of the Mass, the use of symbols and vestments. Through these differences, they learned how Anglicanism can vary in other parts of the Communion.

Across the three Encounters, it was clear that mutual learning did take place.[23] People were able to learn from each other in many areas, including traditions and churchmanship. Their thinking also had been challenged or in some way affected by the *indaba* experience. Several were challenged by the importance of making space for others irrespective of their differences or of seeing the image of God in others. Some also had challenging moments during the Encounters. As one observed, "Sometimes I was tempted to go into 'defense' mode! Sometimes I wanted to leave or not continue to be part of *Continuing Indaba*." Yet this participant continued on to the end because something valuable had been found in Continuing Indaba.

CONTINUING RELATIONSHIPS AND PRACTICING *INDABA*

An area of significant learning, for three out of four participants, was about their own diocese and its mission. More than four out of five (83 percent) had learned new ideas or possibilities for addressing challenges or concerns across dioceses in

---

[23] The interviews conducted during and after the last two Encounters and the questionnaires filled out by the participants provide evidence of this mutual learning and of having been affected by the *indaba* experience.

their church. This was the most highly rated of eight areas of learning explored in the survey.[24] It suggests that Continuing Indaba had brought new and creative insights for the participants and that the Pilot Conversation had a strong learning effect.

As a result of the *indaba*, some participants reflected on truth. One had this to say: "I have been challenged to realize that truth is relative; my truth is not your truth and your truth is not my truth and maybe our truths are not truths at all." Another participant wrote on the final questionnaire, "I first thought that homosexuals are sinners but have a change of mind."[25] After Continuing Indaba, 96 percent of the participants felt more comfortable talking with others with views different from their own. About eight in ten felt more curious about understanding why others held those different views. These responses suggest that *indaba* had a major impact.

Some participants had already begun to practice *indaba* while the Pilot Conversation was ongoing. In the Mbeere diocese, the *indaba* process had been used to reduce tensions and to build relationships that could lead to the clan reconciliation service, which was significant. This also meant that the diocese had embraced *indaba* as a tool of reconciliation. The diocesan groups in the *indaba* Pilot Conversation also had a rare opportunity to interact with a much larger group beyond the church and to experience the enthusiasm for reconciliation among people who had been strongly affected by the clan divisions.

As another example, one diocese observed that it already followed a process similar to *indaba*. By establishing priorities for its clergy school, using a facilitator, it created a very participatory outcome for the school. The diocese also went one step

---

24 The mean rating for this type of learning, among eight possible types offered by the question, was 3.8 out of a possible 4.0. Respondents rated each type separately, from strongly disagree (0.0) to strongly agree (4.0). They also were able to add any other type of learning they experienced in their response to the question.

25 A response to a question in the final survey after the Limuru *indaba* Conversation.

further, encouraging clergy to choose to belong to a mission group that would carry on the process. People have started introducing the mission priorities and are beginning conversations and listening across the diocese. There also has been a youth *indaba* and an *indaba* process developed to help resolve issues affecting parishes, congregations, and other aspects of the diocese. On interfaith matters, Christians also have been encouraged to listen while others speak, for the sake of wider unity.

Before the Encounters began, one of the convenors had this to say in an interview about his expectations:

> I am excited and I feel hopeful, very positive and
> hopeful. I am aware that there are difficulties.
> The opportunity to be brothers and sisters
> despite these difficulties gives me a feeling of
> hope and good about the Anglican Communion.
> . . . Overall I hope that we will discover and be
> able to celebrate our common humanity. We will
> continue to find that we are a communion and a
> community. It is possible, really, really possible
> to be together despite our differences. There can
> be a genuine appreciation of one another. There
> is no contradiction in terms to be on opposing
> sides. We can genuinely hold together.

His comments expressed the feelings of all three bishops in this all-African Pilot Conversation. It was about walking together in fellowship despite differences and learning from each other.

Building relationships takes time, however. The Encounters turned out to be the most important step in establishing and deepening the relationships among participants. The first Encounter in Saldanha Bay helped them establish relationships, and these strengthened over the Ho and Mbeere Encounters. Daily worship, Bible study, interpersonal and group interactions, and visits in different parts of the dioceses also helped deepen relationships. During these Encounters, participants discussed having relationships between parishes, hosting exchange programs, and continuing to stay in relationship with one another after the Pilot Conversation formally ended.

Despite the tensions, the participants had built strong relationships across their diocesan groups, as well as individually. At both the third Encounter and the *indaba* conversation, participants mentioned how difficult it was to imagine that their walk together as a Pilot Conversation was coming to an end. Their question was, what next? Plans were made to continue the relationships, including a visiting clergy exchange.[26] Most of the participants viewed *indaba* as a learning process and a gift from God that should be shared beyond the Anglican Communion. As one observed:

> The question is how are we going to be advocates of *indaba* in creating awareness across the ecumenical movement; that we live together despite our differences.[27]

---

26 Coevaluator field notes (Nesbitt).

27 A response from a short interview after the Limuru *indaba* Conversation.

~ **6** ~

"If I Had a Cow like That . . ."

A Quest for Mutual Mission in Western Tanganyika, El Camino Real, and Gloucester

~~~

FROM EL CAMINO REAL IN CALIFORNIA'S SILICON VALLEY, home of Apple, Facebook, and Google, to Western Tanganyika, a rural region of Tanzania where residents can't always count on having electricity, the contrasts in wealth, culture, and consumption defy most people's imagination. Along with the third team from Gloucester, England, the groups formed an intriguing triangle of tradition and vision where participants could reflect on their mission together in a new way.

Their journey began at the 2008 Lambeth Conference, when three bishops met through *indaba*: a new female American bishop, a seasoned male English bishop, and a male Tanzanian bishop nearing retirement. Not only did their views vary on topics such as homosexuality, but they also mirrored the diversity of beliefs on women and ordained leadership.[1] *Indaba* had helped them realize that they wanted to continue the conversation despite their differences, and they formed a partnership to do so. Joining the Continuing Indaba project, they were curious to know what difference it might make to their partnership.

With the Diocese of Western Tanganyika (DWT) bishop's retirement, the Pilot Conversation offered a fresh beginning for the new bishop. Together, the three convenors decided to focus on the following themes for their Encounters:

- how to deepen unity in the church;
- how to create a multigenerational church that proclaims the gospel in contemporary culture;
- how mission is resourced and sustained; and
- how to combat poverty.

The bishops' hope for the *indaba* journey was that the partnership would grow, with fresh motivation and perhaps a new way forward.[2] They also hoped for mutual learning and deeper understanding. Through the Encounters, they expected that their teams would learn how others went about evangelism and mission work, which might offer fresh insights to improve their own activity. Each bishop chose to participate as a member of the team. They and their team link persons formed a close leadership group that planned and made adjustments during the Encounters, which helped smooth some surprising events along the journey.

---

[1] At that time, the Church of England could not ordain female bishops, and the Diocese of Western Tanganyika did not ordain women at all.

[2] Interviews with each bishop were conducted at the beginning of the Continuing Indaba project.

Overall, the two Western teams were about evenly gender-balanced, although this changed as different participants were rotated on and off the teams from one Encounter to another. The Tanzanian team had only two women. Teams were relatively balanced across the age spectrum, with about a quarter being young adults.

Participants packed their bags and began this Pilot Conversation with confidence. All were very interested in participating, according to the initial survey, and were more likely than teams in other Pilot Conversations to describe themselves as highly enthusiastic (93 percent did so). Some had been involved in the partnership before Continuing Indaba; they felt mostly unconcerned about the Encounters and their *indaba* journey overall. Nearly all expected to have their thinking at least somewhat challenged along the way.

ENCOUNTERING KASULU

Western Tanganyika is a rural part of Tanzania, bordering Burundi to the north and Lake Tanganyika to the west.[3] Kigoma, on the eastern shore of the lake, is the largest town in the region, with about 165,000 people. It serves as the hub for air, rail, and water transportation. Roughly fifty miles northeast of Kigoma, in a region of hills, rivers, and forests, lies Kasulu, the next-largest town with about 37,000 residents.[4] The area's subsistence agriculture depends on growing maize and raising livestock, especially cattle. Since the region has few paved roads, travel is slow and sometimes highly challenging. Its remote location, with limited electricity, also can impede the speed and type of communication that other regions take for granted.

---

[3] The content of this section comes from a report on the Encounter by Continuing Indaba project director Phil Groves, who accompanied the teams on the Encounter. Other content is based on the Encounter timetable, discussion of the first Encounter at the two subsequent Encounters (with evaluators present), and the participant post-Encounter questionnaire.

[4] "Population of Kigoma, Tanzania"; "Population of Kasulu, Tanzania."

The Diocese of Western Tanganyika is the Anglican Church of Tanzania's largest geographic diocese. Kasulu hosts the diocesan office and cathedral, along with a Bible college. It also is home to some government offices and local mosques.

Visiting teams from California and England arrived in Kigoma on Monday, June 20, after a difficult journey. Flight service to Kigoma had been canceled, and last-minute arrangements with charter planes brought the two teams from Dar es Salaam. A new commercial flight service was to begin the day that the teams would depart. On landing, the teams were quickly whisked to a service for the laying of a church foundation stone and a church dinner afterward, not far from the airport.

The next day opened with worship and Bible study, using a form of *Lectio Divina*.[5] This pattern would frame their days together. Participants shared their hopes for the Encounter and a bit about their families, which helped introduce themselves to the wider group. They then split into three groups for visiting churches and building projects, including a health center and a preschool. The visitors usually were greeted with singing, dancing, and often a festive meal of chicken, rice or potatoes, and vegetables, rather than more typical daily fare of *ugali* (a dish made from maize flour) and beans or vegetables.[6] The groups continued their church visits on Wednesday, sometimes being invited to help parishioners with construction or painting projects.

On Thursday, the teams spent the day discussing the four topics that the convenors had chosen for the Pilot Conversation. Two members of each team had been appointed to research how one of these topics related to their own culture and then present it to the group. Although the content was informative, the day was spent in a Western conference format of presentations and discussion. This format may have felt comfortable for visitors, but it eroded the opportunity for authentic encounter. That evening, the participants broke into groups of two or three and visited local homes for dinner.

---

5 See chapter 2. This form was adapted for the partnership by two of its bishops.

6 Personal correspondence from Phil Groves, July 25, 2011.

Friday was planned as another day of sessions, but the agenda was altered for participants in groups of three to visit churches in the region. One group visited as many as thirteen churches that day. The conference format resumed on Saturday to hear remaining presentations on unity of the church. This led to a discussion of human sexuality. It became clear to the project manager, Phil Groves, who was observing the Encounter and was familiar with both Tanzanian and English cultures, that some of the words being used were culturally Western in concept and terminology, such as "gay," "straight," and "sexual orientation." Even "homosexuality," though used in the Bible, differed in meaning across both languages and cultures. Groves asked to speak in order to clarify differences in terms and worldviews that made translation nearly impossible. As he writes, "The realization of the gulf in language was revelatory for some."[7] Encounter had come into the conference.

The remaining presentations would be postponed until the second Encounter. That afternoon, the participants visited a local market and then a youth camp, followed by evening meals with local hosts.

On Sunday, a packed service in the cathedral was followed by a visit to a youth camp and a hurried departure that cut the Encounter short. The teams had received word on Saturday that their departing flight from Kigoma had been canceled. They would need to take a bus overland to Mwanza, on the shore of Lake Victoria at the northern edge of Tanzania, and catch a flight from there. Saying good-bye to their hosts, the visitors set off on a journey that would last more than eight hours. Hot, dusty, and exhausted after riding in cramped minibuses on unpaved roads, they arrived as the ferry was shutting down for the evening. With no other route, they would have to spend the night in the minibuses. The disembarking crew members "were clearly anxious for the safety of the teams, fearing armed robbers," wrote Groves, who was part of

---

7 Phil Groves, "Continuing Indaba Pilot Conversation DWT ECR Gloucester," 5.

the stranded group.[8] The crew decided to make an unscheduled trip to take them across the lake, and the teams arrived in Mwanza that night, tired, shaken, and deeply grateful.

The next morning, the two visiting teams gathered for a brief reflection on their Encounter before their flight home. The harrowing experience forged a powerful bond among those who had made the journey. An area of common ground that emerged was their recognition of a strong, shared faith, which bonded them in Christ. This turned out to be a surprise for some, especially as many had expected more tension over their differences.[9]

REFLECTING ON THE ENCOUNTER

The visiting teams had struggled with the abrupt changes in the Encounter, as well as the differences in cultural expectations and in cultural understandings of time, according to a post-Encounter survey. Some participants, used to a precise schedule, felt stressed when difficult travel conditions delayed their arrival. The differing expectations of exactly when events would begin were a surprise for others. Another aspect of time involved the lengthy pace of site visitations. Several had wished for more time for conversation. Although the scheduling changes shortened the time available for the Encounter, it is possible that dedicated time for group discussions may reveal a cultural difference, since reflective conversations in some cultures may occur amid activities together.

Participants also noted a concentration on projects needing funding, rather than on the experience of daily life in the community. Groves writes:

> They were shown farming initiatives, but not
> led to understand what farming actually meant.

---

[8] Personal correspondence from Phil Groves, April 26, 2016.

[9] Expectations came from the initial survey findings.

That is small scale digging of fields by hand and harvest by hand. They did not see where people actually sleep, how family life is ordered and how the nuclear family is impossible.[10]

Since the partnership before Continuing Indaba had undertaken Tanzanian sewing machine and solar cooking projects, and funded scholarships for five hundred primary school students in a traditional donor-recipient model of mission, a focus on potential projects wasn't unexpected, however.[11]

The problem of language was mentioned by several participants. Teams from the two dioceses that speak primarily English engaged each other in a culturally intimate way, but not all Western Tanganyika team members could easily follow the English conversations. In the fast pace of an open plenary conversation, it wasn't easy for them to ask repeatedly for others to speak more slowly or to clarify what was said.

A common suggestion was to have translators. However, this would have significantly slowed the conversation. Participants also would have tended to talk to the translator instead of to one another. Since one aspect of encounter can involve the struggle to communicate in a language not often used, helping one another in the midst of that struggle can transform relationships. Groves notes that although the seminar format created inequalities of power, the simplicity of *Lectio Divina*'s ample silence, with only a few words shared by each participant, allowed everyone to speak equally.

The personal meaning of the Encounter centered on two themes. The first was a sense of shared humanity and unity through the participants' common Anglican faith, often described as *brothers and sisters of an extended spiritual family*. The second was the need to learn more about their cultural differences and how they affected their beliefs and practices. Overall, participants shared a feeling that "more unites us

---

10   Personal correspondence from Phil Groves, July 25, 2011.
11   Pat McCaughan, "El Camino Real."

than not." A host participant wrote that through Christ, and the *indaba*, those from the most-developed and least-developed countries could sit together and talk (as equals). Most participants returned home feeling they had experienced the adventure of an authentic encounter.

ENTERING EL CAMINO REAL

Stretching along California's central coast from Silicon Valley to San Luis Obispo, the Diocese of El Camino Real is diverse, ranging from San Jose, urban home to one million people at the heart of America's high-tech industry hub, through rich forests and the agricultural fields of the Salinas Valley, and on to the scenic Pacific coastline. Extremes of wealth and poverty, as well as a vast range of cultures and languages, mix in this stretch of geography. This also is one of a very few American dioceses to have a female diocesan bishop.[12]

At the small Monterey airport on a crisp November evening, a travel-weary Gloucester team was greeted with hugs from its hosts. The team from Western Tanganyika, having encountered travel delays, was scheduled to arrive late the next day. Visiting participants would stay with families in the area, while the hosts would either commute from home or stay locally.

The Encounter began the next day with the teams attending the diocese's annual convention to learn about the church's process of governance. That evening, as dinner was being served, three vehicles arrived, and an exhausted Western Tanganyika team was greeted with hugs and warm coats, and then ushered into a packed convention hall amid enthusiastic applause. The convention continued the next morning. In the afternoon, team members visited a nearby supermarket, electronics store, and shopping mall, followed that evening by an orientation to the diocese.

---

[12] At the time of this Encounter, Bishop Mary Gray-Reeves was one of four female diocesan bishops in the Episcopal Church.

On Sunday, participants worshiped in local parishes with their host families. Later, they met to reflect on their experience at the convention. Gloucester visitors remarked on the church's engagement with social issues. A Tanzanian member was surprised by the use of time in the meeting—each person was given two minutes to speak and had to stop when time ran out. Over dinner, a discussion arose about time and the stress that arises because of tight time schedules.

The next day, the group visited Silicon Valley to have lunch at a parish feeding program for low-income and homeless persons. One hundred volunteers helped to prepare food donated from local supermarkets. Participants joined the guests at lunch tables, many engaging them in conversation. A Tanzanian participant, asking a guest where he went to church, was surprised when the the reply was "nowhere." Several Tanzanian members later admitted that they had difficulty understanding the situation of homelessness.

After lunch, the group members completed their presentations from Kasulu, and then toured the firm eBay. The Gloucester participants were familiar with eBay and environmental technology, but the Tanzanians were puzzled by both. That evening, the group went to a professional hockey game, which further puzzled the visiting teams. As they sought to understand the sport, some made comparisons to soccer, which resulted in shared insight and cheers when the home team scored a goal. Lively conversation and informal mixing across cultures deepened their relationships.

Tuesday would be spent in seminar-style conversation. Pondering what they had seen the day before, visitors wondered why people in such a rich land had to rely on charity in order to eat. A Tanzanian participant remarked, "The way you live is a challenge to us." The discussion moved into concern over dependency and the need to transform a "handout" into a "hand up."

That afternoon, they heard a presentation intended to explain the challenge that organized religion faces in engaging youth and young adults today in American culture. Later, the Gloucester team members described the situation in their culture as one where people belong but don't believe; the challenge was to help young people feel passion about their faith. A host team member noted that in Latino ministry, people want to believe without belonging; building community was a struggle because of their lack of time to invest in relationships. Tanzanian members comparatively added that there are baptized people who don't go to church—the internet invites youth to mimic Western culture. In their diocese, if people don't attend for three years, they won't have a Christian burial.

In the evening, the teams traveled to a multicultural parish in San Jose. After being warmly welcomed, they were invited outside by a priest in the First Nations community that is part of the parish.[13] As the visitors joined him to see their sweat lodge under a full moon, a brief ceremony unfolded: they heard Lakota and Nez Perce prayer and song, and felt the warmth of the fire and the fragrant smudging that took place. Silently, they returned to the church, where the Hawaiian community shared their songs and hula. A festive Mexican dinner hosted by a parishioner and her mother awaited them in the parish hall. The multicultural presentations had surprised the host team. As a parishioner described it, "the parish decided to go 'all out'" for the *indaba* guests.

On Wednesday, the teams gathered at a cabin in the coastal hills. The conversation reflected on the previous evening and the First Nations ceremony. A visitor asked if the First Nations parishioners regard themselves as Christian, since Jesus hadn't been mentioned in the ceremony. A host participant said yes, although historically because Native Americans had been murdered in the name of Jesus, the use of Creator was a more common expression of the inclusivity of God. A Western Tanganyika member reflected that Christianity in Africa tends to be very Western, as missionaries had emphasized that African ways needed to change. However, some countries have

---

[13] This community identifies itself as First Nations.

allowed more traditional elements in their Christian worship. This led to a discussion of how people have been harmed by the church's practices.

The women met together for lunch. The Tanzanian women privately had asked if the women could meet, since in their culture, certain topics weren't discussed in mixed groups. Over lunch, the Tanzanian women expressed a strong desire to help women improve their self-esteem, to value their own abilities, and to value educating their daughters. Women on the other teams listened intently and offered support.

After lunch, the conversation moved to technology. The team from Western Tanganyika expressed a desire to learn more about computers and programs, as very few clergy have a computer, and most communication is by mobile phone. An offer was made to share their expertise on evangelism in return for someone to teach them basic computer use. Both British and American team members cautioned against overreliance on technology. Used badly, it could have negative effects, especially among young people. The conversation continued along these lines, with the technologically advanced teams downplaying the value of technology, while the Tanzanian focus was on the ability to choose whether to use it.

Later, the teams traveled to Santa Cruz, where they walked on the beach, waded in the Pacific surf, took photos, and then gathered at sunset around a fire pit for Eucharistic worship. This created minor tension over differing worship customs, but everyone took part.

On Thursday morning, participants gathered in the damp fields of a Salinas farm to follow the workers who picked and packaged romaine and learn more about American agriculture. Team members delicately jumped from furrow to furrow, several expressing amazement at the efficient operations of this family-owned business. Some also felt ambivalent over the steady pace of the automated machinery, as workers were required to keep up with it. A few asked about the discarded romaine scattered in its wake, wondering if it could be put to other uses; the guide replied that it would be plowed into the field, which would cut the amount of fertilizer needed.

The teams went to a downtown Salinas parish for lunch and conversation. Afterward, a facilitator announced that they would be talking about sexuality. He added that they would not try to change one another's minds. A member of each diocesan team shared how sexuality, including homosexuality, is understood within that diocese and the surrounding culture. After an extended conversation, the room quieted. A member of one of the teams shared his story of coming out as homosexual. He spoke slowly and thoughtfully, pausing at times to choke back emotion. Others listened in respectful—and for some, stunned—silence. There was a brief conversation afterward, but many wanted to be alone with their thoughts.[14] That evening, everyone met at the bishop's home for dinner and a good-bye gathering.

The Encounter ended the next morning with a final reflection session and worship. As participants spoke in turn, the emotion in the room became palpable. One participant was touched by the deep sharing from the heart, both by a participant opposed to homosexuality and by the participant who shared his story of coming out. It had brought a realization that people in the American church don't agree about everything. A Tanzanian male participant was surprised to see few people in church, and fewer youth, and by how easy it was to travel from one place to another. A Tanzanian female participant spoke about the women's gathering and the concern over women's low self-image, adding that they weren't trying to change the culture but to open up opportunities for women and girls. One of the younger Tanzanian men replied, "I am willing to take some of the risk to help you."

Some participants had been informed that they would be replaced by others at the next Encounter. This loss of relationship was deeply felt. Good-byes were rushed, as flight

---

[14] For another version of this event, see Groves and Jones, *Living Reconciliation*, 135–41.

cancellations for the Gloucester team resulted in a sudden overland trip to San Francisco to catch another flight. The Western Tanganyika team would stay another day and enjoy the wedding celebration of a local team member getting married that evening, before their long journey home.

GOING TO GLOUCESTER

The striking tower of Gloucester Cathedral marks the River Severn's passage through Gloucestershire as it winds through the southwest English countryside not far from the Welsh border. The river plain gives way to sloping hills and the natural beauty of the Cotswalds to the east. The city of Gloucester, as well as its name, is rooted in the Roman era as a fortification site. The cathedral stands on an early Christian worship site.[15]

Today Gloucester and nearby Cheltenham are thriving centers for business and finance, electronics, technology, and light manufacturing. Each has slightly more than one hundred thousand people and also neighborhoods of significant poverty. Gloucestershire is 95 percent Caucasian, although Gloucester itself has a growing racial and ethnic minority population.[16]

The Diocese of Gloucester has 390 churches, including the historic Gloucester Cathedral and Tewkesbury Abbey, and 116 schools. Slightly less than two-thirds of Gloucestershire residents are Christian, a decline of 12 percent since 2001. The second largest religious group is Muslim—about 1 percent of the population—primarily concentrated in the city of Gloucester. Those claiming no religion make up more than a quarter of the population, nearly doubling since 2001.[17] The attrition of young adults, especially in urban areas, has been a concern of the diocese. It has emphasized ministries for youth and young adults such as Rock the Cathedral, street pastors, interactive

---

[15] "Cathedral History."

[16] "Population Profile (2015)," 22–24.

[17] Ibid., 25–26.

reading and story-telling for children, a Night Shelter, and social housing for young families. Parishes also help with particular ministries.[18]

The reunion of the teams in mid-February was described by a Tanzanian member as a Pentecost, where all were laughing and joyful despite the weariness of travel. As in the other Encounters, Bible study using *Lectio Divina* and worship would frame each day.

The Encounter formally began the next day, Shrove Tuesday, with a Quiet Day in Gloucester Cathedral. The theme focused on reaching out to those who felt spiritual but not religious. The three bishops—from Tanzania, the United States, and Gloucester—offered meditations; participants afterward could roam the cathedral and its grounds in silent reflection. The day offered a soothing way for visiting teams to recover from their journey and orient themselves to their new surroundings and chilly temperatures.

The group later traveled to the countryside, visiting a church rooted in the seventh century, where they reaffirmed their baptismal vows. That evening in Tewkesbury, they reflected on what they had learned over their *indaba* journey. Both British and American participants remarked on differences between their two cultures that they hadn't expected. A Tanzanian participant added, "Now it is as if we are living together, compared to Kasulu." This perception was affirmed by how well the teams mixed across cultures. They sampled pancakes and joined the Shrove Tuesday games with Tewkesbury youth. After a festive dinner together with the dean of Tewkesbury Abbey and his family, he invited them for a private evening tour by candlelight of the cavernous abbey built in the twelfth century.

Wednesday began with a walking tour of low-income areas in urban Gloucester. One group visited a neighborhood with a sizable homeless population, including a shelter that offered

---

18 Field notes from a session on the Diocese of Gloucester and the challenges it faces.

legal support for those seeking asylum in England. The other walking group visited a multicultural community, including an urban farm that helped people from rural regions feel more at home in the city. Afterward, the conversation turned to how the church might minister in those communities and how poverty and marginalization are understood differently across cultures and socioeconomic contexts. That afternoon, the teams visited a school, and then the Gloucester County Office for an orientation to the region. In the evening, teams went to a candlelit Ash Wednesday service in the cathedral.

The group traveled to a dairy farm on Thursday morning to learn more about agriculture in the region. Later, they broke into small groups to talk informally about what they had seen. Some were surprised at how few people were employed on such a large farm because of mechanization. Two Western Tanganyika members commented on how large the cows and sheep had been. One said, "If I had a cow like that, it could change my life. I'd be a rich man." A Gloucester participant explained that they were fed a rich diet, and some also were about to calve. Another participant suggested that those cows might not survive in Western Tanganyika because they depended on the biochemical and technological support that made them so productive.

The cow became a symbol of the role of technology in agricultural capitalism. A Gloucester member noted how the rising cost of technology was affecting its viability, leading to a vivid cross-cultural discussion on technology in agriculture, issues over environmental sustainability, and the vulnerabilities of technological dependency.

On Friday, the group traveled to Cheltenham to visit a school. After lunch, they visited the Rock, a drop-in community center for at-risk youth from a range of backgrounds and faith traditions. Located in a church, it serves as a safe bridge between traditional Christian communities and the region's youth culture, offering a variety of games and exercises to build basic social and life skills. Several youths led the visitors through some trust-building games and joined them in an open discussion. They asked the team members hard questions about the existence of God, creationism and evolution, and why some had wanted to be priests. That evening, the teams accompanied street pastors through parts of Cheltenham.

The next morning, the group returned to the countryside for a walk in the Forest of Dean. Later, the men went bowling in Gloucester while the women met over tea. Initially, one of the younger women had been disappointed that she wasn't going bowling, but her mood changed when she heard the Tanzanian women present their proposal for women's empowerment; she then understood the significance of their meeting together. The proposal made use of existing women's networks (Mothers Union) to train women who could work with other women in the villages on the need to send girls to school. In the discussion that followed, some British and American women asked tough questions about certain details, anticipating criticism from men on the proposal. The Tanzanian women grew frustrated and then disappointed, prompting some women to begin framing their questions and discussion in a positive way and asking the presenters how they could be supportive. The Tanzanian women clearly had something to say. That evening, the group went to a professional rugby match, followed by supper at a Gloucester team member's home.

On Sunday, visiting participants joined local parishes for worship and lunch, then gathered for a final reflection session and dinner at Glenfall House, a nineteenth-century estate given to the Diocese of Gloucester. Small groups struggled with how to prioritize what they thought was important regarding the four Pilot Conversation topics. A Tanzanian member wanted to add the issue of technology, but others saw it as less important. When trying to narrow their choices, one participant suggested voting. Challenged about how they would decide in *indaba* fashion, one member asked the person requesting technology to explain his concern, which prompted another participant to urge that it be included.

The group also heard one of the Tanzanian women present the women's empowerment proposal, which led to a lively discussion. One woman on another team had analyzed the budget for feasibility. Another had mentioned it to her congregation that morning and reported that the women wanted to help. The Western Tanganyika bishop affirmed its importance, and other men became engaged. A Western team member asked for a voice vote on the proposal. Hearing no opposition, he declared their support for the proposal settled.

In closing, participants were asked what had meant the most during the Encounter. Tanzanian members mentioned the street pastors and the home stays. The women appreciated the warm clothing and their host's husband fixing breakfast. American participants affirmed the value of staying with a family and spoke of the Rock's inspiring work. British participants valued their guests' questions and seeing their culture through others' eyes. As in the previous Encounters, several participants had gained new insights about their own dioceses in surprising ways.

HOLDING *INDABA* IN EAST SUSSEX

The three teams made their way to Pilgrim Hall, in East Sussex in southeast England, on Monday, February 27. Several stopped along the way for sightseeing at Windsor Castle and shopping. The orientation to the *indaba* conversation began that evening. They would have to put their group under the care of two facilitators, from Canada and Scotland, and this brought feelings of anxiety. They were assured that the *indaba* process was about a way of talking together and was not intended to harm their partnership.

The *indaba* conversation opened the next morning with a silent reflection on the journey that had led the teams to Pilgrim Hall. The discussion that followed was primarily about building trust in the *indaba* process, as well as with each other.

Some of the conversation guidelines the participants wanted were for every voice to be heard, for no one to walk away when the conversation was difficult, and for equality among lay and ordained voices.

The group broke into diocesan teams to identify three questions that they wanted to discuss in the *indaba*. The Tanzanian team returned with practical questions regarding the future of the partnership and the *indaba* process, while the other two teams' questions were concerned with various social and church issues. This disparity pointed to cultural differences and also to a critical concern within the partnership itself. The facilitators urged the group to explore the meaning of the different lists, which led to frustration. As they continued to discuss how to combine the lists into questions for the *indaba*, someone suggested voting. Two others expressed that they wanted to make sure all voices were heard, which voting would exclude. Voting also would be problematic for the Tanzanian team, as it was outnumbered by the two Western teams. A facilitator added, "*Indaba* is different from partnership; it is about negotiating your understanding." A group consisting of two members from each diocese worked together that evening on a combined agenda for the next morning.

The next day's *indaba* began as a facilitator handed out questions that the working team had put together. As participants read them, several began to ask about the meaning of terms such as "unity in the church" or "flourish." Another concern emerged over different cultural understandings. A Tanzanian member asked about the difference between gender and sexuality—concepts with specific content arising out of Western contexts but not translating easily across cultures or languages.

The *indaba* conversations began with small groups of two members from each diocese discussing the theme of "unity in the church." In the plenary session, each group summarized what it had talked about. For most, the discussion had begun with the role of Scripture, tradition, and reason, but then moved to the issue of sexuality, including homosexuality, polygamy, gender and ordination (authority of women), and globalization. A Tanzanian member explained that in his local language, there was no word for homosexuality. For another group, homosexuality was a hard issue, but they had found a way to say "this is a mystery" to express their lack of agreement with each other and also accept that there were differing understandings.

That afternoon, the plenary session featured a fishbowl *indaba*. Two members from each small group, representing the three dioceses, spoke to each other in a small circle surrounded by the larger group, who listened. Speakers began by sharing what they had discussed in small groups. The conversation was difficult for several team members, who struggled to listen openly without responding negatively to what they were hearing. Afterward, some felt that the fishbowl had given them an extraordinary opportunity to listen and understand in a different way. Several admitted, however, that when they were in the fishbowl, they weren't speaking for themselves. A concern also was raised that the fishbowl may have been intimidating for some; one participant admitted to having wanted to enter the fishbowl but "didn't want to drown."

The next *indaba* conversation focused on how the partnership might continue. Earlier, several had expressed a fear that the partnership might not survive. Team differences in their purpose for participating in *indaba* emerged. For one, it was to have their diocese represented. For another, it was to be a model for a partnership that could change the Anglican Communion. A member from the third team noted that he wanted to see how they could be partners with full sharing: "In my visit to Kasulu, I learned a new way of honoring the other person."

Participants reflected on what they wanted to say to the other two dioceses about their hopes for the partnership. A facilitator urged them to share what was on their hearts. All three teams expressed a desire to continue together. They then began to focus on projects and support for Western Tanganyika, but a facilitator pointed out that the interaction was not equally three-way. The conversation then expanded to whether the teams should consist of the group gathered in the *indaba* or be widened. Would opening it up risk losing the level of trust and safety they had achieved?

The final *indaba* began with a Bible study on the topic of wealth and poverty and a discussion of the Kingdom of God, which brought up the themes of mission and church. The diocesan teams met separately to discuss what was essential to the ongoing life of the partnership and how they intended to take it forward. A participant from the diocese most wanting to move to a mutual mission model had, through an earlier interview, expressed several ways that his diocese might be enriched from projects based on mutual mission—closer relationships, cultural exchanges, and other ties—that would offset whatever funds were invested.

For Gloucester, education, schools, and theological teaching were an important focus. Evangelism, communications, and technology were important for El Camino Real. Western Tanganyika valued an exchange program, perhaps sending missionaries, as well as joint projects and good communication. The team also wanted to continue in prayer. The other two dioceses recognized that tight budgets were going to affect their ability to allocate resources and discussed widening the partnership, perhaps seeking matching funds for projects. The bishops agreed to meet and discuss further how their partnership might go forward together. The *indaba* was tough and pragmatic, as the teams struggled with this transition. Later, a link person announced the dates and locations of future meetings for their partnership, providing relief that the partnership would continue beyond that final session, although funding still was a concern.

In closing, participants were invited to speak about a way that *indaba* had contributed to their partnership and what would they like to say to each other as they departed. A bowl was passed, and only the person holding it was allowed to speak. For El Camino Real participants, *indaba* had provided a blend of experience and talk that gave depth to their partnership, especially in its identity and commitment. Individually, as one participant said, it was an opportunity to learn "what I could never have learned" otherwise. Another commented, "It gave me a deeper understanding of where my life needs to go." And another felt that *indaba* "is God's gift. It is what we do with this gift" that counts.

Gloucester participants commented on the friendships that had formed across differences of view and on personal growth: "Friendship is the way in which we are a blessing to others." Another felt a deep gratitude to God "for our diversity, and for our unity." Yet another said, "This trip has made me realize what I am most passionate about," and one admitted, "It has made me value listening."

Western Tanganyika participants also mentioned the friendships they had made and expressed gratitude for encouragement and confidence. "This has really helped me to grow," said one. Added another, "Just to be here is a learning process. . . . Thank you for all you have given me." Still another echoed, "To have more friends like you has been a real blessing," and continued, "I see God in this group."

Perhaps because they felt confident that the relationship among their three dioceses would continue, the parting was joyful. The Final Conversation closed with a Eucharist concelebrated by the three bishops.

REFLECTING ON THE JOURNEY

The Continuing Indaba journey had a transforming effect on this partnership in many ways. Foremost, it had been built on the classic donor-recipient model of mission, but *indaba* represented an opportunity to examine and alter this relationship, which one diocese especially wanted to do. Discussion of this mission relationship, which surfaced at the *indaba* conversation, shook the partnership to its foundation, unsettling the belief that everyone accepted the donor-recipient model.

Much of the tension during the final *indaba* was about shifting the partnership toward mutual mission. Western Tanganyika, anxious over the potential loss of economic support for valuable projects, described how in their culture, people shared what they had with the expectation that others would do the same, illustrating a more communitarian worldview that clashed with Western notions of autonomy and economic disparity. In mutual mission, funding needed to be part of a mutual exchange, which all saw as of mutual value. Had the *indaba* conversation not occurred in a neutral setting, the conflict could have surfaced in ways that would have been far more difficult to address.

Challenges to a Common Journey

The discussion of technology illustrated the huge disparity between a rural region of Africa and the wealthier regions of Silicon Valley and Gloucestershire. The socioeconomic disparity symbolized by the Gloucestershire cows also pointed to the deeper issue of who was entitled to technology and its benefits. Responses about the vulnerability of technology attempted to mutualize the conversation, but they also risked condescension. This was evident when a Western Tanganyika participant asked for honest conversation rather than a reflective self-critique of technology. The larger point was about people being able to make the choice to use technology or not, rather than having it made for them. This also underlay part of the clash over mission.

Sexuality lurked as a challenge in the midst of the three teams. But the decision to form a partnership had already implied that a common mission journey would be possible, despite their strong differences. Often the topic was approached through the use of code language—words or phrases that carried more than one possible meaning. All three teams were adept at both recognizing and using code interpretations when sexuality began to surface in the conversation. During one Encounter, the use of code language signaled to the leadership that it was time to find a structured way for the topic of homosexuality to surface in conversation.

When a team member shared his story of coming out as a gay man, his revelation potentially threatened both his relationships with members who opposed homosexuality and the level of trust that had been built within the group. But the conflict was transformed by the strength of the relationships that had been built and the careful way in which the leaders formatted the session to allow the conversation. A Tanzanian colleague's gesture of a hand on the speaker's shoulder did not signify a changed belief, but rather a heart that could reach across differences to the humanity of the person speaking.[19]

Challenges of Culture

With two culturally Western teams in a three-way partnership, cultural power arose in several ways. The lengthy seminar-style presentations and discussions, familiar to Western academic and cultural sensibilities, often resulted in participants from those two teams talking to one another while most of the third team sat quietly. In contrast, the site visits often led to lively three-way engagement as participants shared common experiences.

How a conversation was framed was another concern. Many topics assumed a Western scope, such as the challenge of how to increase multigenerational church engagement. In contrast, the conversation following the dairy farm showed clear ways in which all perspectives could be solicited and discussed. Cultural differences appeared in what was appropriate to say

---

[19] This participant who spoke was replaced by a new team member for the next Encounter, so it is unknown how relationships would have been affected over the rest of the journey.

in mixed-gender groups and in what could be said apart from what the bishop thought. Specifically, cultural power was exerted in the tendency not to adjust speaking patterns. Rapid speech, colloquialisms, and lack of pausing between speakers made it difficult for most Western Tanganyika members to enter the conversation on an equal basis. Requests to speak more slowly tended to be forgotten.

Another challenge was cultural stress. But the Encounter in Kasulu bonded the British and American participants and equipped them to understand some of the cultural tension for the Western Tanganyika participants. Ironically, the hours of seminar discussion served as a refuge in which to cope with cultural saturation. For American and British participants, it was a symbol of familiarity when they were in Kasulu. For Tanzanian participants, it allowed them to sit quietly and reflect.

A sense of solidarity emerged across the three teams during the journey despite their many differences. The women from Western Tanganyika had explicitly sought out relationships with the women on the other teams, and an ethos of strong, mutual support arose out of their conversations and informal gatherings. During the *indaba* conversation, solidarity across teams arose out of the frustration with a facilitator who pressed them to discuss an issue they didn't believe was present. The shared frustration enhanced feelings of the partnership's autonomy, which helped it recommit to continuing despite a difficult conversation over how its mission would be lived out.

Leadership and the *Indaba* Process

The three bishops together with their link persons formed the leadership team that met daily during the Encounters and provided a sense of safety for participants. But this top-down leadership model also led to a *front-room/back-room* ethos, with key discussions and decisions made away from the group conversation. Ironically, however, the leaders' inability to control all aspects of the Encounters resulted in breakthrough experiences where insights emerged and occasionally understanding was transformed.

The dual roles of the bishop convenors, who also were participants, at times became problematic. Their enthusiasm to participate resulted in a dominance that may have been unintended. They reinforced this disparity when speaking early and often in conversations, sometimes for a significant amount of the time. Their comments also offered cues to other participants as to what might be safely shared, even though all three bishops urged others on their team to speak their own views. But with sharply differing power relations in an *indaba* designed for equal participation, it was uncertain how much could be achieved.

Throughout the journey, the partnership struggled with adjusting its own identity and process to the expectations of Continuing Indaba. One of the tensions involved the convenors' desire to replace members of their teams at will. New members adapted quickly, but each change meant time was needed to build fresh relationships and group cohesion. Other elements were also problematic, such as the long seminar-style presentations, which took time away from opportunities for authentic encounter.

From the survey data, participants indicated that a deep awareness of a shared Anglican identity had emerged. Shared faith gave them a basis for mutual respect. Their daily Bible study using *Lectio Divina* and worship strengthened this bond. As the bishop of Western Tanganyika later wrote:

> The Bible study has truly put us together. The
> way our [B]ible study was conducted moved my
> heart.[20]

The challenges or tensions most often mentioned had to do with differing cultural understandings and uses of time.

---

20 "Bishop Sadock Makaya."

The teams left the *indaba* with an agenda of future meetings and projects, but further *indaba* work remained over what exactly mutual mission would mean for their partnership and how would it be lived out. The deepened relationships, built through trust and mutual respect, made the transformative discussion possible. Despite its shortcomings, many felt that Continuing Indaba had enriched their partnership. On the closing survey, participants consistently rated their *indaba* experience the most highly of all the Pilot Conversations in all aspects, such as its effectiveness, how much was learned, and how much difference it had made personally. Although *indaba* had involved a risk by opening up conversation on the core issue of mission, it also allowed the teams to negotiate a way forward on fresh ground.

~ 7 ~

Reflections on the Journey

Insights, "*Indaba* Moments," and Meaningful Conversation

~~~

THE QUESTION "WHAT NEXT?" WAS ON THE HEARTS of Pilot Conversation participants as they moved through the formal *indaba* conversations that would mark the end of their Continuing Indaba journeys. They were free to continue their journeys, but it would be their own responsibility to do so. At the end of their Pilot Conversation, three convenors expressed their hope in a letter to Archbishop of Canterbury Rowan Williams that the use of *indaba* would increase across the Anglican Communion:

> The Indaba experience has accelerated our
> bonding; our depth of candor with each
> other; and our sincere caring for each other as
> individuals and as representatives of our own
> dioceses and our respective cultures.[1]

Their partnership that had begun at the 2008 Lambeth Conference would continue. For others, relationships would continue in less formal ways.

A question underlying the Continuing Indaba project was whether the *indaba* process made a difference in helping participants understand one another across their diverse cultures and worldviews. Since the research on the Pilot Conversations was required to conclude at the end of the funded project, the long-term effects could not be part of the formal study. However, participants continued to share their thoughts in conversations, correspondence, news stories, and social media, which offer a glimpse of *indaba*'s value over time.

INSIGHTS AND FINDINGS ACROSS FOUR CONTINENTS

The objectives of the Pilot Conversations formed an ambitious agenda for this experimental journey. The first objective, to create an ethos for mutual listening and understanding across major differences, and the second, to contribute to the development of mutual mission through deepened cross-cultural relationships, are discussed below according to the four areas they represent. A fifth area, transformation, addresses the Continuing Indaba project overall.

Learning to Practice Mutual Listening

Learning to listen in a different way is perhaps the most valuable element for understanding and sustaining community

---

[1] Matthew Davies, "Continuing Indaba Enables 'Gospel-Shaped Conversation.'"

in the midst of strong differences. Participants in every Pilot Conversation struggled with listening openly and patiently, especially in moments of discomfort. When they were able to do so, the reward was profound in the amount of deepened understanding and relationships that resulted, according to survey comments.

The ability to listen to others improved steadily across the Continuing Indaba journey. After the first Encounter, participants reported that they had listened to one another only somewhat well, on average. At the end of the formal *indaba* conversation, about three out of four felt that they were listening *very* well.[2] These perceptions tended to agree with what the researchers observed, especially in the smaller groups. When participants were asked about how effective Continuing Indaba had been in helping develop authentic mutual listening, a majority (62 percent) thought it had been *very* effective; almost all (98 percent) thought that it had been at least somewhat effective. The results were similar for how participants regarded *indaba*'s effectiveness in creating deeper understanding.

The greatest challenges to mutual listening arose in four areas: language, cultural power, personal behaviors, and conversation format.[3] Language raised several concerns. Words sometimes held very different meanings across cultures, which could lead to misunderstandings when those differences were not brought up in conversation. Varying accents required time and concentration for all to understand. When participants spoke rapidly, used colloquialisms or words not understood by all, or spoke too softly, listening became yet more difficult. Some hesitated to speak, anxious over being misunderstood. Small groups, however, were helpful in breaking down these barriers.

Participants noted becoming aware of how culture affected the ways that people spoke. In groups with two teams from the Global North, these teams tended to dominate the

---

[2] Participants rated listening on a scale from "not at all" to "very well." See figure A.5 in the appendix.

[3] These findings were based on survey comments, interviews, and observation.

conversations, which made it difficult for them to hear the voices of others in equal measure. Often they had awareness of others' silence, and some privately expressed frustration at not knowing why others didn't speak. It also wasn't clear that they were aware of the different meanings that silence may have had.

Cross-culturally, silence held many meanings. In some situations, it was used strategically to avoid offending others. In other cases, it expressed a lack of safety or trust. Silence also could be a way of coping with cultural saturation or fatigue. Sometimes it represented not quite knowing what to say. One participant whose primary language was not English commented that she understood what was being said but often didn't know how to reply. This could have to do with how a conversation was framed, as well as the vocabulary used. For some participants, words didn't come quickly or easily, and a fast-paced conversation was difficult to enter. This was especially so for those who didn't speak English daily.

Cultural differences also affected what was said in mixed-gender groups or when a person of significant status such as a bishop was present. When higher-status or dominant members earnestly sought to hear others' views, without criticism, mutual listening improved.

Some personal behaviors also inhibited mutual listening. These included interrupting others, making assumptions, being defensive, and implying the superiority of one's views. As participants journeyed together, and when tensions were absent, these behaviors tended to subside.

How a conversation was formatted affected the ethos of listening as well. Some format pitfalls included not allowing enough time for authentic conversation, not recognizing the amount of fatigue that mutual listening could cause, and occasionally not having facilitation when it was needed. Sometimes group members would take responsibility to try to create a more inclusive ethos by asking for the thoughts of participants who were silent. Other times, facilitators would shift the conversation pattern that had developed. Small groups were important in deepening mutual listening, as they were easier for participants to engage and to make adjustments in how the conversation was unfolding. Taken together, participants often worked hard to overcome these challenges and they achieved a remarkable depth of mutual listening.

Understanding Differences and Transforming Conflict

I believe that there is something vital about this process: When you have met people, and get to know why they hold their viewpoints, it is less easy to be judgmental. I might not agree, but I can see.
—Participant (interview)

Conflict provided opportunities for growth in understanding. When tensions arose over conflicting views, how participants chose to respond helped them move away from a trajectory toward hostility and to a path toward deeper understanding of the surrounding concerns. By the end, nearly nine in ten participants felt at least somewhat more comfortable engaging in conversation with others who held different views; more than half felt much more comfortable doing so. Participants in similar numbers also had become more curious about understanding why others held differing perspectives.[4] However, one in five participants also felt more reluctant to express their own thoughts or feelings; several attributed this to the need to understand the context surrounding differences before speaking.

When relationships were still fragile and trust was lacking, coping tactics sometimes were used to avoid conflict. Silence was a common one. Other tactics included trying to shift a

---

[4] On the closing survey, 57 percent strongly agreed and another 22 percent somewhat agreed with being more curious about understanding why others hold different views.

topic to safer ground or reframing it in a way that avoided sharing personal views. The use of code, where a statement had both face value and undertones with other meanings for those who understood the code, was also a means of talking around a conflict.

Although coping tactics allowed differences to coexist, the conflict remained latent—the "elephant in the room" that some participants mentioned. The formal *indaba* conversation typically made participants aware that differences needed to be aired and acknowledged if the group were to have integrity. At times, facilitators helped difficult conversations surface. Sometimes private conversations during breaks allowed differences to be shared that had felt too risky in a large group. Typically, both informal and small-group conversations led to greater confidence in speaking openly.

At other times, participants simply took the risk of expressing strong differences of view in a way that didn't disrespect others who believed differently. Staying with the group norms, such as speaking personally and asking questions to try to understand one another better, often led to fresh understanding of the contexts surrounding their differences. It also resulted in comments on how meaningful the conversation had been. This was key to bringing conflict to the surface and transforming it in a way that allowed participants to value one another while continuing to disagree on their views.

In the end, nearly nine out of ten participants had felt that differing views or understandings had been at least somewhat openly expressed; about half had felt that they had been very much expressed, according to the data. Nearly all claimed new insight or understanding of those who held different views.[5] They also valued being able to understand those differences better. Yet often the differences were not those that incited tension or where participants felt deeply invested; among these, the results were more modest although still positive.

---

[5] More than 60 percent of respondents indicated on the closing survey that they *very much* had gained insight and understanding of those with differing views, while another 35 percent had gained *some* insight and understanding.

Building Relationships across Differences

Any organization with global participation must be able to balance differences through meaningful relationships where conflicts can be discussed or negotiated with mutual respect. All four Pilot Conversations expressed sizable tensions, yet participants in all consistently emphasized the value of relationships they had built through Continuing Indaba. In the closing survey, several referred to building relationships as their most memorable experience. They were, as one put it on the survey, "deep relationships that cross cultural, social, [and] economic divides."

Developing relationships in the midst of differences was a sizable challenge. The Encounters, by taking participants into an adventure of otherness and vulnerability, where they were dependent on relations of hospitality with the host team, had fostered an interdependence that helped bond the relationships. Hosts held cultural power as they showed guests their dioceses and made them feel welcome. Yet in some cases, hosts took considerable risks, such as inviting speakers with differing views on sexuality in cultures where homosexuality was either not accepted or illegal, even though they made it clear that the gesture was not an endorsement.

To be a gracious guest meant becoming vulnerable, especially when entering an unfamiliar culture and language. Most participants willingly entered into the adventure. For some, vulnerability was difficult and tended to result in private complaints and special requests. But to overaccommodate the interests of some guests risked their not experiencing the discomfort of learning about everyday life in another culture and entering into genuine encounter. Where accommodation in homes was possible, participants sometimes mentioned that it had turned relationships into friendships.

Ancient and biblical forms of hospitality emphasized listening and learning from one's guests. A good host ultimately would receive the guests' blessing. Yet a theme expressed by guests in some Encounters was a longing to be invited by hosts to compare what they were seeing with their own context, a step that also would help them cope with cultural dissonance and vulnerability by sharing comparative knowledge. As one later commented on the post-Encounter questionnaire, "I longed to say, 'I have something to share here, please ask me.'" When sharing did occur, the conversations often led to mutual insight and learning. This mutual exchange of dominance and vulnerability across the Encounters became a crucial aspect of developing relationships of respect across differences.

At the end of the journey, participants rated relationship building the most highly of four areas examined in how useful *indaba* had been. Within this area, four out of five participants valued *indaba* as useful for developing relationships across the Anglican Communion. Three out of four felt that *indaba* also could be useful for building relationships in other aspects of church, interfaith, and civic life.[6]

More than eight in ten participants said they planned to stay in communication. Several groups opened Facebook pages as a way to keep their relationships alive. After the journey, one participant in a news article admitted the temptation to let go of others who thought differently, but then referred to a photo of participants from one of the Encounters and said, "I look at those people and ask, 'Can I do without that person in my life?' and I don't believe I can."[7] Others offered similar reflections about the need to maintain relationships across differences.

Becoming Aware of Mutual Mission

The Encounters helped raise consciousness of different approaches to mission. When hosts shared programs aimed at immediate need, where the emphasis was on charity, many

---

[6] Respondents rated the use of *indaba* for each of the four areas separately (see the appendix).

[7] "Canada."

began to reflect on the difference between serving a need and helping empower those in need. This sometimes led to conversation over tensions between social service, such as feeding programs, and social justice, which involved changing social relations toward greater equality. Participants learned about the constraints on public advocacy that some of their churches faced, as well as differing ways in which they worked quietly, informally, or collaboratively on matters of social justice.

Becoming aware of mutual mission was a slower process for many participants. Yet it occurred in many ways. The Encounters had been modeled on mutual mission, with each team both giving and receiving hospitality, insights, and understanding of its local context and mission activity. However, this mutuality wasn't always matched with equal respect. Several participants in three of the Pilot Conversations had remarked on attitudes of others that regarded their own views as less valuable or less evolved. From survey comments, this donor-recipient attitude was perceived as arrogance and resented. However, it tended to give way toward greater mutual respect over the journey as participants came to understand more about one another's cultural contexts.

Resistance to an ethos of mutuality surfaced in other ways, such as expressions of dominance or coping tactics that maintained barriers. These included personal side trips, demands for different treatment, informal complaints, rapid speech patterns, and side conversations. All made an ethos of cross-cultural mutuality difficult to develop. Such behaviors had begun to abate by the end of the journey, suggesting that mutuality was taking root.

The deepening mutuality of relationships turned out to be key to the possibility of mutual mission. When asked in the final survey what had been learned from the Continuing Indaba experience, one participant noted, "How mission is a natural outflow of the deepening of relationships." Only one Pilot Conversation, with a preexisting partnership, earnestly explored the topic of mutual mission. As difficult as it had been for them, the three bishops involved later wrote:

> The Indaba experience has produced within us an awareness of how we can realistically assist each other in ministry and mission through our international ties now developed at a more grass roots level.[8]

Clearly, *indaba* had offered a place where relationships could deepen, mutual respect could grow, and conversations toward mutual mission could begin.

Changing Viewpoints and Understanding

> *We have created a holy space here, to show how each of us is so valuable.*
>
> —*Participant comment, closing session of indaba conversation*

Indaba had a transformative effect for many participants and afterward for several of their dioceses. For the Pilot Conversation with a preexisting partnership, *indaba* meant a change in the way the dioceses would go about their partnership. The high regard that all Pilot Conversation groups gave *indaba* suggests that it also added value to existing relational bonds, as well as helped participants form new ones.

Transformation began with simple steps. By the end of their journey, four out of five participants responded on the closing survey that they had learned *very much* from their experience of differing cultures and worldviews. They also expressed that they had learned more about their own local and diocesan context, its mission, and its challenges, in addition to

---

8 ACNS Staff, "Continuing Indaba Team Welcomes 'Biggest Change to Mission Policy in 50 Years.'"

learning about the locations they had visited. Nearly everyone admitted that getting to know others across dioceses and cultures had made them think about what they may share across their differences. The journey offered practical outcomes as well, such as a fresh awareness of new ideas and possibilities for mission and for addressing challenges or concerns at home.

The *indaba* journey stirred many participants to think in a fresh way. Nearly four out of five said that their thinking had been somewhat to strongly challenged by the process—from differing views and cultural contexts to their own religious understanding.[9] For some, this meant a shift in their thinking, while many others maintained their views but with a deeper understanding of differing circumstances and viewpoints.

At the start of the journey, some were concerned that Continuing Indaba might seek to change deeply held beliefs, especially on gender and sexuality. This was never an intention of the project. A key assumption of *indaba* was that differences of view would continue to exist; its purpose was to find a way forward in the midst of those differences. Several participants had expressed anxiety over feeling expected to change, although their anxiety lessened as others came to respect their views and contexts. However, the word *change* remained sensitive for some. To reduce this concern, the research focused on whether a shift had occurred in attitudes by asking whether participants had been *affected* by their *indaba* experience. This brought a wider variety of responses.[10]

At the end of the journey, about half of the participants stated that both their understanding and their views had been

---

[9] On the closing survey, more than a quarter of participants admitted to having been *strongly* challenged by the process; another half (52 percent) had their thinking *somewhat* challenged.

[10] Participants also could describe in their own words what *affected* had meant for them. A methodological note: The word *change* had been used for first team surveyed; a participant's negative reaction prompted more neutral wording. However, the results are similar for the differently worded questions. For overall illustration in figure 7.1, responses have been combined.

affected by Continuing Indaba." Nearly another quarter of the participants said that their understanding had been affected, although their views had not. In other words, for some, their hearts had shifted but not their minds. Taken together, about three out of four participants experienced a shift in their understanding.

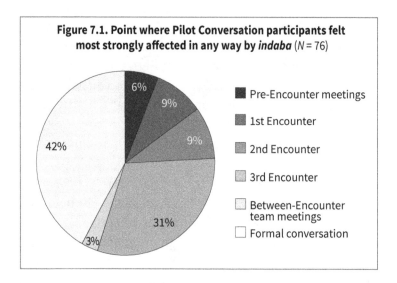

Figure 7.1. Point where Pilot Conversation participants felt most strongly affected in any way by *indaba* (*N* = 76)

For participants who had been affected by Continuing Indaba, typically their first awareness had begun at the pre-Encounter training or at the first Encounter. When asked where they had experienced the *strongest* sense of being affected, it typically was during the third Encounter or the formal conversation (fig. 7.1). This suggests that the Encounters and conversation may have had a cumulative effect. In this way, change came through the shifts in understanding and respect that had allowed relationships to deepen.

---

[11] About a quarter of the participants said on the closing survey that both their understanding and views had been affected *very much*; another quarter said that both were affected *somewhat*.

Sharing in a Global Anglican Communion

At the start of the *indaba* journey, participants had been asked how much they knew about the Anglican Communion. They averaged between knowing a little and knowing something. Except for bishops, few knew very much about it. At the end of the journey, learning what it meant to be part of the Anglican Communion was the most highly rated of all seven learning areas tested.[12] Participants showed an increased awareness and understanding of the Anglican Communion in other survey data as well. Several members commented on feeling part of a worldwide body. One later wrote:

> I have a greater sense of being part of a family.
> As in all families there is not always complete
> agreement but that does not break the bonds
> of kinship. I no longer think of parts of the
> Anglican Communion as separate entities or
> even no-go areas because of their theological
> views.[13]

Comments consistently expressed the value of the Anglican Communion as a way to hold together people from very different contexts in a broad faith tradition with varied understandings and expressions.

Continuing Indaba had understood the success of its project as threefold: remaining in conversation when differences of view were made explicit, creating relationships that might allow people to work together with mutual respect, and strengthening commitments to each other across the Anglican Communion. Participants in every Pilot Conversation remained in conversation, despite moments of high tension, and were able to find places where they could work together in the midst of strong differences. Listening and understanding helped

---

12 Having learned what it means to be part of the Anglican Communion was rated 3.7 on a 4.0 scale (from strongly disagree to strongly agree).

13 Admin, "A Member of the Gloucester Team Reflects on Their Indaba Journey."

build relationships of mutual respect, and of renewed commitment toward the Anglican Communion. Some continuing contact between dioceses and participants reinforced the value of the *indaba* project. In sum, *indaba* did create a capacity for meaningful relationships across strong differences of culture and worldview, and it proved to be invaluable for building relationships across differences based on mutual respect.

INDABA MOMENTS

When participants succeeded at listening openly and intently, inviting others into the conversation who were hesitant to speak, they often experienced special moments of authentic listening and deepened understanding. These moments occurred in all four Pilot Conversations. As one participant later wrote:

> It has made me aware that if I really want to
> understand the perspective of someone else with
> whom I instinctively do not agree, then I need
> to enter their world and see it through their
> eyes. I must also be prepared to allow them to
> enter my world and in both cases that demands
> a vulnerability which does away with barriers of
> race and status, creating a sacred space in which
> the Holy Spirit can open both our hearts and
> minds and enable us to journey together to a
> new place. [14]

Often such moments followed frustration during a difficult conversation and a renewed commitment to try again. In a plenary conversation that nearly polarized into debate, a group came back from the edge with a deeply honest and fascinating conversation over who they wanted to be and how they wanted

---

[14] Ibid.

to function in the world, as distinct teams and in their relationships with each other.

Where *indaba* moments did occur, participants expressed a feeling of having *done indaba*. They often claimed that it was the best discussion they had. They also sensed that a transformation had taken place in both understanding and relationships. Although it was not clear that they knew exactly how to re-create this kind of experience on their own, *indaba* moments tended to occur when the following elements were present:

- topics were framed in a way that all felt they could speak from their experiences and their hearts;
- participants expressed genuine curiosity about what others who weren't speaking actually thought (or what a topic meant in their own cultural context);
- participants took the risk of inviting others to share viewpoints that might make them uncomfortable;
- the pace of speech slowed; and
- participants refrained from interrupting one another.

As one participant later wrote, *indaba* makes a difference only through individuals understanding it and committing to make it work.[15] Despite the frustrations, these moments of authentic understanding and relationship helped participants strive to work together through their difficulties.

THE PRACTICAL ASPECTS OF *INDABA*

The design for the Pilot Conversations had been highly ambitious. It had organized and moved sizable groups to various

---

[15]   Admin, "A Teacher Reflects . . . Telling the Indaba Story."

locations across the world. Some participants complained about the experimental aspects, but they willingly tolerated the challenges and embraced the successes. In the end, participants in all the Pilot Conversations expressed an interest in serving as a model for others.

Although the scope of the Pilot Conversations would be difficult and expensive to replicate, the results have been used to guide smaller, focused *indabas* or *indaba*-style processes. For those thinking about using *indaba*, there are several aspects to consider.

Purpose and Commitment

Indaba can have varied purposes. As the convenors of the all-African Pilot Conversation learned when planning their journey together:

> Indaba process, we discovered that we have
> unique contextual interpretations of the concept
> of Indaba. . . . In Ho, Indaba has a strong element
> of an end in sight, conversation does not go on
> forever; while in Mbeere, Indaba takes place when
> the time is right, and it focuses on the end while
> acknowledging a relevant appropriate process;
> and in Saldanha Bay, Indaba means keeping
> on talking without necessarily focusing on an
> outcome.[16]

Just as some Continuing Indaba participants asked, "Why am I here?" *indaba*'s purpose must be made clear. It shouldn't be so narrow that it's not possible to envision surprising insights and new directions. But like a map, it needs to bring participants back to the primary focus when they begin to lose sight of their direction. It also should offer a sense that deeper listening, understanding, and relationship building will be helpful

---

[16] "Continuing Indaba Bishops Find 'Excitement and Hope' for Communion's Future."

in a particular way. This is especially important when bringing together participants across differing cultures.

Strong commitment to the *indaba* process is essential, especially from the convenors and other leaders. Commitment by participants—to take risks, listen openly, and seek to understand—is also critical for *indaba*'s success. Several participants commented in the final survey that their commitment had helped them struggle to continue instead of giving up during difficult moments.

Indaba Partners and Participants

Partners for *indaba* need to be considered for balance and equality. A challenge for two of the Pilot Conversations was the power imbalance between a Global North majority and Global South minority, which often made it difficult for the majority to engage fully with the perspectives of the minority. Sometimes two teams sharing language and cultural similarities were so dominant that facilitators faced a challenging task of bringing a more balanced awareness within the group. Participants on those teams who were from minority racial and ethnic backgrounds, however, had an easier time engaging cross-culturally and sometimes helped bridge the imbalance.

The two Pilot Conversations most adept at interacting across cultural differences were Hong Kong–Jamaica–Toronto and Ho–Mbeere–Saldanha Bay. Yet even they faced cultural and status challenges to work out along the way. The status challenges that faced all four conversations were hierarchy and power. When bishops were team participants, the status imbalance created challenges for how often or candidly others spoke. Some bishops reduced the disparity by speaking less often, encouraging others to speak their own views, and acting as a member of the group without different treatment. Other power imbalances included gender and in some cases ordained-lay status.

Participants varied in their ability to cope with the

ambiguities and changes of the journey. Although each team had an orientation to Continuing Indaba beforehand, the extent of the orientations had varied. For some, it had been too brief. A few participants also hadn't fully understood the seriousness of the engagement they were undertaking. An introduction to others' cultures is vital, including preparation for how they may be affected by cultural dissonance or shock. Preparation in conversation skills also is necessary for cross-cultural communication, from listening to understand differences to learning how to engage one another across varying accents and proficiencies.

The Role of Encounters

The Encounters were powerful and moving experiences for many participants. They were particularly helpful for visitors from more liberal cultures to understand differing contexts and risks to the church on matters that challenged the cultural norms, such as gender roles, sexuality, caste, or evangelism. As one evaluator, Joanna Sadgrove, wrote:

> Recognition of the courage that the church
> was taking in certain places and the challenges
> the church faced was reported as a sometimes
> humbling experience for visitors, enabling a
> deeper understanding of how perceived divisions
> are impacted by context.[17]

Sadgrove also emphasized that when participants ate, walked, and traveled together, informal conversations and relationships would develop. For example, on an Encounter follow-up questionnaire, a participant commented on how meaningful a car ride with five other participants had been:

---

[17] Dr. Joanna Sadgrove drafted the section on Encounters in the Summative Evaluation Report for Continuing Indaba. See Mkunga Mtingele et al., "Continuing Indaba and Mutual Listening Project, 2009–2012," 66.

> We were able to engage in a frank sharing of
> the differences we each faced in dealing with
> issues around sexuality. It was a spontaneous
> conversation—unplanned—in which everyone felt
> free to express themselves and listened well.

Through the Encounters, participants had come to understand others' contexts, which helped build the trust necessary for *indaba*. Without Encounters, the effect of the *indaba* conversation would have been considerably limited. Even with tight budgets and limited time, some form of Encounter immersion into differing cultural contexts—different neighborhoods, congregations, or other forms of diversity relevant to the purpose and scope of the *indaba*—should occur.

Formal *Indaba* Conversation

While it was hoped that the Encounters would bring about a deeper understanding of cultural differences that might improve mutual listening, the formal *indaba* conversation was intended to put participants' listening skills to the test in an unplanned, authentic discussion on matters of deep concern to them. The hope was that they might move beyond mutual listening and understanding, toward a sense of shared purpose and continuing relationships.

How meaningful the conversations were for participants varied, according to the responses on the closing survey. Two out of three found them to be very meaningful, and another quarter found them somewhat meaningful. For some, the *indaba* conversation was the most memorable aspect of the journey, the place where the experiences of the Encounters helped make possible deep conversation and *indaba* moments. It also was an important turning point for two groups. Some who felt less positive at the time wrote more enthusiastically about it later. Others offered helpful critique in the hope of improving the process for future *indabas*.

The *indaba* conversation was not easy for any of the groups. Each one experienced moments of sizable discomfort, yet all persisted. A major frustration involved lack of clarity at the beginning over the *indaba* process. Often participants assumed that *indaba* would begin with conversations on the topics to be discussed, and they expressed frustration over how long the initial steps took to identify norms that were important to create safe space for speaking from the heart and to decide on what they really wanted to discuss. Few recognized that how they were to talk and respect one another across differences of language, culture, and worldview, as well as what they all thought were topics needing to be addressed, were actually *indaba* conversations. This needs to be clarified so that they are viewed as parts of the *indaba*.

Three areas are key to the *indaba* conversation and its outcomes: the formats used for *indaba*, conversational practices, and facilitation. These need careful attention.

Indaba *formats*

Indaba was at its best when its format included both smaller groups and plenary conversation. In small groups, participants could move from listener to speaker more quickly than in plenaries. Their intimacy helped participants feel less vulnerable, especially across language and cultural differences. They allowed members to adjust to differing accents, gather their thoughts, and consider at a deeper level what was being expressed. Participants could try out ideas, ask questions, and mention things that had touched them deeply or had moved them to tears. Transformation, through the touching of one another's hearts and minds, typically took place in smaller groups.

The size and structure of small groups varied. Those of six to eight participants often were helpful, although they occasionally were affected by power relations that inhibited conversation for some members. Dyads and triads were nearly always useful, especially when each person could speak or listen without interruption, and then ask questions of one another. A format where two or three dyads or triads would combine as a larger group was especially effective in bringing fresh voices together while retaining feelings of intimacy and trust.

Constituency groups, based on a trait that participants might share in common, met the most resistance from those who held some form of dominance in the overall group. Yet they brought new ideas back to the overall group, and those who had spoken little often began to join the plenary conversations. The women's constituency groups opened the way for the full participation of some women who were unaccustomed to speaking candidly in mixed-gender groups or in the midst of clergy. Young adult groups also made important contributions.

Summaries of small-group discussions, when brought into the plenaries, often ignited conversations that otherwise might not have occurred. Many participants also liked the plenary sessions, where consensus and differences were heard by all, and where group decision-making took place. Yet overly long plenary sessions risked falling into the pattern of a few participants speaking while the others remained silent. Speaking in turn during plenaries, such as through use of a talking stick, gave everyone the opportunity to speak at their own pace and resulted in more thoughtful reflections. However, it limited the ability to ask a question, affirm, or follow up on a comment made, which tended to flatten rather than deepen the conversation. Another solution lay in good conversational practices.

Conversational practices

Often good conversational skills were assumed rather than practiced, and agreed-upon norms too easily were forgotten in plenary discussion. In at least one Pilot Conversation, had the norms been reviewed after being set forth by the group, the *indaba*'s effectiveness could have been improved. Conversational practices that encourage others to speak are vital for all voices to be heard. Curiosity also needs to be expressed about different perspectives and the cultural contexts in which they are lived out. When Pilot Conversation participants stepped beyond their own contexts to ask others about theirs, the conversation always was enriched.

Other necessary practices involve greater awareness of the challenges of conversing in another language. For half of the *indaba* teams, English was their second, third, or fourth language, and not one they used daily. Native English speakers often tended to forget this in their own eagerness to participate. The ability to be sensitive to how often one speaks, whether one's words or phrases are easy to understand, and whether the pace of speech allows others to comprehend and think about what has been said all open up conversational space for hearing differences and deepening understanding.

Facilitation of indabas

By the time participants had arrived at the formal *indaba* conversation site, many wanted a deeper engagement with one another but were not sure how to bring this about. Facilitators sought to identify where a group might want to go in its conversation but perhaps couldn't articulate it, and then help the group into a discussion that it didn't know how to have on its own. Facilitators also provided a safe, impartial framework for conflict to emerge that otherwise could have threatened group relationships.

Pairs of facilitators representing differing cultures worked with each formal conversation. Cofacilitation was most effective when the facilitators came from vastly different cultural contexts; not only did this widen the repertoire of understanding, skills, and styles to help the group move forward, but the facilitators also modeled cross-cultural collaboration and communication for the participants. The pair's cultural diversity often helped participants respond in fresh ways that kept the group moving.[18]

---

[18] For one Pilot Conversation, both facilitators came from Western cultures because of a scheduling conflict. Greater cultural diversity would have been helpful.

Overall, facilitation helped participants think creatively about the concerns on their hearts and voice them in an ethos of trust. As one participant commented on the closing questionnaire:

> The Final Conversations were the best. We recognized that it took a very long time to get there and that we do not just want to walk away. What was especially important is that by the third encounter we had formed meaningful and safe relationships, but there were areas we couldn't touch, and pain we couldn't touch, and risks we couldn't take through self-facilitation. Having a facilitated final conversation made us take risks at a deeper level and we left with not only a richer experience of each other but a deeper and more meaningful set of relationships.

Yet *indaba* facilitation faced many challenges. Cofacilitators who didn't know one another had to rapidly develop a unified working relationship. It also took time to understand what the group had experienced in its journey, including anxieties and concerns. In one conversation, participants wanted the facilitators to take an assertive role and tell them what to do, which the facilitators resisted by keeping the group focused on collaborative discussion and decision-making. Occasionally, facilitators didn't realize that a group wasn't able to grasp what they were trying to help it see or do, which resulted in mutual frustration.

For groups that had developed close relationships during the Encounters, a different challenge involved the acceptance of external facilitators who hadn't shared the experience of their journey. In some groups with bishop participants, handing over leadership to external facilitators brought tension that at times affected the conversation. Facilitators had to be able to deflect anyone seeking to dominate or control a discussion. If tensions ignited, they had to discern when to let the group work through them and when a shift was needed to help the group better manage them. In comments and summaries, facilitators had to use the words of the group, and not their own, so as not to influence the conversation and its outcomes.

Some local facilitators were helpful during Encounters, but others weren't as adept at the skills needed for cross-cultural facilitation. Sometimes participants acted as facilitators, and several small groups generated a collaborative internal style where facilitation was mutually shared. These tended to be more successful when the task simply was to help everyone speak and stay engaged in the topic. Self-facilitation was more challenging when deep emotions arose or intervention was needed to help clarify statements that were misunderstood or framed in a way that offended. At times sensitive conversation was avoided altogether in self-facilitated groups by keeping the discussion at a conceptual level or by digressing from the topic. This underscores the need for professional facilitation to be available to help authentic conversation occur in an ethos of mutual respect. Taken together, these experiences emphasize the importance of facilitation for an *indaba*'s outcome.

Adaptation of *Indaba* for Different Uses

One of the concerns following the Pilot Conversations was that some might try *indaba* without a deep sense of what made it different from other types of gatherings and conversations. In traditional *indaba*, the process was embedded in the community—its customs, culture, and how *indaba* had been used in the past. Members were familiar with its purpose, the norms that guided it, and how the process would unfold. Many might correctly say that the processes used at the 2008 Lambeth Conference and in the Pilot Conversations were not authentically *indaba*, but core aspects made the process work in ways that typical Western group processes did not. What was essential for an adapted *indaba* process to be effective?

A core leadership team of Continuing Indaba staff,

consultants, facilitators, and others offering wisdom and familiarity with *indaba* worked to identify what was basic to an *indaba*-style conversation and made it work well. Continuing Indaba staff developed training materials and guides, based on the research findings and on suggestions from facilitators, evaluators, participants, and others who had been involved in the Pilot Conversation journeys.[19] For *indaba*'s use in the Anglican Communion, the three basic aspects of an *indaba* process were identified: biblical reflection on the importance of relationship, conversation on significant matters, and inspiration for both local and global missions.[20] The process had five steps, which formed the framework of the Pilot Conversations:

1. *Sharing the vision*: Collaboratively developing the *indaba* journey and setting its themes, then clearly communicating its purpose to all involved.

2. *Gathering*: Inviting and preparing participants for the *indaba* process.

3. *Encounter*: Enabling participants to personally experience one another's contexts to help them understand the others' worldviews and form deeper relationships on which trust can develop.

4. *Genuine conversation*: Using facilitated conversation to help participants listen and speak authentically and openly.

5. *Going out*: Living out *indaba* through actions in communities, and enabling all to walk together in common purpose or mission. [21]

---

19 Guides include an overview and practical steps on holding a Continuing Indaba event and "Eight Principles" that the Diocese of Derby had found to be essential to an *indaba* Encounter based on its team experience. The guides are available at http://continuingindaba.org/process-guides/. Also see "8 Principals [*sic*] of Indaba."

20 "The Indaba Process."

21 Ibid.

Indaba *and Western cultures*

Those from Western cultures need to take special care in adapting *indaba*. It cannot be burdened with Western emphases on efficiency, regulation, argumentation, and other practices that limit its transformative potential. Differing ways of communicating can challenge many Western norms for group participation, but they also hold potential for new insight. For example, time needs to be available for sharing stories as a way of building relationship or making a point. These are essential for cross-cultural understanding and comprehending differences.

Another concern for cross-cultural *indaba* is the temptation to fuse Western notions of individual equality with postcolonial assumptions of cultural equality. This was a difficulty in the Pilot Conversations, where the assumption had been made that individuals, as equals, would express their authentic personal views. This Western expectation of individual autonomy clashed with other cultural norms where hierarchy and status differences are respected, and where personal identity is deeply entwined in family or communal identity. It affected who spoke in the plenaries and what they said. Even in small groups, some participants were anxious about speaking until they knew what their bishop had said. As a result, it wasn't always clear when a comment represented a personal view or one held by a diocesan team or the community from which a participant came.

Overall, modified forms of *indaba* can bring results across sizable differences in culture and status, as the Pilot Conversations illustrated. But they depend on status-leveling comments and behaviors from higher-status members to encourage others to participate more openly. This was true for every team in the Pilot Conversations. Another important element is the use of small groups where participants share similar status, which can deepen personal conversations. Yet another involves having external facilitators who are familiar with differing cultural norms within a group and can keep a conversation balanced and in motion. For instance, one of the facilitators adeptly cued bishops and a key lay leader, culturally recognizing their status while treating them as group participants, which likely hastened how they put others at ease. What is most valuable, however, is for a team from the differing cultures or backgrounds involved to design together how the *indaba* will be adapted and enacted so that all voices can be heard.

Practical considerations

A number of considerations for adapting *indaba* arise out of the Pilot Conversation experiences. Some contribute to *indaba* working well; others can help avoid pitfalls. Here are some of the key attributes of a successful *indaba*:

- Preparing participants beforehand in listening and conversation skills, especially for cross-cultural differences.

- Making space for personal encounters with differences. Experiencing the *other* is invaluable for deepening mutual listening and understanding, whether in cultures across the world or in next-door neighborhoods; in the lives of young adults or senior citizens; or in varying economic, spiritual, or other contexts where divisions arise.

- Encouraging different ways for participants to help others understand the contexts that inform their beliefs and worldview, such as through storytelling, explaining artifacts and symbols, and using other experiential methods.

- Being sensitive to the group's needs. If an Encounter or other intense experience occurred just before the *indaba* conversation, participants may need time for reflection so that they can enter the *indaba* with clarity and focus.

- Being sensitive to the group's level of energy. Exhaustion from travel, communicating in another language, and cultural dissonance needs to be considered in planning the format and rhythm of the *indaba*. Intensity and exhaustion can help produce candor and commitment, but these also risk inhibiting deep listening and respectful conversation.

- Sharing ritual events where people come together for a common purpose across their differences. Depending on the purpose and the group, these may include prayer, meditation, worship, scriptural reading, and personal reflection, as well as meals and other group occasions. Ritual can reinforce relationships, build cohesion, and ground conversation in shared experience.

- Reflecting together on which conversational practices will lead to safety and mutual respect, and abiding by them throughout the *indaba*.

- Desiring to listen and learn as much as to speak and share. No one voice should dominate the conversation.

- Mutually listening to understand one another's views; the purpose is to understand, not to critique.

- Making space for everyone to speak. Seek ways to invite silent voices into the conversation or change how a conversation is framed so that others can participate more easily.

- Making sure that all voices involved in a concern are part of the conversation.

- Asking about one another's contexts or cultures and what a topic or concern means from their standpoint.

- Creating space for new topics to emerge. Sometimes a latent or deeper concern may arise that needs significant time for conversation. Part of *indaba* is allowing for conversation to move in sometimes surprising directions.

- Sharing summaries of small-group discussions with the overall group and giving participants an opportunity to correct or add anything they want to have heard. This allows a common narrative to emerge.

- Facilitating large groups, using professional and cross-cultural skills, and supporting mutual facilitation in small groups so that all voices are heard, understood, and respected, especially where topics are controversial or emotions may arise.

- Summarizing a discussion at its end. A facilitator can help the group identify what was missed or misunderstood, and then move toward a next step or action depending on the *indaba*'s purpose.

- Remembering that informal conversations during breaks and over meals can be places where questions are asked or meanings clarified that contribute to the *indaba*.

- Having an observer or evaluator, who can help identify *why* an *indaba* is working or not so that adjustments can be made if needed and outcomes confirmed.

Indabas are organic. They take on a will of their own in the direction they collectively move. The roles of leadership and facilitation are to help every member fully contribute and be heard so that the group direction represents the creative synergy of all. Members have a key role as active participants through mutual listening and inviting one another into conversation. This can lead to surprising insights and is the ground on which pathways can appear that offer new directions for the future.

MEANINGFUL CONVERSATION AND THE PATH AHEAD

Continuing Indaba helped four cross-cultural groups have meaningful conversations and build the kind of relationships that seldom occur across vast differences of culture and worldview. Clearly, this was not *indaba* in its traditional form, but the adapted *indaba* did create a unique bridge across cultures. Participants struggled to listen, encountered differing worldviews, and yet managed to find common ground for staying together in the midst of sometimes strong disagreement. *Indaba* had created authentic encounter for many, and more than seven in ten participants felt they had learned something about themselves from the process.[22] They arrived home, most ending in a different place of understanding than where they had begun. All had gained new experiences and relationships.

The experimental nature of the journey helped identify ways in which *indaba* might provide a path for others. Some participants expressed that they had experienced something special and perhaps rare, in words not unlike the authentic "I and Thou" of which the Jewish scholar Martin Buber wrote.[23] *Indaba* helped create a better ethos of listening and offered a way for people to hear and begin to understand the differing

---

22   The closing questionnaire asked participants what they had learned about themselves from Continuing Indaba, as well as whether they had gained new insights or understandings of their own perspectives or viewpoints.

23   Martin Buber, *I and Thou.*

cultural conditions and histories that have affected how a shared faith tradition is lived and expressed in different ways. Commented one participant in an interview at the end of the formal *indaba* conversation:

> If we have the courage to encounter each other's
> genuine humanity we can easily live with
> the differences. This is the root of liberation
> theology. . . . There is potential for indaba to do
> that; to redefine the ecclesiology of the Anglican
> Communion. Therefore there is the potential
> that the Anglican Communion will survive. . . .
> The fact that the Anglican Communion enabled
> such a dialog is phenomenal.[24]

Mutual listening and understanding can enrich and deepen the belief that a common journey together is possible.

---

[24] Rev. Fr. Julian Hollywell SCP, Vicar of Spondon, interview with author, quoted with permission.

~ 8 ~

Other *Indabas* across the Anglican Communion

This is a rare opportunity and a benefit that will live well beyond the Indaba process itself.

—Participant comment[1]

∿∿∿

WHAT HAPPENED AFTER THE PROJECT ENDED would indicate the overall success of Continuing Indaba. Would commitments have become strengthened across the Anglican Communion? Would people have moved away from polarizing attitudes over deeply held differences? Would relationships have been built in which differences could be maintained and respected?

---

[1] Written comment in response to evaluation reflection questions following second Encounter.

Would *indaba* have incited creative thinking over new ways of moving forward together? Would the communal approach that *indaba* embodied be adapted for use elsewhere?

When participants returned home from the Pilot Conversations, some pondered how they would make use of what they had learned from their experiences. The teams involved in one Pilot Conversation continued their partner relationship with planned visits. Other participants shared their reflections on Facebook and wrote about their experiences for the Continuing Indaba website and elsewhere. A few later made informal visits or participated in clergy exchanges. Some advocated or helped plan new *indabas* at home. The experience had been a catalyst in many participants' lives, sparking the desire to share new ways of relating across differences.

Even before the Pilot Conversations had ended, the impact of the Encounters had led some of the participating dioceses to experiment with new ways of using *indaba*. Participants were sharing and discussing their experiences, and telling others about *indaba* through preaching and local presentations. Two participants had linked their parish preschools. *Indaba* was tried in a monastery, a clergy school, a provincial youth camp, and in partnership with villages or other groups to reduce tension and build relationships. Most commonly, *indaba* was used in congregations and dioceses, in councils and meetings, and for listening and discussing sensitive issues.[2]

In fall 2012, when the results of Continuing Indaba were shared with the Anglican Consultative Council (ACC 15), two resolutions were passed supporting *indaba*'s ongoing use. After intense debate over the purpose of *indaba*, the first resolution (15.39) formally clarified it to be "a process of honest conversation that seeks to build community, energize mission, and provide a context in which conflict can be resolved."[3]

---

[2] These examples come from participant descriptions on the closing questionnaire of how *indaba* had been used in their dioceses and participant interviews during the Encounters.

[3] "Resolutions ACC 15."

The other resolution (15.21) encouraged the Anglican Communion to engage with the theological resources developed through Continuing Indaba and hear the stories of those involved in the Pilot Conversations. It requested that resources and guides on using *indaba* be developed and shared for those wanting to try the process, which were then posted on the Continuing Indaba website. In addition, it requested that commitment be made to facilitator training and evaluation. Director Phil Groves continued to offer advice for adapting *indaba* to different purposes.

A VARIETY OF PURPOSES FOR *INDABA*

Since 2012, *indabas* have been adapted for a range of purposes within the Anglican Communion and beyond. Some have sought to soften and transform conflicts. Others have focused on having the participants get to know and understand one another across cultural and geographic differences. Yet others have sought to build relationships, bring about reconciliation, engage in mutual learning, and share a mission or purpose. The following examples offer a glimpse of the differing ways in which *indaba* is changing relationships in the Anglican Communion, within its churches, and most of all, among its participants.

Diocesan *Indabas*

Diocese of New York

After the Pilot Conversation involving a team from New York ended, the new diocesan bishop, the Rt. Rev. Andrew Dietsche, faced a diocese that was deeply fragmented. Tensions across urban, suburban, and rural districts as well as across demographic groups threatened its future direction. Wealthy New York City parishes felt burdened by small rural and ethnic congregations that business practices suggested would need to be closed. He believed that people needed to get to know one another across the diocese before thoughtful decision-making could take place that affected one another's lives and the diocese's future.

Bishop Dietsche called for a diocese-wide *indaba*. Some of the Pilot Conversation participants had imagined this possibility, as they were amazed to realize during the New York Encounter that they had been unaware what neighboring congregations were doing in the community, and their experience had engendered a strong desire to get to know one another. Two members of the New York team drew from their *indaba* experience to help design a process for the diocese. The *indaba* would consist of four-person teams, reflecting the diversity of each participating congregation.

Teams from fifty-four congregations in the diocese met for the first time in September 2013 to plan their Encounters. They represented a mix of urban, suburban, and rural; wealthy and struggling; white, multiracial, and ethnic congregations. Each team was partnered with two others across different congregational contexts. Over the next several months, each team hosted its partners for a weekend with its congregation. Participants also stayed in the homes of team members and others in the congregation. This personal form of hospitality turned out to be one of the most challenging aspects of the *indaba* but also was critical to its success.

The format of the weekend Encounters involved a Saturday morning introduction, where the guests learned about the host congregation, its challenges, and its hopes for the future. The afternoon focused on the congregation's connections with the surrounding community. Evening was a time for personal conversations with the hosts and their families. After Sunday worship and social time, a facilitated conversation allowed team members to share their reflections and ask questions, *indaba* style. Each congregation also was to pray for one another throughout the year.[4]

---

4 "Toward a Shared Understanding of our Common Life," 3–4.

At the end, a concluding celebration was held for all *indaba* participants. Several congregations continued to journey together in ministry, mission trips, and other activities. As one participant commented, "*Indaba* removed stereotypes about the Diocese and made it possible for us to think of doing mission together."[5]

When the time came for the diocese to talk about the hard choices facing small, economically marginal congregations, some from wealthier parishes that had participated in the *indaba* freshly understood these congregations' tangible missions and the ministry they were doing and willingly began to search for ways to work together in partnership and mutual mission. A comment often echoed was "These are our friends."[6] Future steps needed to keep that in mind. The *indaba* had knit the diocese into a cohesive body. Another outcome of the *indaba*'s success was the use of *indaba* conversations by the Evangelical Lutheran Church in America (ELCA) in its Metro New York Synod.[7]

The New York *indaba* led to interest in further diocesan *indabas*. In 2014, an *indaba* was held for individuals who had wanted to participate but whose congregations weren't able to form a team. Clergy and laity met in separate *indaba* groups, following the Encounter design of visiting one another's congregations. A third *indaba*, in 2015, returned to the congregational team format. It also included two teams from the first *indaba* that wanted the structure to help deepen their relationships.[8]

The Ven. William Parnell, archdeacon, who oversaw the diocesan *indabas*, expressed surprise over how well *indaba* had worked. "Indaba has given people the tool to be engaged with others who aren't like them. How often do we as the church give people the tools to do that?" He also noted that the *indaba*

---

5   Ibid., 8.

6   Personal conversation.

7   "Toward a Shared Understanding," 7.

8   Ibid., 5; interview with the Ven. William Parnell, archdeacon, Diocese of New York, December 2014.

consisting of individuals had been difficult to sustain. The team approach, which brought together communities of participants, strengthened commitment, and maintained a group presence, was better suited to *indaba*.[9]

Parnell advised others thinking about doing an *indaba* to talk with people who have planned or been part of one. "Insist that people get in each other's space, including their personal space," he said, emphasizing the importance of radical hospitality and Encounter. "Be fully present. Also, don't turn it into another church meeting. And, focus on having fun together. Allow it to transform your parish or diocesan life."[10]

Mergers, partner relationships, and the use of alternative spaces and formats for mission and ministry continue to be explored as strategic planning moves forward in the diocese. What *has* changed is that congregations in the diocese are considering one another as "us" rather than "them."

Diocese of Auckland (New Zealand)

Like New York, the Diocese of Auckland faced several challenges to its future. "How can we be in mission and ministry if we are essentially congregations that are islands unto ourselves with little or no understanding of each other?" the diocesan bishop, The Rt. Rev. Ross Bay, and assistant bishop, The Rt. Rev. Jim White, asked in their joint address to the 2014 diocesan synod.[11] Rapid demographic growth also meant that the church had no presence in some districts. With rural and some urban churches financially hurting, little money was available for outreach. A free-market approach of self-funding would not help the church grow or develop a sense of togetherness or shared identity. The bishops turned to *indaba*.

---

9 Interview with the Ven. William Parnell, archdeacon, Diocese of New York, December 2014.

10 Ibid.

11 A diocesan synod is similar to a diocesan convention: an annual meeting where business of the diocese is conducted. "Bishops' Charge to the Second Session of the Fifty Fourth Synod of the Diocese of Auckland," 4.

Congregations were invited into an *indaba* process during Lent 2015. Each was matched with two others, differing in size and location. Each was to host a weekend Encounter to allow participants to get to know one another better and gain understanding of the particular challenges and richness of each context. The five-person congregational teams each included someone ordained and someone under twenty years old if possible. Similar to the New York *indaba*, the visits began on Saturday afternoon, with brief worship and an introduction to the congregation, its mission, and its ministry context. That evening provided social time with the hosts, as guests stayed in local homes for the night. Following Sunday morning worship and time afterward with the congregation, the teams concluded that afternoon with a closing reflection together.[12]

Themes emerging out of the *indabas* included the power of hospitality, a sense of relationship and family amid the diverse congregations, shared vulnerability, shared challenges for the future, and the value of Local Shared Ministry (also called Total Ministry).[13] In the 2015 Advent letter to the diocese, one of the bishops noted that some congregations had planned to meet again and stay in touch as a way to contribute to one another's lives.[14] Next steps involved building further relationships and collaboration within the diocese and possibly holding *indabas* with other dioceses.

Indaba and Governance

Indaba has represented a bold, new step for use in governance. Churches and other groups often have relied on parliamentary process for official meetings and decision-making. Although decisions can be efficiently made through parliamentary means, sometimes the will of the majority can ignore the voices of the minority, resulting in resentment or opposition rather than

---

12 The purpose and format are described in ibid.
13 "Auckland Bishops Deliver Charge."
14 "Bishop's Letter Advent 2015."

widespread support for a decision. Caucuses may meet to negotiate a solution, but they often barter positions rather than
probe the interests or contexts surrounding their differences.
Decisions that need broad affirmation may benefit from the
depth and contextual understanding that *indaba* offers.

In some situations, *indaba* has been used in combination
with parliamentary process. Business may be suspended while
participants move into *indaba* to focus on a specific question
or concern. An *indaba* process also may run parallel to the
parliamentary process, with insights from *indabas* that affect
resolutions and decision-making brought into the governance
meeting.[15] *Indaba* can even become the model for governance
in some contexts.

Shortly after the Pilot Conversations ended, the Church of
England had urged its dioceses and parishes to use *indaba* in
building global relationships. One of the participants from the
Derby team spoke passionately to the church's General Synod
about her experience.[16] The Diocese of Saldanha Bay also considered how it might use *indaba*. Bishop Raphael Hess wanted
to use it in diocesan meetings alongside constitutional processes. In doing so, the diocesan synod became conversation-
based with inclusive facilitated discussions on key topics. As
Hess noted in *Living Reconciliation*, leadership using *indaba*
principles may be slower, but it is more patient and collaborative by making sure that different voices have been heard.[17]
Indaba-style processes also are likely to result in decisions that
unite a community rather than continue to face resistance.

Indaba in a diocesan convention

In 2013, Iowa Bishop Alan Scarfe and others visited their
new companion, the Diocese of Nzara in South Sudan. While
watching the diocesan synod, he was struck by the style of

---

[15] "Continuing Indaba and Governance Processes."

[16] A General Synod is similar to a General Convention: a churchwide meeting
where business is conducted. Admin, "Church of England Commits Itself to
Continuing Indaba."

[17] Groves and Jones, *Living Reconciliation,* 176–78.

conversation. People spoke to each other directly, using an *indaba*-type process to work toward a conclusion without the parliamentary practices commonly used in the West. He also pondered over how he might find a way to use *indaba* at his own diocesan convention that fall.[18]

During the Iowa convention, two small-group *indaba* sessions were held. In the first, participants reflected on models for young adult ministry in the diocese. The second took on the topic of reimagining the church. A scribe for each *indaba* group noted the ideas brought up, which were given to a review group to identify shared themes and vision. Those were returned to groups for a facilitated discussion.

The conversation on young adult ministry had been especially difficult because of tensions over the direction that it should take. *Indaba* brought out the importance of building relationships in community, the need for multiple forms of leadership development, and the necessity of hearing the voices of young adults, which had been missing from the conversation. A priest stated in his sermon the next day that the *indaba* conversations had helped participants see "that we cared about the same things, and wanted to find a win-win solution."[19] He felt that the *indaba* was invaluable in helping them find a direction that was more creative than the either-or choice they had faced.

The first *indaba* spilled into the conversation on reimagining the church, bringing up the need to consider what might really matter to young adults in order for them to feel part of it.[20] As participants struggled with speaking honestly and openly, both deep connection with tradition and the desire for change were heard and acknowledged, as well as the need to balance both in moving forward.[21] A media report of the event

---

18 This case study draws on the following sources: Groves and Jones, *Living Reconciliation*, 185–87; "Indaba Process Honors All Voices at Convention," 1–2; Kathleen Milligan et al., "Reflections on Indaba," 1–2.

19 The Rev. Benjamin S. Webb, "Inspiring Our Mission."

20 Ibid.

21 Milligan et al., "Reflections on Indaba," 2.

noted that participants were able to talk with others they never would have met. They valued having all of their voices being represented in the summary documents as well.[22]

Indaba small-group conversations have become part of the annual diocesan conventions. They also have been used in congregations to generate new ideas and directions for mission and ministry and for deeper self-understanding. According to Bishop Alan Scarfe, "Indaba reminds us that every one's voice is vital, and always has been."[23]

Indaba *principles for listening in the Anglican Church of Australia*

Indaba principles were used to aid in deeper listening to issues facing the Anglican Church of Australia's 2014 General Synod. Parliamentary process had offered little opportunity to understand the differing theological views on questions that underlay some of the legislative resolutions. Members were superficially cordial across their differences but otherwise did not engage one another. Bible study and prayer also had been limited.[24]

A pilot event was held with the Standing Committee and key stakeholders to help them get a sense of the value of this new process. For the General Synod, small-group conversations inspired by *indaba* were integrated into the meeting along with its parliamentary business. Twenty-five small groups of ten persons each, representing the diversity of the church, met daily for Bible study and facilitated conversation. The aim was to do the following:

- allow more members to share their personal views across differences and to be heard in an ethos of safety and trust;

---

22 "Indaba Process Honors All Voices at Convention," 2.

23 Personal correspondence, April 13, 2016. Used with permission.

24 Garth Blake, "Sixteenth Session of General Synod."

- help one another understand the places where they agreed and where they differed, in a manner that might deepen their relationships; and

- consider initiatives for the church's life and mission in coming years.[25]

Each day, the small-group discussions had a slightly different emphasis. These included sharing hopes for the church's ministry and mission; concerns about the church's current ministry and mission and what might underlie such concerns; and practical steps toward realizing the hopes that had been mentioned the first day.

The groups reviewed notes taken on their discussions, which then became part of a program record containing experiences, ideas, and suggestions for the church to consider. Many commented on how much they liked the small-group discussions in combination with the meeting's formal parliamentary process, according to one of the organizers. One participant called it the birth of a new style of General Synod possible for the future.[26]

A different process in the Anglican Church of Canada

Trying to find a way to stay together across differences has been a Canadian cultural ideal. After facilitating an *indaba* group at the 2008 Lambeth Conference, Archbishop Colin Johnson returned to the Diocese of Toronto with enthusiasm to try *indaba* in the diocesan synod. Afterward, he was surprised at how 750 people had come to a virtual consensus without a legislative vote; only a handful had disagreed, he noted. In an interview, he described it as a "transformative event" where everyone had been able to express their point of view.[27]

Indaba was introduced churchwide at the 2010 General Synod. It emphasized mutual listening as a way to discuss the

---

25 Marilyn Redlich and Garth Blake, "Small Group Discussion Programme—GS16."
26 Ibid. 3; personal correspondence.
27 Personal interview, June 13, 2016, used with permission.

place of gay and lesbian people in the church, rather than the divisive debates of previous conversations.[28] It also helped participants feel that they had been heard with understanding by others holding sharply differing views. At the end, they arrived at a consensus statement that even many with strong positions felt they could bear.

A "circle of listening" process is now used in the church, influenced by both *indaba* and the sacred circles of Indigenous People. The process emphasizes mutual listening and authentic conversation, yet respects the differences of sacred circles and *indaba* for their own peoples and contexts. Archbishop Johnson pointed out that these processes have changed the ethos of listening and decision-making in the diocese to be more inclusive and oriented toward finding consensus, rather than simply being based on a majority vote.

Indaba also has been credited with having built deeper understanding and appreciation for Indigenous People's differing ways of leadership and governance. A respectful partnership has formed in the church, which has included provision for self-determining territory and governance, apology for the church's historical abuse, and recognition of their distinctive spirituality as both Christian and Aboriginal.[29] The circle of listening process has allowed for deeper dialogue and understanding to inform the decisions being made.

Indaba and the Next Generation

The energy and insights that younger members brought to the Pilot Conversations had helped their teams build relationships across differences. Most were curious, engaged, and more willing to take risks. Through *indaba*, their voices were heard and given respect. A South African youth *indaba* was held shortly after the Pilot Conversations ended, to learn how more young people might be engaged in the life of the

---

28 Marites N. Sison, "Canada."
29 "Anglican Council of Indigenous Peoples."

church.[30] Two youth coordinators wrote that youth wanted to be listened to, wanted safe places to speak, wanted authenticity and mentoring from elders, and wanted to be part of the decision-making. They emphasized the need to include young people as potential partners in the church, as youth are vital to its mission and future.[31] *Indaba* offered a way to do just that.

In Hong Kong, the challenges facing youth involvement in the church are somewhat different. Over the years, growing societal differences between younger and older generations have brought tensions. During the Pilot Conversations, the church had held a province-wide youth *indaba* where young people shared concerns on their hearts (see chapter 4). It had been helpful for church leaders as they considered how to maintain relationships with youth, and also was valued as a way to bring greater harmony across generations through mutual listening and accommodation.

During the turbulence of 2014, the church used *indaba* for conversation over growing tensions between young adults, especially those who embraced the Occupy and Umbrella Movements, seeking greater democracy, and elders who were concerned that activism might cause political reaction.[32] The youth expressed frustration over the church's conservative approaches but also heard elders express the historical context that had shaped their views and the wisdom they sought to offer.[33] The mutual listening helped both youth and elders hear and better understand each other's viewpoint in an effort to build trust and relationships.

Tensions on college campuses have risen in many locations over recent years. In the United States, *indaba* was introduced at the 2016 Province VIII college conference for Episcopal chaplains and students. About sixty young adults gathered

---

30   ACNS Staff, "Continuing Indaba Team Welcomes 'Biggest Change.'"
31   Kevin David and Tony Lawrence, "The Place of Young People in the Continuing Indaba Process."
32   Phil Groves, "Report to ACC 16."
33   Phil Groves, "Phil Groves at CCEA."

to learn about *indaba* across the Anglican Communion and to consider how they might design their own college *indabas.* Using an *indaba* process to do so, in small groups they identified and discussed concerns touching their passion that could be addressed in an *indaba.*[34] They also considered the range of voices needing to be part of the conversation, how an *indaba* might take place, and what norms would help make it a safe place to share. Participants took turns listening, speaking, and observing.

Small groups then described their *indabas,* which led to a discussion of the dangers of tokenism, which could cause a minority voice to feel isolated or overbalanced by the dominant group. Some participants suggested a need for *indabas* within constituency groups before more broadly based *indabas* could be safe for topics of deep pain, such as racial relations. Their insights indicate that *indaba* may be helpful for campus ministries in engaging important conversations.

Indaba and Race, Gender, and Sexuality

Indaba *and race*

Shortly after the Pilot Conversations ended, the Episcopal church missioner for black ministries, the Rev. Angela Ifill, convened a planning team for a black clergy *indaba.* About seventy black clergy from North America, the Caribbean, and Africa came together in 2013 for an *indaba* on unity and effective leadership, with the theme of "Visioning: Seed Time and Harvest." The *indaba* opened with a preconference gathering of separate groups for Sudanese, Haitian, and Liberian clergy; those clergy ordained eight years or less; those in large congregations; and those ordained as vocational deacons.[35]

The key topics for the *indaba* included personal and internal

---

[34] The author oversaw the *indaba* process at the conference.
[35] Public Affairs Office. "Episcopal Church Black Clergy Indaba." Additional detail comes from a meeting agenda.

reconciliation; identity; reconciliation with colonial empire; the mission of reconciliation within congregations, neighborhoods, and communities; and working to dismantle structural racism to bring about racial reconciliation. A prominent black scholar or church leader introduced each topic. Following each presentation, participants met in small *indaba* circles around the room for conversation. A leader from each group then summarized the conversation for all to hear. A weaver, acting as a reporter, harvested wisdom from the discussion to share via social media for continuing conversations. Insights from the *indaba* also were compiled into a booklet that participants took with them on the final day.

The *indaba* brought enthusiastic responses. The Rev. Canon Stephanie Spellers, a speaker at the *indaba*, later reflected:

> Everyone I heard marveled at how honest and raw our conversations were. We spoke of empire and colonialism. We spoke of the differences between black experiences based in the US, the Caribbean and Africa. We spoke of class and socio-economic barriers among us and between us and the communities we love. And we spoke in ways few of us had heard before about heartbreak: the heartbreak of racism (in the church and in society), of serving congregations in decline or in conflict, of serving a church that is ambivalent about our very presence.
>
> Even those who had known each other for years said the *indaba* has allowed them to break through to deeper levels of relation, wisdom and even healing.[36]

From that experience, *indaba* has been used in participants' parishes, with transforming effects for at least one in its mission and ministry.[37] Another international black clergy

---

36 Personal correspondence, April 28, 2016. Used with permission.
37 Groves, "Report to ACC 16."

conference with *indaba*-style conversations was scheduled for November 2016.

Indaba-style conversations also have been used to discuss interracial tensions. The Diocese of Virginia, having used such gatherings to address tensions over sexuality a few years earlier, held *indaba*-style listening sessions in 2015 for people to hear about painful experiences of racial tension and division and the many ways that racial divisions affected one another's lives. Everyone was able to speak freely from their own standpoint without fear of being debated or criticized. As Bishop Shannon Johnston remarked in his pastoral address announcing the initiative, "I can tell you from many experiences of *indaba* style sessions that something actually mysterious happens when it is faithfully engaged. It is, indeed, a Holy Spirit phenomenon."[38]

Interracial healing is a long journey, but *indaba*-style listening offered a beginning step for the diocese in its commitment to racial reconciliation.

Indaba *and gender*

When women met together in small groups during the Pilot Conversations, several became empowered to speak more often in mixed-gender plenaries. They offered different viewpoints and sometimes were agents of transformation in the conversations. This led to curiosity over how *indaba* might work among women in other contexts.

Sponsored by Anglican Women's Empowerment (AWE) and Continuing Indaba, the first Anglican all-women *indaba* took place in 2013, bringing together six women from the United States and five from Africa, representing the countries of Burundi, Democratic Republic of the Congo, Kenya, Rwanda, and Tanzania.[39] The *indaba*'s theme was violence against women, and its aims were to deepen understanding and

---

38 The Rt. Rev. Shannon S. Johnston, "Bishop Johnston's Pastoral Address."

39 AWE has a mission of social change by empowering women in leadership.

conversation across different cultures and to develop insights that might result in both local and mutual missions.[40] As in the Pilot Conversations, each woman shared a symbol and a personal story to introduce herself. This was followed by group norm-setting to make the *indaba* safe, Bible study using *Lectio Divina*, and worship that framed the women's days together.[41]

Two Continuing Indaba facilitators, from Botswana and Canada, took turns leading and observing the *indaba*; as they modeled cross-cultural interaction, this helped participants see the possibilities of mutual leadership across cultural differences. The facilitators also tightly structured the process so that mutual conversation might emerge. Women met in small groups to form questions and themes for *indaba* conversation, deciding on three themes related to violence: education, economic empowerment, and breaking the silence. They then were paired, one African and one American, to take turns listening and learning about what violence against women meant in each other's cultural contexts.[42] Later, in plenary sessions, the women shared something they had learned.

The last day focused on creating pathways to healing and wholeness as a means of becoming free from the effects of violence. Again, women listened to each other in pairs and then, in plenary, they spoke in turn about what they had learned and what they thought could be done in their own context to produce healing and wholeness. Before closing, participants met in constituency groups—African and American—to discuss what they might want to say to the other group and also take with them from the *indaba*. After sharing their thoughts in plenary, the *indaba* concluded with worship.

Overall, cross-cultural learning from the *indaba* was remarkable, especially given the *indaba*'s brief time. For African women, some of the most valuable learning had to do with

---

40 Anglican Women's Empowerment, "Fact Sheet." The *indaba* was evaluated by the author, using pre- and post-*indaba* questionnaires, short interviews, and observation.

41 The author observed and evaluated the AWE women's *indaba*. Details in the case study are from field notes.

42 Because there was an odd number of participants, one group formed a triad.

comparatively analyzing violence against women and discussing strategies for eliminating it. American women acknowledged that listening is the most important aspect of working with women, and also that they needed to be aware of their own assumptions and stereotypes underlying their views, according to survey comments. They had let go of a customarily fast, goal-oriented speaking style as they encouraged the African women to share their experiences through open and patient listening for long periods. The American women also began referring to the African women's comments and building on what they had said, evidence that listening and new understanding were transforming the conversation.

Women from both continents strongly agreed that they had felt treated as equals by women from the other continent, according to the closing survey. Getting to know women from different cultures also had made them think about differing ways that they work to improve women's status, as well as what they share in common. Some mentioned feeling part of a global sisterhood. As an African woman commented, "We have started to understand one another so there is a need to strengthen the relationship." Although one out of three American women had already visited African rural areas, others commented on their need to visit in order to better understand the African women's contexts.[43]

The women's *indaba* was especially successful for the African women, who had met as strangers across sizable differences of culture and status. One of the older women, the wife of an archbishop, set a collaborative tone by affirming the younger women and inviting them to speak out. Their shared status as visitors (some for the first time to New York or the United States) also helped foster relationships, evident during meals and informal time, as well as in their interweaving comments, where they referred to what another had said and then built on it.

From the relationships they formed, the African women spoke of following up with practical projects of local and mutual missions to help empower local women and seek to

---

[43] Paula D. Nesbitt, "AWE Women's Indaba," 14, 18.

engage men in the conversation to end gender violence. They also spoke of the value of a women's *indaba* among women, both locally and cross-culturally within Africa, as a way to help break the silence surrounding gender-based violence, raise consciousness, and share strategies for improving women's status and healing.

One of the participants, from the Democratic Republic of the Congo, has drawn on the *indaba* experience to help victims of gender violence speak out publicly against the exploitation of girls.[44] Another outcome has been a friendship between an African and an American woman that resulted in their working together in Burundi; yet another African participant traveled there to spend time with them, and the three women further explored their ministries.

Scholars of gender and globalization have searched for processes that help women converse in a way that respects cultural differences.[45] *Indaba* potentially is such a process. As one African participant in the women's *indaba* summarized, "We generally go to conferences where facilitators have planned the lines of the conversation, but [at the *indaba*] we built [the agenda] ourselves as a group; we said what we wanted to talk about and how we wanted to go through the conversation."[46]

Indaba *and sexuality*

Conflicts over homosexuality had led to the call for a listening process and the use of *indaba* in the Anglican Communion, but sexuality was only one of many topics explored at the 2008 Lambeth Conference and in the Pilot Conversations. As participants found common ground in faith, mission, and other matters, *indaba* helped those holding conflicting views on sexuality to stay in relationship. Since then, some listening processes and *indaba*-style conversations have been held that

---

44 Groves, "Report to ACC 16."

45 Myra Marx Ferree and Aili Mari Tripp, *Global Feminism*.

46 ACNS Staff, "Women's Indaba Success Will Mean Similar Gatherings across Africa, US."

narrowly focus on the status of same-sex relationships in different churches and in the Communion.

The Diocese of Virginia over the years had been distressed as the majority of members from eleven congregations disaffiliated from the diocese and the Episcopal Church. Homosexuality was the visible issue, although it wasn't the only concern.[47] Lawsuits and appeals over church property had added to the tension, felt especially by those who held conservative views but remained in the church. The diocese's use of *indaba*-style gatherings to bridge these deep divisions ultimately allowed its ministry to move forward, even though strong differences of theological understanding remained.[48]

Another use of *indaba* involved a consultation among Episcopal and some ecumenical leaders, as well as leaders from Anglican Communion churches in countries where civil same-sex marriage was legal or becoming so. The 2014 Consultation asked for responses to liturgical and theological resources for blessing same-sex relationships that would be presented to the Episcopal Church.[49] The format included a facilitated *indaba*-style conversation to help participants learn more about differing church responses to legalized civil marriage in other cultural contexts, including concerns about marriage equality.

The *indaba* was valued because of the space created where people could understand and gain new insights on differing international and denominational contexts, especially for those in situations where speaking out still involved taking risks or where issues surrounding marriage equality were highly complex. Interviews indicate that several returned home enthusiastic about *indaba*'s possibilities. Some thought that the *indaba*'s deep sharing had also benefited other parts

---

[47] Mary Frances Schjonberg, "U.S. Supreme Court Refuses to Hear Falls Church Anglican Case." Also see Miranda K. Hassett, *Anglican Communion in Crisis*.

[48] Johnston, "Bishop Johnston's Pastoral Address."

[49] The Standing Commission on Liturgy and Music was charged by 2012 General Convention Resolution 049 to gather responses from church and Communion voices and report back to the 2015 General Convention. This *indaba* is summarized from Paula D. Nesbitt, "Follow-Up Evaluation Report."

of the Consultation. However, a common comment was the need to include wider differences of view for *indaba* to be at its best and to understand fully what else needed to be done. *Indabas* on same-sex relationships were also being planned in two other Anglican Communion churches.

The Scottish Episcopal Church in 2014 held a Cascade Conversation to address the challenging issues of human sexuality as part of a yearlong churchwide discussion. For the kickoff event, about sixty people from dioceses across the church met over two days in six facilitated small groups to listen openly and seek deeper understanding of their differences. The process, designed with input from Continuing Indaba, allowed participants to offer their personal thoughts without fear of being criticized, stereotyped, or pressured toward a decision by those holding strong positions at either end of the spectrum.

At the end of the event, each group crafted a statement that shared their experience. The value of open conversation and importance of mutual respect across differences of view were common themes. "Our respectful listening to each other led to the uncomfortable realization of how difficult and painful our view can be for other people," summarized one group. Another said, "We heard people rather than positions."[50] Participants departed with hope, but they were also realistic about the difficulty of holding strong differences together in unity.

This event led to a subsequent cascading of local conversations across the church, which culminated in a thoughtful discussion in General Synod over two core questions:

- What has shaped your views about same-sex relationships over the years?

- What considerations should the Scottish Episcopal Church take into account when

---

50 "Cascade Conversation."

exploring whether to incorporate same-sex
marriage into its life?[51]

Overall, the conversations had been viewed as more effective
than anything previously tried.[52]

In 2015, the church's General Synod followed a detailed
process, which involved first considering whether it wished to
make any change with regard to same-sex marriage. Following
an affirmative decision, a number of alternatives were explored.
From the discussion, a sizable majority preferred to make a
canonical change and voted to do so. The General Synod discussion was described in a media post as "seldom angry and
at times very moving," although for some it was also painful.
One bishop spoke of the power of the Cascade Conversations
on his own journey. Another bishop involved in the conversations stressed the importance of keeping everyone together, "a
family in one house"; yet taking no action wasn't viable either.[53]

Following the affirmative vote, conversations took place
between those representing the Faith and Order Board and the
College of Bishops to consider measures that would safeguard
those finding a canonical change very difficult. "We have
tried to express the reality that, even if we make a clear decision on canonical change, we remain a church which recognizes and honours its own diversity," said the Most Rev. David
Chillingworth, primus of the church.[54]

The church took the next step in 2016, changing its marriage canon to gender-neutral language, with provisions
made for matters of conscience. The move was credited with
respecting the diversity of views within the church. As one of
the bishops voting against the measure said:

---

[51] "General Synod 2014 Day Two."

[52] "Same Sex Relationships and the Scottish Episcopal Church."

[53] Pat Ashworth, "Scottish Synod Opens Church Door to Same-Sex Weddings."

[54] Personal correspondence following June 23, 2016, interview, used with
permission.

> I feel comfortable with the fact that we have arrived
> at the position in our Church where those of us
> who did vote against the motion can nonetheless
> live with the outcome. . . . We have demonstrated
> how potentially divisive and destructive issues can
> be sensitively and carefully, and with due process,
> come to both a good and indeed the best possible
> outcome for all.[55]

The change must undergo further debate and another, more stringent vote at the 2017 General Synod. Conversation is continuing to discern solutions that will help the church remain a place for varying views.

Other *Indabas*

Indaba has been used across a range of groups and contexts for meaningful conversation about differences. Bishops in Dialogue, inspired by *indaba* at the 2008 Lambeth Conference, began the following year as a grassroots meeting of six Canadian and six African bishops of differing backgrounds and viewpoints. Its purpose was to continue informal conversations, deepen relationships, and increase mutual understanding. Over the years, the bishops have shared experiences and differences on a range of topics, including sexuality, but also on bridge-building, mutual responsibility and interdependence, and mission.[56] According to Bishop of Toronto Colin Johnson, cofounder of the group, the focus more recently has been on reconciliation: how the bishops can learn from one another, what they can share, and the various ways in which each is engaged in a reconciliation process. About forty-five bishops have participated at one or more meetings that have taken place across the world.[57]

---

[55] "Scottish Episcopal Church Takes First Step towards Same Sex Marriage."

[56] André Forget, "Bishops' Consultation Helps Keep Communion Together, Says Canadian Primate"; Garth Q. Counsell, "Bishops in Dialogue."

[57] Interview with the Rt. Rev. Colin Johnson, bishop of Toronto, June 2016.

Phil Groves, Continuing Indaba director, in reporting on *indaba*'s varied uses at the 2016 Anglican Consultative Council, spoke of a process used by Church of North India Moderator and Bishop Pradeep Kumar Samataroy to heal tensions between tribal and dalit peoples in his diocese. The facilitated conversations offered a structure and clarity that helped lead to a resolution. Groves also provided an update on the outcome of Mbeere's *indaba*-style gathering of clan elders and the reconciliation of a long-standing tension between two tribal groups described in chapter 5. Two years later, the elders had told him that *indaba*'s ongoing use in local towns and villages was having a positive effect on both the economy and church growth.[58] Groves noted that bishops from Burundi and Rwanda, having heard the story of transformation, had visited Mbeere to learn more about the process.[59]

In Zambia, the Anglican cathedral hosted a seven-hour *indaba* among the leaders of the country's key political parties in response to growing tension and concerns over potential violence prior to the 2016 general election. The *indaba* was an ecumenical effort involving members of the Council of Churches, Evangelical Alliance, Pentecostal groups, and the Episcopal Conference, and was chaired by a Roman Catholic archbishop. Following the *indaba*, political rhetoric had changed, ending violent language. The participants also had made a commitment to focus on key issues and on peace and to urge followers to support those outcomes.[60] The *indaba* suggests that such a process may have a powerful role across religious and secular institutions in decreasing tensions and seeking solutions.

---

[58] A comparable form of conversation in Kiswahili is *baraza*, used in parts of Kenya (see chapter 1).

[59] Groves, "Report to ACC 16."

[60] Gavin Drake, "Cathedral Indaba Eases Political Tensions in Zambia."

INDABA AS A WAY FORWARD

From an *indaba* conversation between seminary and diocesan leaders in the Anglican Church of Canada, a report observed, "The *indaba* process is one in which much, if not most, of the work is about naming the problem."[61] This feeling was shared by many participants in Pilot Conversations and other *indabas*. Although *indaba* could be frustrating at times, it helped move participants deeper into the heart of the larger issue, which then could be named and work begun to find effective solutions.

For *indaba* to be transformative, differing voices and viewpoints—across statuses and standpoints—need to be heard in order for participants to gain a comprehensive understanding of a conflict or concern. They also must be part of finding the solution. Because of the importance of respecting different views, *indaba* has been accused by outsiders as having liberalizing tendencies. Although both strongly traditionalist and strongly liberal participants have admitted to gaining a deeper understanding of why others held differing views, they also have maintained their own beliefs. Theologically, as two Continuing Indaba participants had put it, they still believed that God would judge the other harshly, but the gospel supported their upholding respectful relationships across their differences.

Coming into the life of the Anglican Communion at a time when the need for new paths to forging relationships across differences of culture and understanding has become urgent, *indaba* has been part of a spirit of the age where listening and respecting differences are key to living together and working collaboratively to address critical issues and concerns. *Indaba* also has inspired creativity across cultures in developing processes that recognize the role of differing views in finding solutions that maintain unity and cohesive community.

---

61   "The d'Youville Report," 14.

~ **9** ~

Indaba and
the Future

DURING A TIME WHEN THE ANGLICAN Communion has been threatened with fracturing over differences in belief, culture, and understanding, *indaba* has played a role in its ability to remain intact. It has helped many understand others' perspectives and actions. It has strengthened their ability to hold authentic conversations despite conflicts over how faith is lived out. It has made possible a commitment to maintain relationships of mutual respect for differing cultural contexts and interpretations of a shared faith tradition. Where this path was followed, common ground and concord have been cultivated along the way despite the diversity of understandings that remain.

The *indaba* journey also has brought new companions, fresh voices, cross-cultural awareness, and some real wisdom for those who have taken the risk. To set aside familiar pathways of conversation, personal biases, and the longing for clarity, certainty, or dominance has been a series of difficult steps. But *indaba* has helped people enter into genuine encounter, where they were able to see how their own solutions might not fit another's context. Many returned home significantly affected in some way—not necessarily in their belief or faith, but in the understanding that surrounds differences in beliefs and practices.

Indaba's spread across the Anglican Communion is not only about finding a viable path to the future together in the midst of profound differences but also about recognizing the limits of exclusively Western approaches to listening, negotiation, and conducting relationships, especially in a global context that no longer depends or wants colonial or imperial power to dominate decision-making and international relations. *Indaba* has become a symbol of this transition—the desire for a wider bridge to maintain relationships and seek ways forward together that recognize and respect authentic differences, identities, and cultures. It has inspired differing uses and formats across the Communion, some called *indaba* or *indaba*-style, and others given a name that represents a different context or culture. Key to all of these is the desire for common ground and mutual respect that allow a group or community to move forward in the midst of their differences.

INDABA'S ROLE IN THE ANGLICAN COMMUNION

Before *indaba*, the Anglican Communion had come to the end of its road using a style of leadership and practices steeped in its colonial past. Starting in the late 1980s, when the need for change became most clear, most of the tensions had arisen out of what Bishop Michael Marshall called an "explosion of Christianity out of the mould of one particular culture . . . into a variety of cultures."[1] This triggered further tensions

---

[1] Marshall, *Church at the Crossroads*, 68.

that are still evident over authority and power, and between individualism and interdependence. Writers from the "two thirds world" at that time had prophetically warned that the future would depend on mutual relationships, working together in mission and ministry, rather than on governance alone.[2]

Ironically, the 1990s growth of networks that brought new partnerships across churches and continents, some seeking to determine the direction of the Communion, also resulted in new cross-cultural relationships that included the dependency of primarily white conservative North Americans on African leaders to maintain their ties with the Anglican Communion as they disaffiliated from the Episcopal Church and the Anglican Church of Canada.[3]

The Global Anglican Future Conference (GAFCON) became a framework for some of these network movements. Yet a number of GAFCON members viewed their involvement as being alongside a full commitment to the Anglican Communion, which frustrated the political movement aims of other members. The dual loyalty also has served as a public way to signify a conservative theological commitment while participating in a theologically diverse Communion. Where *indaba* has brought both members of GAFCON and those holding views they oppose into deep conversation, it has been a difficult but worthwhile journey. Some tensions have eased, further frustrating those seeking to gain from continued tension and a divided Communion.

In many ways, the Anglican Communion found new life and direction because of the bold risks that Archbishop of Canterbury Rowan Williams took in bringing an African process of deep communal listening into the center of the Communion. Not everyone had been pleased with his vision. Some wanting to obtain political dominance felt rebuffed by the removal of processes that might have allowed them to gain

---

2 Samuel and Sugden, *Lambeth*, 157.
3 For more on these networks, see Hassett, *Anglican Communion in Crisis*.

moral and political victories. Williams also had been concerned over the fragile organizational structure of the Communion, calling repeatedly for gracious restraint on further elections of openly gay bishops in the Episcopal Church and elsewhere for the sake of the common good of the Communion. To some, he seemed to put greater emphasis on refraining from elections than on the incursions across geographic boundaries to grant ecclesial asylum to those leaving the Episcopal Church and the Anglican Church of Canada. Williams believed that the structure of an Anglican covenant could address both concerns and that *indaba* might provide deepened understanding that would strengthen the severely frayed bonds of affection that held the Communion together.

A covenant, proposed to bring clarity to Anglican identity and affiliation, played into a long-standing Anglican tension between those desiring dogmatic conformity and others valuing doctrinal mutuality.[4] Concerns arose over the covenant's administrative authority and potential use for political ends. Some argued that an organizational restructuring wasn't necessary if the mutual accountability that arose from strengthened relationships could create the type of respect that would hold the church together in organizational communion despite differences.[5] For others in former colonial churches, the covenant was symbolic of a new postcolonial era where each church would formally sign and uphold it as an equal to all others. The role of *indaba* had been viewed as a way to live alongside the covenant with mutual respect in a postcolonial and globally interconnected world. Yet where the covenant stalled because of its focus on governance, against which the writers two decades ago had warned, *indaba* has depended on relationships based on mutuality, which they had advocated.

By the time Archbishop Williams stepped down, *indaba* had shown promise in how the Anglican Communion might

---

4 Paula D. Nesbitt, "Doctrine," 385.
5 For a diverse collection of essays, see Mark Chapman, *The Anglican Covenant*.

hold together through mutual listening, understanding, and respect across deeply painful differences. Moreover, with the use of *indaba*, many felt that the Communion might become a truly global organization, valuing diversity of understanding and practice, yet maintaining a common integrity of Christian faith, ministry, and unifying mission. As he stepped down, the covenant's future was uncertain, but *indaba* already was making transformative change.

Reshaping Communion through Relationships

For Anglicans, the journey had begun over differing understandings and practices of their shared identity and tradition. For many, the Anglican Communion was a means of sharing mission and relationships in a tangible, global way. The religious bond, much like extended kinship, has intensified conflicts in some cases, but it also has made partners want to find a way to remain together if at all possible. *Indaba* has provided safe space for difficult conversations that at times have been painfully honest, where underlying issues could be probed. It also has helped bring about what Indian scholar Felix Wilfred has identified as the role of global mission: dialogue and the mutual sharing of religious and spiritual experience, leading to both mutual understanding and awareness of the presence of God across boundaries and differences.[6]

But *indaba* also means certain responsibilities for its participants. Some have been difficult for Westerners. To meet as equals across cultures and historical inequalities, the Enlightenment understanding of tolerance—which respects individual autonomy to make choices so long as they don't infringe on others' rights—needs to be balanced with a relational understanding of tolerance as an experience of living together with differing views, deepened friendship, and a

---

6 Felix Wilfred, "From World Mission to Global Christianities," 24.

willingness to allow give and take.[7] Mutual accountability affects individual decisions by considering others as relational stakeholders in whatever is to be decided. This does not mean that people must support what they believe to be morally unjust simply because others believe that it is just. But it does mean that others need to be considered and that decisions need to be explained or pastorally addressed, with earnest respect shown for those who may find them difficult.

Communal-oriented societies also have challenges, such as staying in relationship with those whose actions may violate their beliefs about morality and the social order. In the Pilot Conversations, the extended-family metaphor often was used to characterize the relationship of participants who strongly disagreed but nonetheless felt a kinship bond. This type of relational understanding allowed an African man to put a hand on the shoulder of an *indaba* colleague as he told his story of coming out as a gay man. It also helped Toronto and Jamaican participants to understand the complexities of social justice advocacy in Hong Kong and the different, more private way that concerns were approached and negotiated. Differences of view remained, but the relational bonds stayed in place.

Because the acceptance of difference is embedded in the very notion of *indaba*, it models a way to remain in relationship despite varying beliefs and worldviews. With *indaba* and *indaba*-style processes in use, the Anglican Communion's structure is resilient enough to accommodate the diversity in its midst and serve as an organizational canopy that supports the bonds of relationship. In this manner, *indaba* has helped reshape the way that people understand and value their relationships with one another across the world.

Moving beyond Agreement

At the start of the Pilot Conversations, some participants had yearned for others to agree with their views, since agreement

---

7 On this balance, see ibid., 21.

would affirm deeply held beliefs and their correctness across cultures and contexts. For others, it was very personal, such as being an ordained woman or a gay man in the midst of those who believed that their status was an apostasy. Over the Encounters, participants became aware that the situations surrounding their differences were far more complex than they had realized and were often affected by how cultures and societies had been formed, as well as how they lived out their faith. *Indaba* allowed for discussion without the integrity of one's belief being threatened by others' beliefs, because of the mutual respect and commitment participants shared in seeking to understand their differences and remain in relationship.

More important than agreement has been the ability to work together on missions and actions toward shared goals and mutually beneficial outcomes. Here, differences of view actually become an asset to broaden the understanding of tasks or challenges. Next steps or solutions then can address the complexity of a concern and its underlying issues. Thus diversity becomes necessary for social creativity and the imagination needed to adapt and survive peaceably in a transitional world. *Indaba*-style processes have offered a forum for different cultures and viewpoints to bring forth fresh ideas that can be explored and perhaps incorporated. Previous agreements or accords can be revisited and discussed in *indaba* as needs or concerns arise, without anxiety that a just solution might be undone, provided that all key voices are represented and heard fairly. Through such a process, social change can become stabilized.

Relationships built on the bedrock of mutual respect and trust, rather than on mutual agreement alone, can enrich and deepen the belief that a common journey together is possible. In 2016, Anglican Communion leaders held two challenging meetings about its future: the first among the primates (leaders) of the member churches and three months later the Anglican Consultative Council (ACC), composed of laity, clergy, and bishops from the churches. The previous primates' meeting in 2011 had involved *indaba*-style conversations, after which a participant had suggested that *indaba* was "becoming the way the Communion talks to itself."[8] Unfortunately, seven primates had refused to participate in 2011 because of the presence of the Episcopal Church,[9] which meant that their voices were not part of the conversation.

At Archbishop Welby's urging, several who had stayed away did participate in 2016, but the meeting did not involve an *indaba* format. Much could be said about the difficulty of the conversation, the differing understandings of authority in the churches' governance processes, and whether the use of *indaba* might have affected the outcome. But for several who attended, the strength of relationships and the understanding of particular contexts, which *indaba* had helped make possible over the years, allowed difficult words in recommending disciplinary steps for the Episcopal Church (because of its decision to change its church canon on marriage) to hold symbolic value but not altogether destroy those relationships.

At the ACC meeting, the primates' report was received. But the ACC recognized *indaba*'s ongoing potential to play a transformative role across the Communion by passing a resolution (16.11) embracing its use to strengthen relationships in local churches, help transform conflicts involving strong differences, encourage new approaches for churches (provinces) to renew their relationships and commitments with each other, and communicate more widely how Anglicans understand and practice reconciliation to help transform conflict and end violence around the world.[10]

Through *indaba*, the Anglican Communion has an opportunity to struggle with some of the critical issues of living

---

[8] Anglican Communion News Service, "ACNS4827."

[9] A second openly gay/lesbian bishop had been elected in the Episcopal Church the preceding year. ACNS Staff, "Primates Not Attending Dublin Meeting Have Reiterated Their Commitment to the Communion." Also see Andrew Goddard, *Rowan Williams*, 183.

[10] This is a paraphrase of Resolution 16.11's key points, which can be found in "Resolutions ACC 16."

peaceably in globally interrelated societies. *Indaba*'s model of seeking an overall unity that is grounded in diversity, where both differences and tensions can be better understood and addressed, can help build the type of interdependent relationships needed today. With respect to the *indaba* process for political leaders hosted at Lusaka cathedral (chapter 8), Zambian president Edgar Lungu told Archbishop Welby, "When we fail to agree in the political arena we call on the Church and the Anglican church has stood out—they really help us to talk to each other."[11]

INDABA AND RECONCILIATION

Justin Welby, who took office as the archbishop of Canterbury in 2013, was relatively unknown in ecclesial circles. He had been a bishop for only one year, yet he brought many years of secular leadership experience and a different perspective. Having overseen Coventry Cathedral's famous reconciliation ministry, he was deeply moved by it. He also had been involved in the design of *indaba*'s use in the Anglican Communion and later endorsed it, saying, "It has dared to invite us into a space where differences and disagreement are acknowledged in the diversity and unity of the family of God."[12]

Reconciliation became one of Archbishop Welby's three priorities for the Anglican Communion. As he described it:

> Reconciliation doesn't mean we all agree. It
> means we find ways of disagreeing—perhaps very
> passionately—but loving each other deeply at the
> same time, and being deeply committed to each
> other. That's the challenge for the church if we
> are actually going to speak to our society, which
> is increasingly divided in many different ways.[13]

---

11 Drake, "Cathedral Indaba," 3.
12 Justin Welby, foreword to *Living Reconciliation*, xiii.
13 Justin Welby, "Reconciliation."

Indaba had played a role in helping lower tensions in the Communion to the point that reconciliation might be imaginable as a next step. The Mbeere clan reconciliation (chapter 5) serves as a vital illustration of how the *indaba* process can help make reconciliation steps possible.

Faith and Reconciliation

Biblically, reconciliation indicates a changed relationship, one that formerly had been marked by alienation. The word often is used to express the desired relationship between humanity and God. In the Christian understanding, the church and its members as the body of Christ enact the reconciling mission of Christ in the world.[14] Reconciliation balances human diversity in a manner that allows all to work together for a shared purpose. Differences among individuals allow them to function as different parts of the body. Importantly, differences must not be denied or suppressed if authentic reconciliation is to be achieved.

As the Pilot Conversations ended, a participant answered the closing questionnaire question "In the future, I can see how *indaba* could be used in my . . ." by drawing a giant bracket and writing, "Reconciliation of Communities and Families." This participant had spontaneously made the connection between *indaba* and reconciliation. In the years since, Continuing Indaba has emphasized *indaba*'s potential as a process that can help churches, communities, and people across the Anglican Communion explore and move into a journey of reconciliation, ultimately themselves becoming agents of reconciliation.[15] This has been set forth in the book by Phil Groves and Angharad Parry Jones titled *Living Reconciliation*, which identifies key steps for living a faith journey of reconciliation and shows how *indaba* can have a role in the process.

In the Pilot Conversations, a shared Anglican faith tradition

---

14 See 1 Corinthians 12:12–27; 2 Corinthians 5:18–20.
15 "Continuing Indaba: A Guide," 4.

provided common ground for participants as they listened and explored how others worshiped and lived out their faith across cultures. Understanding of differences is a critical step for any reconciliation. In the end, nine out of ten participants felt that the process had helped give them a better understanding and appreciation of the varying ways in which Anglican faith and mission were lived out across their contexts.[16] On the closing survey, some expressed a sense of reconciliation in how their faith had been affected, with one saying *indaba* had provided "greater awareness of others, and [was] a wondrous exercise in 'respecting the dignity of every human being.'" Said another, "Though different, we belong to one body." And yet another admitted, "It reinforce[d] for me the fact that WE NEED EACH OTHER. One issue is not enough to divide us. There is a lot more that unites us." All had thought that the *indaba* journey had meant at least something to their faith, which for the majority had been affected very much.

Some participants also began to wonder about the possibility of *indaba* for interfaith encounters and conversations. At the end, according to the closing survey, nearly eight in ten Continuing Indaba participants thought that it could be useful to build relationships and discuss differences. The majority also thought that it could help reduce interfaith tensions. One participant pondered after the 2014 New York *indaba*, "What would it be like if [we] did an *indaba* . . . to build bridges between faith traditions and other aspects in [the] community?"[17]

Some interfaith-based reconciliation efforts by other organizations have sought to identify common ground where a moral vision can be shared for a way forward, involving not only moral and spiritual aspects but also social and political

---

[16] On the closing survey, 89 percent had thought that Continuing Indaba was effective in building a better understanding of common ground as Anglicans; of those, a majority (52 percent) had thought that it had been *very* effective. For understanding differences, nearly two-thirds (66.3 percent) had thought that it had been *very* effective.

[17] Personal interview, December 2014.

discussions.[18] Pope Francis also has spoken regularly of a "culture of encounter" to bring about right relationships in human society.[19] From the lessons of Continuing Indaba, deep listening and encounter across faiths might lead to greater mutual appreciation and respect. However, it must be done carefully. After working with Northern Ireland Catholics and Protestants during the 1990s, Cecelia Clegg, design consultant for Continuing Indaba, emphasizes the importance of encouraging people to express their different religious identities so that they are visible and respected.[20] This ensures that common ground is not assumed where it does not exist and that any steps toward building relationships are owned together. From an interfaith standpoint, reconciliation can be understood as bringing differences into a relationship of mutual respect.

A New Meaning for Reconciliation

Reconciliation often has been understood as an act where parties set aside their differences and return to full relationship. Although this type of reconciliation is possible in some situations, in others reconciliation requires a long journey for all concerned. As a process, it typically involves many steps, sometimes over many years or a lifetime, occasionally over generations. In situations of deep alienation and pain, *indaba*-style listening within constituency groups (those sharing a common status) can offer a safe framework for exploring shared and differing experiences. For dominant groups, constituency *indabas* also serve as a place to reflect on how they have treated others, as the men's group had done in one Pilot Conversation.

Further steps include hearing the pain of one another's truths, such as in a facilitated process; engaging in personal and spiritual reflection; and desiring to let go of revenge or the type of anger that can consume one with enmity. The

---

18   Owen Frazer and Richard Friedli, "Approaching Religion in Conflict Transformation."

19   Thomas J. Eggleston, "Culture of Encounter," 1.

20   Clegg, "Between Embrace and Exclusion," 151.

process of forgiveness, personally and collectively, is part of the long journey, as is the process of conversion (*metanoia*), where behavior is transformed and restorative acts make possible the building of new relationships. *Indaba* can serve as a helpful format for several of these steps.

Some have asked whether reconciliation is possible in certain situations. Where groups have removed themselves from the other or have demonized another as the enemy, or where bloodshed has torn apart families, communities, and societies, hard reconciliation work lies ahead for all. "Reconciliation doesn't happen when an oppressor decides to be nice. Reconciliation begins when an oppressed people reclaim their humanity," observes Bishop Mark MacDonald, the national indigenous bishop of the Anglican Church of Canada.[21] For those who have been gravely wronged or abused to speak up can take great courage. Anglican bishops in Canada, after being humbled by what they had learned about the abuse of First Nations and Indigenous Peoples in church-run residential schools and other aspects of society, realized the need to continue learning about the injustice. Supporting the call to action that came out of the Canadian Truth and Reconciliation Commission, they have committed themselves to walk in partnership with Indigenous People to rebuild relationships both in the church and in the country (chapter 8).[22]

At the 2016 Anglican Consultative Council, Archbishop Welby set forth an inclusive vision of the process of a reconciliation journey, saying:

> As Anglicans we are called to be something
> special, a people of reconciliation, finding
> authority through relationships, transcending
> complexity and difference, relishing diversity,
> loving each other. A monument, a beacon to the
> hope of Christ. In a world that burns with hellish

21 Susan Kim, "Reconciliation about Reclaiming Indigenous Identity."
22 "Canadian Bishops Embrace Indigenous 'Calls to Action' as 'Hope for a Brighter and Better Future.'"

> darkness visible, may we above all see not just
> what we are, but what we can be when we turn
> aside to the Pearl of the Kingdom, a pearl only
> seen clearly when we love one another.[23]

This understanding of reconciliation emphasizes that authority over one another must be grounded in a mutual respect for the diversity that others bring to the whole of human society. Reconciliation culminates as respect becomes transformed into the kind of compassion and love that make the well-being or flourishing of everyone the primary concern. For the Anglican Communion, this is the end toward which *indaba* has journeyed.

INDABA AND BEYOND

In 2008, *indaba* yielded few Google search results. Most were linked to the Anglican Communion's use of *indaba* at the 2008 Lambeth Conference and a notable reference to an annual Design Indaba held in South Africa. Now, in 2016, more than 3 million results appear, showing a wide range of uses for *indaba*. Some are Anglican related, but most show the rapid spread of *indaba* in secular contexts ranging from business and commercial branding to use in negotiations such as the UN conferences on climate change.

Indaba in Climate Negotiations

Indaba was used at the 2011 United Nations Climate Change Conference (COP17) held in Durban, South Africa, which sought a treaty to limit carbon emissions. It was brought into the meeting partly because the conference was located in the region of Zulu-speaking people and partly because it was

---

[23] In his opening address, Archbishop Welby refers to Matthew 13:45–46, the parable of the kingdom of heaven being like a pearl of great value. "Archbishop Welby Briefs ACC Members on the Primates' Gathering and Meeting."

a process that would help the negotiators and other parties be sure that all views were heard and fairly considered. The hope was for participants to reach beyond their own national interests to find a global solution that was in the interest of everyone.

"We hope Parties will use the Indaba to talk to each other, not pass each other," expressed Maite Nkoana-Mashabane, president of COP17, in her opening address at the conference.[24] When a delegate later asked her who were the elders, meaning those who would be participating in the *indaba*, she responded, "You all are," and gestured to the delegates of 192 nations.[25] She also explained that she had introduced the process to help build trust, which was lacking among participants, as well as to increase transparency in the conversations.[26]

The *indaba* process put diplomats who represented key countries into a standing circle to talk with one another, with this inner circle surrounded by those from other countries. Those in the standing circle were to talk personally about the areas where they could not compromise and also to offer possible solutions to the others in the circle.[27] Although a treaty was not reached at the conference, there was agreement to create a legally binding accord by 2015. Complaints arose because the meeting took an extra thirty-six hours for the nations to come to an agreement, but it also was praised as the first time that the countries had acted beyond their own self-interest in reaching that step.[28] COP17 was considered a significant milestone compared with the previous climate change conferences.

Indaba was used again at the 2015 UN Climate Change Conference, which faced a deadline to work out the agreement promised by the 2011 meeting. Time was running out,

24 Maite Nkoana-Mashabane, "Opening Address by Minister Maite Nkoana-Mashabane at the High-Level Segment of COP17/CMP7, ICC, Durban, 06 December 2011."

25 Eric J. Lyman, "Durban Turns to Zulu Tradition of 'Indaba' to Help Bridge Gaps in Climate Talks."

26 Maite Nkoana-Mashabane, "Statement."

27 John Vidal, "Paris Climate Talks."

28 Jonathan Shopley, "Durban's Indaba Delivers a Deal That Might Just Work."

and many were concerned that no agreement would be reached before delegates went home. Chairing the UN negotiations, French foreign minister Laurent Fabius chose to try *indaba* again, as a way to focus the discussion on the most difficult concerns. Starting with nine hundred points of disagreement on the eve of the scheduled final day of the summit, he called for "an indaba of solutions" to find, as he put it, "landing zones on compromise" as a way forward in those places where deep tensions still remained.[29] The series of *indaba* meetings ran for three nights. Two facilitated *indabas* were held, each with eighty chairs surrounding a large table, to be occupied by one key negotiator from each country. Each night, participation was first-come, first-served, as there were fewer spaces than countries represented.[30] However, all countries did have an opportunity to be heard.

According to Pia Ranada, an eyewitness to an *indaba* that began at midnight, the mood was urgent.[31] Fabius facilitated, urging delegates to focus on the three remaining difficult issues. Diplomats signaled their desire to speak by propping up their countries' nameplates. Many told stories of how their countries were affected, such as the "melting mountains" of Nepal or the disappearing beaches of the Maldives whose very survival was at risk. When roadblocks appeared, Fabius told the delegates involved to have a facilitated small-group conversation in a separate room to seek a way forward. Small-group participants were to share those areas where they would not compromise, but they also had to present possible solutions for others in order to move forward together.[32]

An agreement was finally reached. All countries had to give up something. Although not ideal, the agreement was a breakthrough after more than twenty years of climate-talk

---

[29] Pia Ranada, "#COP21."

[30] Tom Arup, "Paris UN Climate Conference 2015."

[31] The following details are from Ranada's eyewitness account in "#COP21."

[32] Adrian Segar, "The Simple Consensus Process That Saved International Climate Change Conferences."

frustration.[33] A West African diplomat cited the *indaba* format as being effective in bridging differences and being "participatory yet fair," urging that it be used more often when negotiations are difficult.[34]

Indaba in Other Contexts

Although the Anglican Communion may have been the first global adaptation of *indaba* for a religious organization, and the UN climate talks were perhaps the politically most wide-reaching application of *indaba*'s potential to transform conflict in a way that differences are respected while all participants move forward together, *indaba* has been adapted in many ways—some historically and others more recently.

One of the earlier uses of *indaba* outside traditional communities was in South African scouting. In 1952, the first World Indaba for Scout Leaders was held to bring together leaders from about fifty countries across the world to build relationships and exchange ideas on young adult scouting (Rover Scouts).[35] Local *indabas* for scout leaders and young adults have been held over the years in locations ranging from Britain to Nicaragua to Malaysia.

More recently, the use of the word *indaba* has grown rapidly in South African business and commerce, typically to signify a conference or gathering for the open exchange of ideas. Design *indabas* have been held for more than two decades. They began in 1994 as a "roadshow" to bring together a fragmented community of design professionals at a transformative time in South African history.[36] Held in Cape Town, they have become annual cultural events of creative interchange across the design world. Annual tourism *indabas* and mining *indabas* are now being held in South Africa too.

---

33 John Vidal et al., "How the Historic Paris Deal over Climate Change Was Finally Agreed."

34 Quoted in Vidal, "Paris Climate Talks."

35 "First World Indaba for Scout Leaders in Britain."

36 "Design Indaba Conference 1995."

The word has been used for other applications globally as well. Indaba Music is an online community for musicians to collaborate or share their work.[37] *Indaba* also has become the name of a software program, developed by a group of "transparency-oriented" nongovernmental organizations to integrate data collection across different global locations and platforms as a sort of collaborative workplace.[38]

Some have expressed reservations over the widespread use of *indaba* outside of its traditional context in the historical regions of the Zulu and Xhosa peoples. Where the word *indaba* is used for purposes having little to do with its original intention as a distinct cultural practice, or perhaps contrary to it, concern has arisen that it may be corrupted into a global fad that renders it meaningless. However, it has proved a valuable aid when people both with roots in tradition and from other communities have drawn on the wisdom of the best cultural practices in offering *indaba* to try to find a common way forward when reliance on Western processes has not succeeded, such as when Archbishop Makgoba suggested *indaba* to the Anglican Communion and COP17 president Maite Nkoana-Mashabane used it for the climate change conference. Others have sought inspiration from *indaba* in order to identify or create processes within their own cultural contexts that could bring about a similar type of transformation, such as the circles of listening used in the Anglican Church of Canada.

For some, such as in the Anglican Communion, the explicit use of the term *indaba* has implied respect for a different cultural process and symbolizes its value where Western processes have historically dominated. This contrasts with the belief of a few in the Communion that *indaba*'s influence has been infused into the organization's cross-cultural bloodstream and thus it no longer needs to be explicit, which can lead to both forgetfulness of what the "other" has brought and corruption of the very processes that have made *indaba* so effective. The

---

[37] Indaba Music, https://www.indabamusic.com.
[38] "About Indaba."

challenge for all is to remember and respect *indaba* and its cultural tradition in whatever adaptations are made and in its intended purpose.

A Wider Transformation in Relationships

Indaba has served many roles in the Anglican Communion. It has deepened relationships across cultures and other differences; helped transform conflict into a context where people can remain in conversation together in the midst of their differences; and brought about mutual respect and movement toward mutual mission and reconciliation. It also has helped bring an end to a legacy of Western dominance and an elitist attitude toward other parts of the world and their cultures. Unity has become possible across profound diversity of cultures and continents.

Indaba provides a social framework for a process of authentic communication to take place. Deep, open listening to understand must precede any form of authentic response. Listening affects understanding, which can lead to either reconsidering or reaffirming a perspective or position. An authentic response lets the speaker know that he or she has been heard. In a wider context, authentic communication is rooted in the deep listening and discernment needed for moral reflection. The response that follows becomes the ground for ethical action, through justly treating others with dignity and respect despite disagreements. From a religious standpoint, it could also be said that it becomes the basis for prayer, through open listening to discern divinely inspired insight or understanding of another situation that may bear on one's own thinking. And also for ministry, it provides understanding of how people choose to respond and serve together in community.[39]

Where authentic communication occurs, it transforms a mere sharing of information or positions into active mutual engagement. However, it also means that collaboration must

---

39 Paula Nesbitt, "Prayer and Ministry."

replace one-way messaging: those holding dominant or hierarchal power must be open to listening authentically and giving others' views full consideration. This represents the potential for a wider transformation in both local and global human relationships.

CONCLUSION

With human migration, communities across the world are likely to become ever more pluralistic—culturally, religiously, and politically. This diversity can be a source for growth rather than a cause of controversy or division. But for communities of faiths—or nations—to hold together in the future, they need to engage with one another's differences in a way that seeks to understand them more fully and respectfully so that relationships are built where trust can develop. This is key to shared mission or purpose. Religious groups of various faiths have an important role to play in offering compassionate support and dignity, as well as intentional encounters that seek to build relationships of respect across sometimes vast differences.

Canadian sociologist Peter Beyer has suggested that religious groups may respond in one of two ways to globalization trends. The first is to take a conservative or fundamentalistic stance, where religion is interlocked with identities that may be threatened by global change. The second involves a reorientation toward the whole or global, valuing the cultures within the whole.[40] The first option leads to increasing conflict over purity of faith, behavior, and ultimately identity. The Communion wisely has chosen the second option, through both *indaba* and reconciliation.

The second type of response is particularly difficult for those who have built their faith on a single understanding—whether traditional or liberal—as it entails understanding and forming relationships that respect the integrity of different

---

[40] Peter Beyer, introduction to *Religion in the Process of Globalization*, i–xliv.

contexts and views. It also calls for considering one another in choices and decisions. This is the transformation of empire into a world shared equally by all; in theological terms, it is both the covenant of Noah and the New Covenant, respecting the faith and integrity of all.

The challenge is to find common ground where communities can cohere while preserving the integrity of distinct identities and beliefs without degenerating into postmodern relativism. Just as any authority of Scripture must look at the whole, not selectively focusing on one passage or detail while ignoring other passages that offer a different understanding, we must look beyond conflicting ways of how we live out our beliefs to the larger narrative of life that is shared by all. Through *indaba* and similar processes, we can seek to hear and better understand the many differing perspectives of this narrative and build a community of global relationships that will allow us to have a viable future together.

About the Evaluation Research

Continuing Indaba and Mutual Listening Project

~~~

THIS APPENDIX DESCRIBES THE RESEARCH evaluating the Pilot Conversations aspect of the Continuing Indaba and Mutual Listening Project. Because of the project's experimental and cross-cultural aspects, a combination of process- and outcomes-based evaluation was used. Since the researchers were not involved in the project's design or changes that were made along the way, the methods needed to be able to accommodate unexpected shifts in participants, logistics, and other matters. Such contingencies affected how rigorous the investigation could be without the controls needed for consistency across contexts and participants over time. To adjust for situations affecting the research, we gathered similar data in multiple ways. These also provided a way to cross-check and verify our findings.

The researchers collaborated closely throughout the project. Three planning meetings were held at the start to discuss how to gather data effectively in a cross-cultural manner. Their cross-cultural discussions helped them set aside assumptions and limitations in understanding what they were observing. An outstanding example of the value of this type of collaboration occurred during a formal *indaba* conversation. One of the researchers was approached by a participant who was upset over the use of the word "change" on a questionnaire, interpreting it as a liberal bias to the project. This participant would not have commented to the other researchers because of differing cultural norms. As a team, we discussed alternative wording, and the researcher vetted a new possibility with the participant. This resulted in a substitution on subsequent questionnaires that we felt would not compromise the data-gathering. The research team also met after the last *indaba* conversation to compare observations for consistency and complementarity across cultural and disciplinary perspectives.

DATA COLLECTION

The researchers introduced the purpose of the evaluation to the Pilot Conversation participants at the beginning of the project. Participants were given human subjects protocol information, consistent with typical standards for protocols at American and British research universities. Participants could freely refuse to be interviewed or complete questionnaires, and if recording equipment was used, they could request that it be turned off. All participant comments were cited anonymously, with any publicly identifiable content removed, unless written permission was given or they had been previously published in news media. Some participants sought out evaluators, offering comments or requesting interviews, including some private critiques that made helpful observations.

Survey Research

Chapter 2 describes the use of survey questionnaires during the project. They were distributed at the beginning of the Pilot Conversation, between Encounters, and at the end of the formal *indaba* conversation. The opening questionnaire was translated into Kiswahili, which three of the participant teams knew. The closing questionnaire was administered on-site, at the end of the formal *indaba* conversation, with at least one of the two researchers fluent in Swahili available to assist with translation or to answer questions if needed. The questionnaires were available both online and in paper format. Data from the paper questionnaires were later manually entered into the online database. Since questionnaires included closed-ended and open-ended formats, both quantitative and qualitative analyses were possible.

Table A1. Questionnaire Response Rates

Pilot Conversation	Baseline (opening survey)	Post-Encounter 1	Final (closing survey)
New York–Derby–Mumbai	43%	33%	91%
Toronto–Hong Kong–Jamaica	54%	50%	91%
Saldanha Bay–Ho–Mbeere	67%	17%	100%
Western Tanganyika–El Camino Real–Gloucester	63%	44%	96%
Total	69%	37%	95%

The percentage of team participants who filled out questionnaires varied across the project (table A1). Participant illness, attrition, and new members added to teams affected both the respondent pool and the response rate, including the ability to compare data across the questionnaires. Some who filled out the initial questionnaire did not identify their Pilot Conversation, resulting in their responses being treated as missing when grouped by Pilot Conversation.

Participant demographics are shown in table A2. Because of some changes made in participants, the percentages are approximate. Overall, the changes did not affect the general demographic pattern.

Table A2. Participant Demographics

Gender (Final questionnaire, N = 85)

Female	39%
Male	61%

Location (Final questionnaire, N = 86)

Africa	34%
Asia	15%
United Kingdom	17%
North America	26%
Central America/Caribbean	8%

Order (Final questionnaire, N= 86)

Lay	45%
Priest/deacon	43%
Bishop	12%

Age (Baseline questionnaire, N = 64)

Under 40	31%
40–49	23%
50–59	33%
60 and over	15%

Interviews

All leaders of the Pilot Conversations—convenors (bishops) and link persons—were interviewed at the start of the project and at least once before the end. An effort was made to interview every participant at one or more points during their *indaba* journey. Interviews took place during unstructured time surrounding the sessions. Some interviews involved semistructured questions that were asked across participants; other interviews were unstructured, following participant comments and reflections. Of the two Encounters in which evaluators could not be present, a special effort was made during the next Encounter to interview participants and gather their reflections on what had occurred.

Interviewing was important for cultural contexts where surveys were not common or language differences made questionnaires difficult, but it also turned out to be helpful to participants across cultures. All appeared to value the opportunity to share their thoughts. Many offered remarkable insights. And all helped the evaluators develop a richer understanding of their experiences.

Observation

The core of the data-gathering occurred through observation of the *indaba* Encounters and formal conversations. All Encounters except two were observed by an evaluator. Two or more evaluators were present for each of the formal conversations. During the Encounters, evaluators occasionally moved from a strict observer role when invited explicitly by the group to participate or when refraining from doing so would be disruptive. When this occurred, such as taking part in *Lectio Divina* or being explicitly asked to contribute a brief comment, they maintained a neutral presence so as not to shift the group's thought or direction.

At first some participants had felt that the presence of evaluators inhibited what they said. As trust built during the process, however, this became less of a concern. At the same time, others affirmed that the evaluators' presence brought a measure of safety; they wanted the conversation heard by an impartial source. A point of tension arose in one Pilot Conversation as some participants expressed concern about the evaluators writing a report over which the group would have no control. Although a summary report was written independently as a condition of the grant, participant data were aggregated and personally identifying content removed. The report was made available on request from the Anglican Communion Office. [1]

EVALUATION FINDINGS

Although the survey research compared overall measures on how effective the *indaba* project was in achieving its aims, field research and interviews carried more weight in developing a detailed analysis of the process. All data formats were compared to identify findings that were consistent. Overall, the similarities in responses across Pilot Conversation teams were striking. Minor differences appeared, such as whether the formal *indaba* conversation was rated more highly than the third Encounter, but no sharp disparities emerged. This suggests a reliability of the process and the data across cultural context and participant experience.

The evaluation focused on several areas for assessing the effectiveness of how *indaba* was adapted for the project. Chapter 7 discusses the findings that show how *indaba* was effective in maintaining a conversation style grounded in listening and seeking to understand rather than to debate. Figure A1 shows participant views on how effective they thought Continuing Indaba was on various aspects such as mutual listening and understanding differences. Participants were increasingly comfortable with differences over time, when comparing data from the opening and closing surveys.

---

[1] Mtingele et al., "Continuing Indaba and Mutual Listening Project," 3–4.

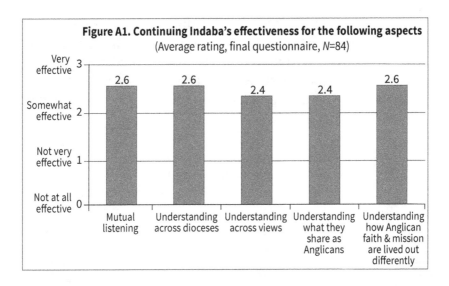

Figure A2 shows participant perceptions at the end of the Pilot Conversation journey. Most differences were not the kind that resulted in tension, however. In conversation over differences that aroused tension, participants were more adept at managing the level of tension than knowing exactly how to replicate those moments when they transformed it into deeply productive conversation.

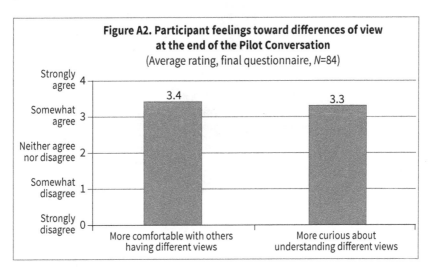

Awareness of differences also had value for participants in a range of ways (fig. A3), such as in personal reflection, identifying common ground across differences, and in meaning-making as part of the same faith tradition. Participants also gained new insights or understandings from encountering differences (fig. A4).

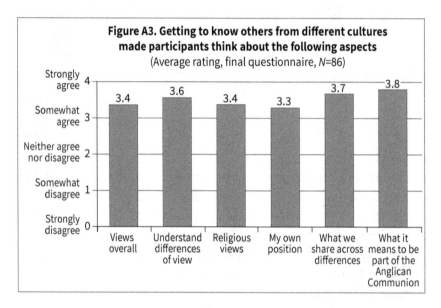

Figure A3. Getting to know others from different cultures made participants think about the following aspects
(Average rating, final questionnaire, N=86)

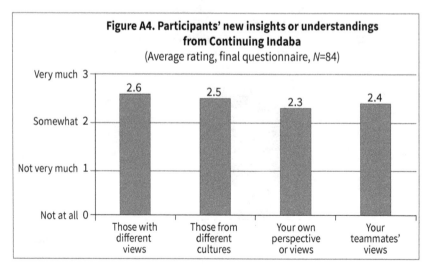

Figure A4. Participants' new insights or understandings from Continuing Indaba
(Average rating, final questionnaire, N=84)

The ability to understand and value differences depended upon participant skills in listening to understand when differences or tensions emerged. Mutual listening improved over the project (fig. A5), although for one group, the third Encounter was slightly more powerful than the formal *indaba* conversation. As a trend, however, all improved listening skills over time.

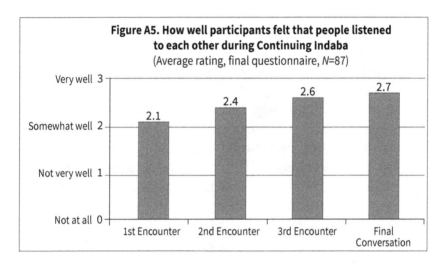

Figure A5. How well participants felt that people listened to each other during Continuing Indaba
(Average rating, final questionnaire, *N*=87)

Moving participants beyond mutual listening toward a common purpose, another objective, was evaluated by the extent to which participants sought to remain in relationship across strong differences of view and culture and how they acted that out during the formal *indaba* conversations. The value of relationships with others who differed in both culture and viewpoints produced the strongest overall finding in both the survey and field data.

Engaging participants in mission issues that lead to action was not possible to evaluate for results, based on the time limit of the project. Rather, it was analyzed through discussions that were initiated by participants about mission rather than by team leaders, particularly as they compared similarities and differences across their cultural and geographic contexts. Both the survey and conversation data suggest that the *indaba* experience was useful in strengthening mission awareness and, for some, movement toward mutual mission. Survey data also addressed learning new ideas of possibilities for mission and how *indaba* might be used in the future to strengthen mission locally and globally (fig. A6). Chapter 7 discusses findings on both building relationships across differences and mutual mission.

The use of *indaba* as consistent with Anglicanism, or the Anglican Way, was evaluated through a series of survey questions regarding participants' faith and understanding of the Anglican Communion. The survey data showed that Continuing Indaba did hold meaning for participants' Anglican faith, particularly in understanding the diversity of how Anglicanism was expressed across contexts and cultures, as well as differences in how others understood it and lived it out. Participants marked the effectiveness of Continuing Indaba for building understanding of how Anglican faith and mission are lived in different cultural contexts among the most highly of all effectiveness measures tested (fig. A1). Several comments referred to *indaba* as a spiritual experience. Anglicanism, with its openness to diversity of belief and expression, perhaps was particularly well suited for a process such as *indaba*, as figure A6 also suggests.

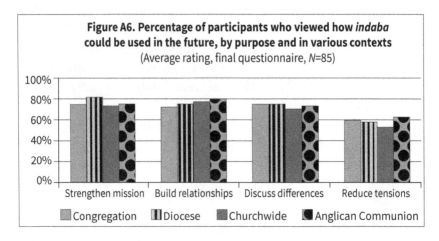

Figure A6. Percentage of participants who viewed how *indaba* could be used in the future, by purpose and in various contexts (Average rating, final questionnaire, *N*=85)

Finally, the evaluation sought to determine which aspects of Continuing Indaba could be useful beyond the scope of this project. Figure A7 shows participants' views on the usefulness of the *indaba* process for secular and interfaith contexts.

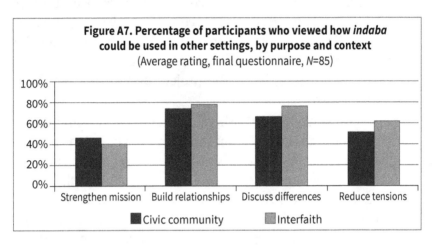

Figure A7. Percentage of participants who viewed how *indaba* could be used in other settings, by purpose and context (Average rating, final questionnaire, *N*=85)

To replicate the Continuing Indaba and Mutual Listening Project would be profoundly difficult and expensive. Besides the cost for teams to travel around the world, as well as host one another, the time commitment required, about one month within a twelve-month period, limited who was able to participate. However, the spontaneous adaptation of aspects of Continuing Indaba for other uses, when the Pilot Conversations were under way and subsequently, suggests that *indaba* holds value for encountering others' differing contexts and creating space for mutual listening to understand one another more fully, as well as for discussing differences and the way forward. These things were at the core of the various adaptations discussed in chapter 8. Just as *indaba* is unique to its traditional cultural contexts, the Continuing Indaba Pilot Conversations were unique in their own way. Both offer opportunities to share aspects that hold potential for adaptation, provided that the core aspects of listening, learning, understanding, and respect across differences are safeguarded.

The Value of Evaluation

"I didn't realize how valuable evaluation was. Without it, you can't prove that you are doing any good," Continuing Indaba director Phil Groves had remarked after the research project had ended and the report was completed. The evaluation offered a collective narrative of common tendencies amid the many differing views and experiences of participants. It also identified both strengths of the project and areas that could have been improved.

Above all, it has helped others consider how to build effectively on what was learned from the Pilot Conversations project in order to adapt *indaba* and similar processes of mutual listening and understanding to their own needs. As chapter 8 shows, *indaba* has continued to help various groups negotiate a journey across differences and toward a common goal or purpose, while respecting and even appreciating the value of having varying viewpoints in their midst.

~ BIBLIOGRAPHY ~

"About Indaba." *Amida.* http://indaba.amida-tech.com/ (accessed April 10, 2016).

ACNS Staff. "Continuing Indaba Team Welcomes 'Biggest Change to Mission Policy in 50 Years.'" *Anglican Communion News Service.* August 3, 2012. http://www.anglicannews.org/news/2012/08/continuing-indaba-team-welcomes-biggest-change-to-mission-policy-in-50-years.aspx (accessed May 16, 2016).

———. "Primates Not Attending Dublin Meeting Have Reiterated Their Commitment to the Communion." *Anglican Communion News Service.* January 22, 2011. http://www.anglicannews.org/news/2011/01/primates-not-attending-dublin-meeting-have-reiterated-their-commit-ment-to-the-communion.aspx (accessed June 27, 2016).

———. "Women's Indaba Success Will Mean Similar Gatherings across Africa, US." *Anglican Communion News Service.* March 5, 2013. http://www.anglicannews.org/news/2013/03/womens-indaba-success-will-mean-similar-gatherings-across-africa,-usa.aspx (accessed August 13, 2016).

Admin. "Church of England Commits Itself to Continuing Indaba." *Continuing Indaba.* July 17, 2012. https://continu-ingindaba.org/2012/07/17/cofe_commitment/ (accessed June 12, 2016).

———. "Essence of Indaba." *Continuing Indaba.* September 18,

2013. https://continuingindaba.org/2013/09/18/essence-of-indaba/ (accessed October 21, 2016).

———. "An Interview with Bishop Moses of Mbeere in Kenya on Continuing Indaba." *Continuing Indaba.* http://continuingindaba.org/2012/07/24/an-interview-with-bishop-moses-of-mbeere-in-kenya-on-continuing-indaba/ (accessed December 29, 2015).

———. "A Member of the Gloucester Team Reflects on Their Indaba Journey." *Continuing Indaba.* August 3, 2012. http://continuingindaba.org/2012/08/03/a-member-of-the-indaba-team-reflects-on-their-journey/ (accessed August 13, 2015).

———. "A Teacher Reflects . . . Telling the Indaba Story." *Continuing Indaba.* August 8, 2012. http://continu-ingindaba.org/2012/08/08/a-teacher-reflects-telling-the-indaba-story/ (accessed August 11, 2012).

"Africans Critical of Western Policies," *Lambeth Daily* 10 (July 1988): 1, 3.

Anglican Communion News Service. "ACNS4827: The 2011 Standing Committee Daily Bulletin—Day 1." March 26, 2011. http://archive.wfn.org/2011/03/msg00167.html.

"Anglican Council of Indigenous Peoples." *Anglican Church of Canada.* http://www.anglican.ca/about/ccc/acip/ (accessed June 22, 2016).

Anglican Women's Empowerment. "Fact Sheet." Women's Indaba, February28–March 3, 2013. Unpublished. New York: Anglican Women's Empowerment.

"Archbishop Welby Briefs ACC Members on the Primates' Gathering and Meeting." *Anglican Communion News Service.* April 8, 2016. http://www.anglicannews.org/news/2016/04/archbishop-welby-briefs-acc-members-on-the-primates-gathering-and-meeting.aspx (accessed April 9, 2016).

Arup, Tom. "Paris UN Climate Conference 2015: Negotiations Turn to Zulu-Style Meetings." *Sydney Morning Herald.* December 11, 2015. http://www.smh.com.au/environment/un-climate-conference/

paris-un-climate-conference-2015-negotiations-turn-to-zulustyle-meetings-20151210-glkwg9.html (accessed April 11, 2016).

Ashworth, Pat. "Scottish Synod Opens Church Door to Same-Sex Weddings." *Church Times*. June 13, 2015. https://www.churchtimes.co.uk/articles/2015/12-june/news/uk/scottish-synod-opens-church-door-to-same-sex-weddings (accessed June 24, 2016).

"Auckland Bishops Deliver Charge." *Anglican Taonga*. September 3, 2015. http://www.anglicantaonga.org.nz/Features/Extra/Auckland-bishops-deliver-charge (accessed June 13, 2016).

Battle, Michael. *Ubuntu: I in You and You in Me*. New York: Seabury Books, 2009.

Beam, Christopher. "Mumbai? What about Bombay?" *Slate*. July 12, 2006. http://www.slate.com/articles/news_and_politics/explainer/2006/07/Mumbai_what_about_Bombay.html (accessed July 2, 2015).

Bellah, Robert N., Richard Madsen, William M. Sullivan, Ann Swidler, and Stephen M. Tipton. *Habits of the Heart: Individualism and Commitment in American Life*. Berkeley: University of California Press, 1985.

Beyer, Peter. Introduction to *Religion in the Process of Globalization*, i–xliv. Würzburg: Ergon Verlag, 2000.

"Bishop Sadock Makaya: Telling the Story." *Continuing Indaba*. September 8, 2012. http://continuingindaba.org/2012/09/08/bpsadock/ (accessed August 13, 2015).

"Bishops' Charge to the Second Session of the Fifty Fourth Synod of the Diocese of Auckland." *Anglican Diocese of Auckland*. http://www.auckanglican.org.nz/Anglican/media/Images/PDF/Synod-charge-2014.pdf (accessed June 13, 2016).

"Bishop's Letter Advent 2015." *Anglican Diocese of Auckland*. http://www.auckanglican.org.nz/latest-news/breaking-news/bishop-s-letter-advent-2015 (accessed June 13, 2016).

Blake, Garth. "Sixteenth Session of General Synod:

Programme." Report to the Standing Committee, Anglican Church of Australia. October 22, 2012.

Bolsover District Council. "Employment Topic Paper." March 2013. http://web.bolsover.gov.uk/reportsagendas/Reports%5Creport15053.pdf (accessed July 1, 2015).

"Bombay: History of a City." *British Library.* http://www.bl.uk/learning/histcitizen/trading/bombay/history.html (accessed July 2, 2015).

Buber, Martin. *I and Thou.* 2nd ed. Translated by Ronald Gregor Smith. New York: Charles Scribner's Sons, 1958.

"Canada: Indaba Process Leads to Deeper Understanding." [Diocese of Toronto, Anglican Church of Canada.] *Episcopal News Services.* March 30, 2012. http://episcopaldigitalnetwork.com/ens/2012/03/30/canada-indaba-process-leads-to-deeper-understanding/ (accessed June 10, 2015).

"Canadian Bishops Embrace Indigenous 'Calls to Action' as 'Hope for a Brighter and Better Future.'" *Anglican Communion News Service.* October 27, 2015. http://www.anglicannews.org/news/2015/10/canadian-bishops-embrace-indigenous-calls-to-action-as-hope-for-a-brighter-and-better-future.aspx (accessed April 8, 2016).

"Cascade Conversation: Listening across the Spectrum." *Scottish Episcopal Church.* May 1, 2014. http://www.scotland.anglican.org/cascade-conversation-listening-across-spectrum/ (accessed June 19, 2016).

"Cathedral History." *Gloucester Cathedral.* http://www.gloucestercathedral.org.uk/history-heritage/cathedral-history/ (accessed September 29, 2015).

Chapman, Mark, ed. *The Anglican Covenant: Unity and Diversity in the Anglican Communion.* London and New York: Mowbray, 2008.

———. Introduction to *Christ and Culture: Communion after Lambeth,* edited by Martyn Percy, Mark Chapman, Ian Markham, and Barney Hawkins, 1–27. New York: Morehouse, 2010.

Chapman, Mark, Barney Hawkins, Ian Markham, and Martyn

Percy. Editors' preface to *Christ and Culture: Communion after Lambeth*, xvii–xviii. New York: Morehouse, 2010.

"City Population." *Republic of Ghana.* 2010 Census. http://www.citypopulation.de/Ghana-Cities.html (accessed August 14, 2016).

Clegg, Cecelia. "Between Embrace and Exclusion." In *Explorations in Reconciliation: New Directions for Theology,* edited by David Thombs and Joseph Kiechty, 140–53. Abington, UK: Ashgate, 2006.

———. "Instructions for Final Conversation." Unpublished paper. December 2011.

"Continuing Indaba: A Guide." *Continuing Indaba.* https://continuingindaba.files.wordpress.com/2013/11/an-indaba-starter-guide-a5-booklet.pdf (accessed April 5, 2016).

"Continuing Indaba: Celebrating a Journey." Progress Report, May 2012. *Continuing Indaba.* http://continuingindaba.files.wordpress.com/2012/05/continuing-indaba-report.pdf (accessed June 6, 2016).

"Continuing Indaba: What Is Indaba?" *Anglican Communion Office.* http://www.aco.org/ministry/continuingindaba/whatis/whatis.cfm (accessed March 28, 2014; site discontinued).

"Continuing Indaba and Governance Processes." *Continuing Indaba.* https://continuingindaba.org/resources/continuing-indaba-and-governance-processes/ (accessed June 6, 2016).

"Continuing Indaba and Mutual Listening in the Anglican Communion: A Project Sponsored by the Most Reverend Rowan Williams, Archbishop of Canterbury." Unpublished document, n.d.

"The Continuing Indaba and Mutual Listening Project." *Anglican News Service.* May 6, 2009. http://www.anglicannews.org/news/2009/05/the-continuing-indaba-and-mutual-listening-project.aspx (accessed March 26, 2014).

"Continuing Indaba Bishops Find 'Excitement and Hope' for Communion's Future." *Episcopal News Service.* November 23, 2010. http://www.episcopalchurch.

org/81799_12584_ENG_HTM.htm. Accessed November 25, 2010.

Counsell, Garth Q. "Bishops in Dialogue: Historical Background." *Anglican Church of Canada.* http://www.anglican.ca/wp-content/uploads/Historical-Background-to-Bishops-in-Dialogue.pdf (accessed June 30, 2016).

David, Kevin, and Tony Lawrence. "The Place of Young People in the Continuing Indaba Process: Why We Need to Include Them and How." *Continuing Indaba.* http://continuingindaba.org/2012/06/07/youth-and-indaba/ (accessed March 19, 2016).

Davies, Matthew. "Continuing Indaba Enables 'Gospel-Shaped Conversation.'" *Episcopal News Service.* July 30, 2012. http://episcopaldigitalnetwork.com/ens/2012/07/30/continuing-indaba-enables-gospel-shaped-conversation/ (accessed November 13, 2015).

———. "Listening Process a 'Gift' to Church." *Episcopal Life* 20, no. 9 (September 2009): 1–2, 8.

"The Derbyshire Churches in Partnership with the Church of North India." http://www.northindia-derbyshirechurches-partnership.org.uk/aboutus.htm (accessed March 13, 2012).

"Design Indaba Conference 1995." *Design Indaba.* http://www.designindaba.com/events/design-indaba-conference-1995 (accessed April 10, 2016).

"Diocese of Mbeere." *Anglican Church of Kenya.* http://www.ackenya.org/dioceses/mbeere.html (accessed December 28, 2015).

"The Diocese of Saldanha Bay." *Anglican Church of South Africa.* http://www.dioceseofsaldanhabay.org.za/ (accessed December 19, 2015).

"Disestablishment of the Church." *Diocese of Jamaica & the Cayman Islands (Anglican).* http://www.anglicandioceseja.org/?page_id=381 (accessed January 16, 2016).

"Distinctive Facilitation." *Continuing Indaba.* https://continuingindaba.files.wordpress.com/2013/11/distinctive-facilitation.pdf (accessed December 28, 2015).

"Diversity." *Toronto Facts, City of Toronto*. http://www1. toronto.ca/wps/portal/contentonly?vgnextoid=dbe867b42d 853410VgnVCM10000071d60f89RCRD (accessed January 8, 2016).

Douglas, Ian T. "Equipping for God's Mission: The Missiological Vision of the 2008 Lambeth Conference of Anglican Bishops." In *Christ and Culture: Communion after Lambeth*, edited by Martyn Percy, Mark Chapman, Ian Markham, and Barney Hawkins, 167–82. New York: Morehouse, 2010.

———. "The Exigency of Times and Occasions: Power and Identity in the Anglican Communion Today." In *Beyond Colonial Anglicanism: The Anglican Communion in the Twenty-First Century,* edited by Ian T. Douglas and Kwok Pui-Lan, 25–46. New York: Church Publishing Incorporated, 2001,

Drake, Gavin. "Cathedral Indaba Eases Political Tensions in Zambia." *Anglican Communion News Service*. April 25, 2016. http://www.anglicannews.org/news/2016/04/cathedral-indaba-eases-political-tensions-in-zambia.aspx (accessed June 12, 2016).

Draper, Jonathan. "Continuing Indaba: Seeking Reconciliation in the Anglican Communion." In *Creating Space,* edited by Phil Groves and Jonathan Draper, 14–31. 2nd ed. London: Anglican Communion Office, 2010.

Duraisingh, Christopher. "Toward a Postcolonial Re-visioning of the Church's Faith, Witness, and Communion." In *Beyond Colonial Anglicanism: The Anglican Communion in the Twenty-First Century,* edited by Ian T. Douglas and Kwok Pui-Lan, 337–67. New York: Church Publishing Incorporated, 2001.

Durkheim, Emile. *The Elementary Forms of the Religious Life.* New York: Free Press, 1965.

"The d'Youville Report." National Gathering on Theological Education. *Anglican Church of Canada*. January 2010. http://www.anglican.ca/wp-content/uploads/2010/02/dYouville-Report.pdf (accessed March 30, 2016).

Eggleston, Thomas J. "Culture of Encounter." *Houston Catholic Worker* 34, no. 3 (June–August 2015): 1, 7–8.

"8 Principals [*sic*] of Indaba: Diocese of Derby." *Continuing Indaba.* July 13, 2012. http://continuingindaba. org/2012/07/13/continuing-indaba-in-the-diocese-of-derby/ (accessed March 20, 2016).

Ellis, J. B. *The Diocese of Jamaica: A Short Account of Its History, Growth and Organization.* Project Canterbury. London, Society for Promoting Christian Knowledge, 1913. http://anglicanhistory.org/wi/jm/ellis1913/03.html (accessed January 16, 2016).

"The Emergency Loya Jirga Process" *United Nations.* 2002. http://www.un.org/News/dh/latest/afghan/concept.pdf (accessed March 12, 2014).

Ferree, Myra Marx, and Aili Mari Tripp, eds. *Global Feminism: Transnational Women's Activism, Organizing, and Human Rights.* New York: New York University Press, 2006.

"First World Indaba for Scout Leaders in Britain." *Trove: National Library of Australia.* August 25, 1952. http://trove. nla.gov.au/newspaper/article/82770260# (accessed April 10, 2016).

Fletcher, Wendy. "Living Church after the Fall: A Canadian Case Study." In *Creating Space*, edited by Phil Groves and Jonathan Draper, 152–67. London: Anglican Communion Office, 2010.

Forget, André. "Bishops' Consultation Helps Keep Communion Together, Says Canadian Primate." *Anglican Communion News Service* [*Anglican Journal*]. July 4, 2016. http://www.anglicannews.org/news/2016/07/bishops-con-sultation-helps-keep-communion-together,-says-canadian-primate.aspx (accessed July 6, 2016).

Frazer, Owen, and Richard Friedli. "Approaching Religion in Conflict Transformation: Concepts, Cases and Practical Implications." In *CSS Mediation Resources, Center for Security Studies.* Zurich, Switzerland: September 2015. http://www.css.ethz.ch/content/dam/ethz/special-interest/

gess/cis/center-for-securities-studies/pdfs/Approaching-Religion-In-Conflict-Transformation2.pdf (accessed June 28, 2016).

"GAFCON Jerusalem 2008: Statement on the Global Anglican Future." *VirtueOnline.* June 29, 2008. http://www.virtueonline.org/portal/modules/news/article.php?storyid=8509#.Uzs2HaJ788M (accessed April 1, 2014).

"General Synod 2014 Day Two." *Scottish Episcopal Church.* June 13, 2014. http://www.scotland.anglican.org/general-synod-2014-day-two/ (accessed June 19, 2016).

Githuku, Sammy. "Conflict and African Spirituality: Agĩkũyũ Perspective." In *Creating Space,* edited by Phil Groves and Jonathan Draper, 108–19. London: Anglican Communion Office, 2010.

Goddard, Andrew. *Rowan Williams: His Legacy.* Oxford, UK: Lion, 2013.

Green, Kirsty. "Fall in Christians, Increase in Muslims as Census Figures Reveal Religion Shift." *Derby Telegraph.* December 12, 2012. http://www.derbytelegraph.co.uk/Fall-Christians-increase-Muslims-census-figures/story-17565098-detail/story.html#ixzz3Xn0Lli786 (accessed April 19, 2015).

Groves, Phil. *Global Partnerships for Local Mission.* Cambridge, UK: Grove Books Limited, 2006.

———. "Phil Groves at CCEA: What Do I Know?" Presentation to Council of Churches in East Asia. October 16, 2015. http://living-reconciliation.org/2015/10/phil-groves-at-ccea-what-do-i-know/ (accessed March 19, 2016).

———. "Continuing Indaba Pilot Conversation DWT ECR Gloucester." Unpublished report. June 2011.

———. "Report to ACC 16." *Continuing Indaba.* https://continuingindaba.org/2016/04/01/report-to-acc-16/ (accessed June 6, 2016).

Groves, Phil, and Jonathan Draper, eds. *Creating Space.* London: Anglican Communion Office, 2010. http://continuingindaba.org (accessed May 20, 2016).

Groves, Phil, and Angharad Parry Jones. *Living Reconciliation.* Cincinnati: Forward Movement, 2014.

"Guidelines for Local Facilitators of Encounters." Continuing Indaba Project. Unpublished document. London: Anglican Communion Office, 2011.

Handford, Clive. "Celebrating Common Ground." In *Christ and Culture: Communion after Lambeth*, edited by Martyn Percy, Mark Chapman, Ian Markham, and Barney Hawkins, 42–54. New York: Morehouse, 2010.

Hassett, Miranda K. *Anglican Communion in Crisis: How Episcopal Dissidents and Their African Allies Are Reshaping Anglicanism.* Princeton, NJ: Princeton University Press, 2007.

"History of the Diocese." *Anglican Diocese of Ho.* https://sites. google.com/site/anglicandioceseofho/about-ipc (December 26, 2015).

"History of Locko Park and Hall." *Locko Park.* http://www. lockopark.f9.co.uk/Locko%20history.htm (accessed July 9, 2015).

"Hong Kong: The Facts." *Government of the Hong Kong Special Administrative Region.* http://www.gov.hk/en/about/ abouthk/facts.htm (accessed January 11, 2016).

"Hong Kong Sheng Kung Hui: A Brief Introduction." *Hong Kong Sheng Kung Hui.* http://www.hkskh.org/content. aspx?id=10&lang=1 (accessed January 11, 2016).

"Indaba in Toronto: A New Outlook on Ways We Serve God!" *Echo* [Province of Hong Kong Sheng Kung Hui] 272 (July 2011): 8–11.

"The Indaba Process." *Continuing Indaba.* http://continu-ingindaba.org/process (accessed May 28, 2016).

"Indaba Process Honors All Voices at Convention," *Iowa Connections* [Episcopal Diocese of Iowa] 3, no. 10 (December 2013): 1–2.

Johnston, Shannon S. "Bishop Johnston's Pastoral Address." *Diocese of Virginia.* http://www.thediocese.net/ council/2015/pastoral (accessed June 9, 2016).

Kim, Susan. "Reconciliation about Reclaiming Indigenous Identity: Bp MacDonald." *Anglican News Service.* June 24, 2015. http://www.anglicannews.org/news/2015/06/reconciliation-about-reclaiming-indigenous-identity-bp-macdonald.aspx (accessed June 17, 2016).

Lambeth Commission on Communion. *The Windsor Report 2004.* London: Anglican Communion Office, 2004. http://news.bbc.co.uk/nol/shared/bsp/hi/pdfs/18_10_04_windsor_report.pdf (accessed August 4, 2015).

Langer, Arnim, and Ukoha Ukiwo. "Ethnicity, Religion and the State in Ghana and Nigeria: Perceptions from the Street." CRISE Working Paper 34, Center for Research on Inequality, Human Security and Ethnicity, Department of International Development, University of Oxford, October 2007. https://lirias.kuleuven.be/bitstream/123456789/316986/1/workingpaper34.pdf (accessed December 26, 2015).

Lederach, John Paul. *The Little Book of Conflict Transformation.* Intercourse, PA: Good Books, 2003.

Lee, Frankie. "'He' Theology." In *Creating Space,* edited by Phil Groves and Jonathan Draper, 133–51. 2nd ed. London: Anglican Communion Office, 2010.

Levitt, Peggy. "God Needs No Passport." *Harvard Divinity Bulletin* 34, no. 3 (Autumn 2006): 44–57.

Lyman, Eric J. "Durban Turns to Zulu Tradition of 'Indaba' to Help Bridge Gaps in Climate Talks." *Energy and Environment Blog, Bloomberg BNA.* December 5, 2011. http://www.bna.com/Durban-turns-zulu-b12884908469/ (accessed April 16, 2016).

Makgoba, Thabo. "Addressing Anglican Differences: Spirit and Culture at the Foot of the Cross." June 10, 2010. http://archbishop.anglicanchurchsa.org/2010/06/addressing-anglican-differences-spirit.html (accessed July 9, 2016).

———. "An Anglican Microcosm." In *Creating Space*, edited by Phil Groves and Jonathan Draper, 58–70. London: Anglican Communion Office, 2010.

[Makgoba, Thabo]. "Essence of Indaba." Initiated for the 2008 Lambeth Design Group. http://www.aco.org/vault/Reflections%20document.pdf (accessed March 8, 2014; site discontinued).

Marshall, Michael. *Church at the Crossroads: Lambeth 1988.* San Francisco: Harper & Row, 1988.

Masolo, D. A. *Self and Community in a Changing World.* Bloomington: Indiana University Press, 2010.

McCaughan, Pat. "El Camino Real: Listening Is Key to Ongoing Partnerships with Gloucester, Western Tanganyika." *Episcopal Church.* July 1, 2010. http://www.episcopalchurch.org/library/article/el-camino-real-lis-tening-key-ongoing-partnerships-gloucester-western-tang-anyika (accessed April 24, 2016).

Milligan, Kathleen, Suzanne Peterson, Elizabeth Popplewell, and Meg Wagner. "Reflections on Indaba." *Iowa Connections* [Episcopal Diocese of Iowa] 4, no. 3 (March 2014): 1–2.

Mtingele, Mkunga, Paula Nesbitt, and Joanna Sadgrove. "Continuing Indaba and Mutual Listening Project, 2009–2012." Summative Evaluation Report. Unpublished. March 19, 2012.

Mtuze, P. T. *Introduction to Xhosa Culture.* Alice, South Africa: Lovedale Press, 1991.

"Mumbai." *New World Encyclopedia.* http://www.newworldency-clopedia.org/entry/Mumbai#cite_ref-26 (accessed July 2, 2015).

Neill, Stephen. *Anglicanism.* 3rd ed. New York: Oxford University Press, 1977.

Nesbitt, Paula D. "AWE Women's Indaba: Evaluation Report." Unpublished. April 25, 2013.

———. "Covenant or Conflict at Canterbury: Organizational Challenges and Futures for the Anglican Communion." Paper presented at the Joint Meeting of the Society for the Scientific Study of Religion and the Religious Research Association, Louisville, KY, 2008.

——. "Doctrine." In *Handbook of Anglican Studies,* edited by Ian Douglas and Martyn Percy, 384–99. Oxford, UK: Oxford University Press, 2015.

——. "Follow-Up Evaluation Report." *Standing Commission on Liturgy and Music Consultation on Same Sex Marriage.* July 7, 2014. https://extranet.generalconvention.org/staff/files/download/10739 (accessed March 22, 2016).

——. "The Future of Religious Pluralism and Social Policy: Reflections from Lambeth and Beyond." In *Religion and Social Policy,* 244–61. Walnut Creek, CA: AltaMira Press, 2001.

——. "Prayer and Ministry: The Moral and Ethical Dimensions of Communication." Master of Divinity thesis, Harvard Divinity School, 1987.

Nkoana-Mashabane, Maite. "Opening Address by Minister Maite Nkoana-Mashabane at the High-Level Segment of COP17/CMP7, ICC, Durban, 06 December 2011." *International Relations and Cooperation, Republic of South Africa.* http://www.dirco.gov.za/docs/speeches/2011/cop17_1207.html (accessed April 9, 2016).

——. "Statement." *Ad Hoc Working Group on the Durban Platform for Enhanced Action.* May 17, 2012. https://ufccc.int/files/press/statements/application/pdf/20120517_adp_open_mnm.pdf (accessed April 11, 2016).

Ntlali, Ebenezer. "Indaba: A Southern African Concept." In *Creating Space,* edited by Phil Groves and Jonathan Draper, 53–57. London: Anglican Communion Office, 2010.

Odour, John Mark. "Exploring the Baraza Model for Conflict Resolution: The Luo Drumbeat." In *Creating Space,* edited by Phil Groves and Jonathan Draper, 76–89. London: Anglican Communion Office, 2010.

"Official Programme & Event Guide: The Lambeth Conference." Anglican Communion Office. Hampton: RunningMan Publishing, 2008.

"Population of Kasulu, Tanzania." *Mongabay.com.* January 17, 2012. http://population.mongabay.com/population/tanzania/158214/Kasulu (accessed August 16, 2015).

"Population of Kigoma, Tanzania." *Mongabay.com.* January 17, 2012. http://population.mongabay.com/population/tanzania/157738/Kigoma (accessed August18, 2015).

"Population Profile (2015)." *Gloucester City Council.* http://www.maiden.gov.uk/InstantAtlas/Equalities/summary.pdf (accessed September 29, 2015).

Proceedings of the Anglican Congress, Toronto, 1963. New York: Seabury Press, 1963.

"Profile of the Diocese." *Diocese of Toronto: Anglican Church of Canada.* http://www.toronto.anglican.ca/about-the-diocese/profile-of-the-diocese/ (accessed January 16, 2016).

Public Affairs Office. "Episcopal Church Black Clergy Indaba: Visioning: Seed Time & Harvest." *Episcopal Church.* May 28, 2013. http://www.episcopalchurch.org/posts/publicaffairs/episcopal-church-black-clergy-indaba-visioning-seed-time-harvest (accessed March 26, 2016).

Putnam, Robert. *Bowling Alone: The Collapse and Revival of American Community.* New York: Simon & Schuster, 2000.

Ramswami, Sushma. "Under the Banyan Tree: Indian Analogues to Indaba." In *Creating Space,* edited by Phil Groves and Jonathan Draper, 120–32. London: Anglican Communion Office, 2010.

Ranada, Pia. "#COP21: A Peek inside 'Indaba' Meetings of Paris Climate Talks." *Rappler Blogs.* December 12, 2015. http://www.rappler.com/rappler-blogs/115718-cop21-indaba-solutions-laurent-fabius (accessed April 11, 2016).

Redlich, Marilyn, and Garth Blake. "Small Group Discussion Programme—GS16: Report to the Standing Committee." Anglican Church of Australia. Unpublished report. October 27, 2014.

Reflections Group, "Lambeth Indaba: Capturing Conversations and Reflections from the Lambeth Conference 2008: Equipping Bishops for Mission and Strengthening Anglican Identity." August 3, 2008. http://www.anglicancommunion.org/media/72554/reflections_document_-final-.pdf (accessed August 14, 2016).

"Resolution 1: The Ordination or Consecration of Women to the Episcopate." *Anglican Communion.* http://www. anglicancommunion.org/resources/document-library/ lambeth-conference/1988/resolution-1-the-ordination-or-consecration-of-women-to-the-episcopate?author=Lambet h+Conference&year=1988 (accessed July 5, 2016).

"Resolutions ACC 15." *Anglican Consultative Council.* http:// www.anglicancommunion.org/structures/instruments-of-communion/acc/acc-15/resolutions.aspx#s39 (accessed March 11, 2016).

"Resolutions ACC 16." *Anglican Consultative Council.* http:// www.anglicancommunion.org/structures/instruments-of-communion/acc/acc-16/resolutions.aspx (accessed June 15, 2016).

"Saldanha Bay Local Municipality (WC014)." *The Local Government Handbook: A Complete Guide to Municipalities in South Africa.* http://www.localgovernment.co.za/locals/ view/229/Saldanha-Bay-Local-Municipality#overview (accessed December 19, 2015).

"Saldanha: Main Place 163008 from Census 2011." *Adrian Frith.* http://census2011.adrianfrith.com/place/163008 (accessed December 19, 2015).

"Same Sex Relationships and the Scottish Episcopal Church." *Cascade Conversation: A Brechin Bulletin Special Edition.* June 2014. http://www.thedioceseofbrechin.org/media/ resources/Cascade_Conversation_June_14_Special_Bulletin. pdf (accessed June 19, 2016).

Samuel, Vinay, and Christopher Sugden. *Lambeth: A View from the Two Thirds World.* London: SPCK, 1989.

"Sanctum." *Fresh Expressions.* September 27, 2010. https:// www.freshexpressions.org.uk/stories/sanctum (accessed July 18, 2015).

Schjonberg, Mary Frances. "U.S. Supreme Court Refuses to Hear Falls Church Anglican Case." *Episcopal News Service.* March 10, 2014. http://episcopaldigitalnetwork.com/ ens/2014/03/10/u-s-supreme-court-refuses-to-hear-falls-church-anglican-case/ (accessed June 19, 2016).

"Scottish Episcopal Church Takes First Step towards Same Sex Marriage." *Anglican Communion News Service.* June 10, 2016. http://www.anglicannews.org/news/2016/06/scottish-episcopal-church-takes-first-step-towards-same-sex-marriage.aspx (accessed June 10, 2016).

"Section I.10: Human Sexuality." *Anglican Communion.* http://www.anglicancommunion.org/resources/document-library/lambeth-conference/1998/section-i-called-to-full-humanity/section-i10-human-sexuality?author=Lambeth+Conference&year=1998 (accessed July 8, 2016).

Segar, Adrian. "The Simple Consensus Process That Saved International Climate Change Conferences." *Conferences That Work.* January 18, 2016. http://www.conferencesthatwork.com/index.php/tag/climate-conferences/ (accessed August 14, 2016).

Shamala, Lucas Nandih. "Approaches to Peacemaking in Africa: *Obuntu* Perspectives from Western Kenya." In *African Traditions in the Study of Religion, Diaspora and Gendered Societies,* edited by Afe Adogame, Ezra Chitando, and Bolaji Bateye, 13–23. Farnham, UK: Ashgate, 2013.

Shopley, Jonathan. "Durban's Indaba Delivers a Deal That Might Just Work." *Carbon Neutral.* http://www.carbonneutral.com/resource-hub/company-blog/durbans-indaba-deal (accessed April 9, 2016).

Sison, Marites N. "Canada: New Style of Respectful Listening and Dialogue Presented in Same-Sex Blessings Debate." *Episcopal Life Online.* June 11, 2010. http://www.episcopalchurch.org/library/article/canada-new-style-respectful-listening-and-dialogue-presented-same-sex-blessings-debate (accessed December 5, 2016).

Skeat, Walter W. *A Concise Etymological Dictionary of the English Language.* New York: G. P. Putnam's Sons, 1980.

Solheim, James E. *Diversity of Disunity? Reflections on Lambeth 1998.* New York: Church Publishing, 1999.

"South Africa: The Most Revd Njongonkulu Ndungane Speech at Bishop's Forum in Cape Town." *Anglican Communion*

News Service. May 15, 2007. http://www.anglicannews.org/news/2007/05/south-africa-the-most-revd-njongonkulu-ndungane-speech-at-bishops-forum-in-cape-town.aspx (accessed August 14, 2016).

Sumner, David E. *The Episcopal Church's History, 1948–1985.* Wilton, CT: Morehouse, 1987.

10th Anniversary of the Province of Hong Kong Sheng Kung Hui. Hong Kong: Anglican Province of Hong Kong Sheng Kung Hui, 2008.

Tinker, George E. *Missionary Conquest: The Gospel and Native American Cultural Genocide.* Minneapolis: Fortress Press, 1993.

"Toronto Backgrounder. 2011 National Household Survey: Immigration, Citizenship, Place of Birth, Ethnicity, Visible Minorities, Religion and Aboriginal Peoples." *City of Toronto.* May 9, 2013. http://www1.toronto.ca/city_of_toronto/social_development_finance_administration/files/pdf/nhs_backgrounder.pdf (accessed January 8, 2016).

"Toward a Shared Understanding of Our Common Life: A Report on Indaba in the Diocese of New York, 2011–2015." *Episcopal Diocese of New York.* http://www.episcopalny.com/download/public-documents/diocesan/Indaba-Report.pdf (accessed March 19, 2016).

Trisk, Janet. "Indaba and Power." In *Creating Space,* edited by Phil Groves and Jonathan Draper, 71–75. London: Anglican Communion Office, 2010.

Vidal, John. "Paris Climate Talks: Governments Adopt Historic Deal—as It Happened." *Guardian.* December 12, 2015. http://www.theguardian.com/environment/live/2015/dec/12/paris-climate-talks-francois-hollande-to-join-summit-as-final-draft-published-live?page=with%3Ablock-566c21d9e4b052107bd8b4fb (accessed April 11, 2016).

Vidal, John, Suzanne Goldenberg, and Lenore Taylor. "How the Historic Paris Deal over Climate Change Was Finally Agreed." *Guardian.* December 13, 2015. http://www.

theguardian.com/environment/2015/dec/13/climate-change-deal-agreed-paris (accessed April 11, 2016).

The Virginia Report: The Report of the Inter-Anglican Theological and Doctrinal Commission. London: The Anglican Consultative Council, 1997. http://www.anglicancommunion.org/media/150889/report-1.pdf (accessed August 14, 2016).

Virtue, David W. "Lambeth: Indaba Sex Talk Fails to Satisfy Longing for Clarity in Communion." *VirtueOnline.* August 1, 2008. http://www.virtueonline.org/portal/modules/news/article.php?storyid=8777#.U3ut1nbb474 (accessed May 20, 2014).

Webb, The Rev. Benjamin S. "Inspiring Our Mission: Mutual Listening towards Common Purpose." *Trinity Episcopal Church.* October 27, 2013. http://trinityic.org/cpt_sermons/inspiring-our-mission-mutual-listening-towards-common-purpose/ (accessed March 20, 2016).

Welby, Justin. Foreword to *Living Reconciliation,* edited by Phil Groves and Angharad Parry Jones, ix–xviii. Cincinnati: Forward Movement, 2014.

———. "Reconciliation." *Justin Welby, the Archbishop of Canterbury.* http://www.archbishopofcanterbury.org/pages/reconciliation-.html?page=4 (accessed April 5, 2016).

Wilfred, Felix. "From World Mission to Global Christianities: A Perspective from the South." In *Concilium 2011/1: From World Mission to Inter-religious Witness,* edited by Linda Hogan, Solange Lefebvre, Norbert Hintersteiner, and Felix Wilfred, 13–36. London: SCM Press, 2011.

Windsor Continuation Group, "Report to the Archbishop of Canterbury." Mustang Island. December 17, 2008. http://www.anglicancommunion.org/commission/windsor_continuation/WCG_Report.cfm (accessed March 26, 2014).

ABOUT THE AUTHOR
AND CONTRIBUTORS

The **Rev. Dr. Paula Nesbitt** as a sociologist of religion has researched three Lambeth Conferences on-site (1988–2008) and coordinated the evaluation research team for the Continuing Indaba project. Currently a visiting scholar at the Graduate Theological Union, she has focused her research on topics that involve the contemporary role of transnational religious organizations, the clergy and occupational change, social inequality in cross-cultural relationships, gender, and communication. She has taught in both seminaries and universities, including ten years as a visiting associate professor in sociology at the University of California, Berkeley. She previously had directed the Carl M. Williams Institute of Ethics and Values at the University of Denver. A priest in the Episcopal Church, she also has served as a research consultant with various religious and secular organizations, including Continuing Indaba and the Anglican Communion Office. Her publications include three books and numerous articles.

The **Rev. Canon Dr. Mkunga H. P. Mtingele** has a doctorate in leadership and conflict management and a master of arts in theological studies from Open University, United Kingdom; a postgraduate diploma in theological studies from St. John's College, Nottingham, United Kingdom; and a bachelor of laws with honours from the University of Dar es Salaam, Tanzania. He has worked as a state attorney in the

Ministry of Justice, general secretary of the Anglican Church of Tanzania, and currently general secretary of the Bible Society of Tanzania. He served on the Anglican Consultative Council (1993–99) and currently serves on the Global Council of United Bible Societies.

Dr. Joanna (Jo) Sadgrove is a specialist in religion, identity, and cross-cultural encounter whose academic background encompasses philosophy, theology, anthropology, and geography. Her early work focused on Uganda; more recently, she has worked on Central and Southern Africa and the Caribbean. She has published on homosexuality in Uganda and the Anglican Communion, sexual behavior and religious belonging, and religious identities and cross-cultural change. She currently works as a research and learning advisor for the Anglican mission agency United Society Partners in the Gospel (USPG) and as a research associate in the Centre for Religion and Public Life, University of Leeds, United Kingdom.

CPSIA information can be obtained
at www.ICGtesting.com
Printed in the USA
LVHW010532080120
642858LV00001B/4/P